# EMPIRE'S CHILDREN

CHILDREN'S LITERATURE AND CULTURE
VOLUME 16
GARLAND REFERENCE LIBRARY OF THE HUMANITIES
VOLUME 2005

# CHILDREN'S LITERATURE AND CULTURE

JACK ZIPES, *Series Editor*

# EMPIRE'S CHILDREN

## EMPIRE AND IMPERIALISM IN CLASSIC BRITISH CHILDREN'S BOOKS

M. DAPHNE KUTZER

GARLAND PUBLISHING, INC.
A MEMBER OF THE TAYLOR & FRANCIS GROUP
NEW YORK & LONDON
2000

Published in 2000 by
Garland Publishing, Inc.
A member of the Taylor & Francis Group
29 West 35th Street
New York, NY 10001

10  9  8  7  6  5  4  3  2  1

**Library of Congress Cataloging-in-Publication Data**

Kutzer, M. Daphne.
    Empire's children : empire and imperialism in classic British children's books /
M. Daphne Kutzer.
        p.   cm. — (Garland reference library of the humanities ; v. 2005.
    Children's literature and culture ; v. 16)
    Includes bibliographical references (p.   ) and index.
    ISBN 0-8153-3491-5 (acid-free paper) — ISBN 0-8153-3895-3 (pbk. : acid-
free paper)
    1. Children's stories, English—History and criticism.   2. Imperialism in
literature.   3. Colonies in literature.   I. Title.   II. Garland reference library of
the humanities ; vol. 2005.   III. Garland reference library of the humanities.
Children's literature and culture ; v. 16.

PR830.I54 K88 2000
823'.809358—dc21

                                                                        00-042681

Printed on acid-free, 250-year-life paper.
Manufactured in the United States of America

*To Kathie, with love*

# Contents

# Series Editor's Foreword

Dedicated to furthering original research in children's literature and culture, the Children's Literature and Culture series includes monographs on individual authors and illustrators, historical examinations of different periods, literary analyses of genres, and comparative studies on literature and the mass media. The series is international in scope and is intended to encourage innovative research in children's literature with a focus on interdisciplinary methodology.

Children's literature and culture are understood in the broadest sense of the term *children* to encompass the period of childhood up through late adolescence. Owing to the fact that the notion of childhood has changed so much since the origination of children's literature, this Garland series is particularly concerned with transformations in children's culture and how they have affected the representation and socialization of children. While the emphasis of the series is on children's literature, all types of studies that deal with children's radio, film, television, and art are included in an endeavor to grasp the aesthetics and values of children's culture. Not only have there been momentous changes in children's culture in the last fifty years, but there have been radical shifts in the scholarship that deals with these changes. In this regard, the goal of the Children's Literature and Culture series is to enhance research in this field and, at the same time, point to new directions that bring together the best scholarly work throughout the world.

Jack Zipes

# Acknowledgments

I would like to thank a number of people who have helped me in the course of writing *Empire's Children*. Thanks to Larry Soroka for his help with mountaineering history and with historical sources; Ann Tracy for her help with Latin translations and with the Bible; Tom Morrissey for friendship, patience, and cheerleading; Alexandria LaFaye for the crucial loan of a book at a critical moment; my students in ENG340 in the spring of 1999, who helped me in my thinking about Burnett and who listened to part of this book in progress. I would also like to thank the librarians at Feinberg Library at Plattsburgh State, Bailey-Howe Library at the University of Vermont, and the New York Public Library for patient help with odd requests. A special thanks to Steve Major of Market Makers in Burlington, Vermont, who bailed me out of computer catastrophe at the eleventh hour—he has my eternal gratitude. Thanks to all the friends and colleagues who patiently listened to me think aloud in venues ranging from parking lots to potlucks. And finally, thanks to Kathie Sullivan, my personal reference librarian, for everything she does for me in my life.

# Terminology and Territory

A story, even a children's story, is more than just a story, no matter how simple it may seem. Stories grow out of particular cultures and societies and reflect the values of those societies. Shakespeare's history plays reflect Elizabethan politics as much as they do politics of King John's time, or King Richard's; Defoe's *Robinson Crusoe* tells us as much about the rise of the eighteenth-century mercantile class as it does about shipwreck. "To imagine a story . . . is to imagine the society in which it is told."[1] Stories of individuals and of individual experience nonetheless are part of a large body of stories, which together can form a kind of national allegory, an imaginative picture of the dreams, desires, and fears of a particular culture. Children's texts, often ignored by literary critics, form a crucial part of any such national allegory: children are the future of any society, and the literature adults write for them often is more obvious and insistent about appropriate dreams and desires than the texts they write for themselves. Roderick McGillis has argued that "Children and their books are ideological constructs"[2] and that one way children's publishers continue to make money is by "perpetuat[ing] the values and cultural conceptions of the ruling group."[3]

*Empire's Children* examines a series of British children's texts from the late nineteenth century to the beginnings of the World War II, texts that reflect imperialism and empire as a normal part of the world and often encourage child readers to accept the values of imperialism. Finding a critique of empire in a children's text is rare. In fact, as Patrick Brantlinger has noted, "Much imperialist discourse was . . . directed at a specifically adolescent audience, the future rulers of the world."[4] Brantlinger's interest is largely in the works of popular writers like Marryat, Henty, and Kingston, but the more serious writers for children, even writers of domestic fiction like Frances Hodgson Burnett, also indulged in imperialist discourse. In his discussion of imperialism and literature, Brantlinger notes that ideology need not be self-conscious, and that although "emphases and even theories about the Empire fluctuated greatly, imperialist discourse, like the actual expansion of the Empire, was continuous, informing all aspects of Victorian culture and society."[5] Edward Said takes this argument even further in *Culture and Imperialism* when he argues that the novel was "immensely important in the formation of imperial attitudes, references, and experiences."[6]

Yet for all the attention focused on imperialism and adult texts, little critical attention has been paid to imperialism and its intersections with literature intended for those "future rulers of the world." A special edition of the journal *Ariel* in 1997 was devoted to postcolonialism and children's literature; Roderick McGillis's *A Little Princess: Gender and Empire* (1996) explores empire in one book by one author; and Perry Nodelman's 1992 essay, "The Other: Orientalism, Colonialism, and Children's Literature," makes some tantalizing connections between Said's influential *Orientalism* (1979) and children's literature. And there is, of course, Martin Green's *Dreams of Adventure, Deeds of Empire* (1979), which includes some important discussion of children's texts. But not much has been done to trace the presence and influence of empire in classic works for children, the works adults most encourage children to read, which influence lesser works of literature and which become part of the canon of children's literature. Empire is everywhere in classic children's texts of the late nineteenth century, and its presence continues well into the twentieth. It appears as major setting and, arguably, as character in Kipling's fiction; functions as *deus ex machina* in the works of Burnett and Nesbit; raises troubling questions for Lofting; invades children's play in the works of Milne and Ransome; and can even be found between the lines of books published into the 1970s and 1980s, by Susan Cooper and Lynn Reid Banks, among others.

Empire's ubiquitous presence in children's texts is no surprise. Empire was everywhere in British culture of the period, playing an important role in everything from Christmas pantomimes to music hall songs to children's periodicals to advertising. Empire Day meant a half-holiday from school; seaside entertainments often provided a "native village" tableau, as did imperial exhibitions like Wembley (1924–25); Baden-Powell's Scouting movement grew directly from his military experience in South Africa; Cadet Corps became familiar and popular in public schools; there were school-sponsored Empire Tours in the 1920s; the Empire Marketing Board used images of empire and nationalism to sell goods. Empire was woven into the fabric of British life, and hence into the fabric of British children's fiction. Sometimes imperial imagery takes the foreground, as it does in Kipling's story "The Flag of Their Country" in *Stalky & Co.,* where the boys listen to a speech on patriotism; sometimes it is in the background, as in the figure of the Indian uncle in Nesbit's Bastable stories; sometimes it is encoded so deeply it becomes nearly invisible, as in Milne's stories of the animals in the Hundred Acre

Wood. Just as British public schools explicitly fostered the imperial ideal in students, British juvenile fiction implicitly supported the same imperial ideal.[7]

Another reason for the widespread appearance of empire in children's texts of the period is connected to the question of the production and use of children's fiction. Children's books are written by adults, for children, who until fairly recently had little opportunity to shop for their own books, depending upon adults to supply them with reading material. Perry Nodelman has asserted that "child psychology and children's literature are imperialist activities,"[8] with adults as the imperialists trying to shape the "other" of childhood to their own desires and needs. This is also the underlying thesis of Jacqueline Rose's influential *The Case of Peter Pan: The Impossibility of Children's Fiction* (1984), one of whose claims is that innocence is not "a property of childhood but . . . a portion of adult desire."[9] Adults who produce children's books are nearly always conscious of conveying morals and values to their young audience, and want to ensure that those morals and values are culturally acceptable. This was as true for the Puritans who produced children's books of "courtesy" and manners as it is for the producers of the Berenstain Bears books, with their emphasis on sharing and truth-telling and tolerance.

Overtly political values tended to appear in school texts, but they also appear, in coded form, in children's fiction. There was no literary conspiracy to convince children that empire was a good thing and should continue, but for much of the Edwardian period, and in later times as well, this was the accepted truth that seeps into children's fiction. As J. D. Stahl and others have asserted, "children's literature [is] one of the most forceful means of acculturation [and] reflects the cultural aims of imperial policy."[10] Few would reject the idea that children's books help acculturate children, and I hope to support Stahl's contention that, consciously or unconsciously, some of the most revered of British children's texts support the culture of imperialism—not the politics of imperialism, but the ethos that both produces imperialism and is engendered by imperialism.

If all literature reflects the culture from which it arises, children's literature has some peculiarities setting it apart from adult fiction. First, whereas adult fiction may—indeed, often does—question the reigning cultural code of behavior, children's fiction rarely does so. The role of children's texts, both fictional and nonfictional, is to help acculturate children into society and to teach them to behave and believe in acceptable ways. Second, adults who write children's books are often nostalgic for an ideal childhood that, in all probability, never existed. The world of many children's books, particularly from the late nineteenth century and on, is filled with cheerful games, happy times, and little anxiety: children's books all provide, to some degree, the arcadian paradise of Milne's Hundred Acre Wood. This paradisical world does not bear much relationship to the real world of children, but it certainly answers the adult's need to find a kinder, easier, imaginative world to live in. I believe this is one of the reasons Kipling's *Stalky & Co.* was received with such vituperation by the critics: Kipling presented his readers with real boys, boys cruel enough to kill cats and physically torture school rivals, but boys who were admirable nonetheless—indeed, admirable in part *because* they could kill cats and inflict pain upon other human beings. Adult critics did not want to see the realities of boys' school lives, because those lives did not meet the psychological needs of the adults.

The presentation of childhood as an ideal, innocent kingdom of its own is linked to a third crucial difference between children's texts and adult texts: adults may be aware that a long-accepted cultural code is crumbling, that the world is shifting in unnerving and poorly understood ways, but they want both to shield children from these changes and encourage them to continue believing in and practicing cultural beliefs and codes that are no longer unquestioned in the adult world, perhaps in an unconscious desire to maintain those earlier cultural codes. In this sense, children's fiction is highly conservative, interested in preserving the past rather than in preparing children for a realistic adult future. As an example, in 1924 E. M. Forster provides, in *A Passage to India*, a critique of the failures of the British in India. Children's books of the period, and well beyond this period, still unquestioningly celebrate empire and encourage child readers to live by old imperial rules, not by the rules of a new and shrinking modern Great Britain. The arcadian paradise of children's fiction provides an imaginative space where social and cultural disruption is not only impossible, it is barely acknowledged.

The underlying assumption of *Empire's Children* is that children are colonized by the books they read, and were perhaps more easily colonized in a period where books carried more authority than they do in today's world, where books must compete with film, video, music, and the Internet, all of which convey cultural values in more immediate ways than do books for contemporary children. What I mean by this is that, just as Britain tried to impose Western cultural ideals and behaviors in Africa, India, the Caribbean, and elsewhere, British adults try to impose adult cultural ideals of thought and behavior upon children. Just as colonial subjects were voiceless—their lives are described for us by Westerners, not by themselves—children are also voiceless, depending upon adults to describe their lives for them. I do not see this as any sort of evil conspiracy by adults, but as a natural response to the need to civilize and assimilate the "other" of childhood into the "subject" of adulthood. What I argue throughout this book is that, for the most part, empire is presented as natural and good to children, and that although diluted, this presentation of empire continues well into the twentieth century, although gradually empire is encoded as nostalgia for a more arcadian and ordered English life.

Looking at adult visions of childhood, and adult desires for their children, provides a mirror for adult desires and longings for themselves. If political and social circumstances seem troubling or wrongheaded to adults, if the world seems to be going in the wrong direction, adults can hope that the next generation will restore the world to its proper balance—and these hopes often appear in children's books. Just as some parents try to relive their youthful dreams through their offspring, urging sons and daughters to become the scholars and athletes they themselves were not, an entire culture can try to relive past glory through its children. It is this relationship that *Empire's Children* explores.

Before going any further, however, some definition of terms is in order. The words *empire, imperialism* and *colonialism* are tricky terms. Does "empire" refer only to formal British colonies of white settlers, such as Australia and Canada, or does it include various protectorates and treaty ports with a majority indigenous population, like the Cape Colony or Kowloon? Does "imperialism" refer to formal acts of territorial acquisition, or to the ideology that lies behind such acquisition—or both? Is "colonialism" to be reserved only for permanent white settler colonies, or can it be more broadly used to refer to the British impulse to populate foreign territories with less-permanent settlements of white soldiers and administrators? In general, I mean "imperialism" to have a broad and inclusive definition, to include the advocacy and glorification of military force to both expand and maintain the empire; the promotion of the racial superiority of white Europeans, and especially Englishmen, over darker-skinned non-Europeans; the waving of the flag of patriotism and nationalism; the civilizing of the spiritually and morally "dark" areas of the world. Without the ideology of imperialism, expansion of empire is impossible, and it is this ideology that is omnipresent in classic British children's books.

Colonialism, on the other hand, is a somewhat narrower term. Edward Said's distinctions between imperialism and colonialism are pertinent here. He sees imperialism as being "the practice, the theory, and the attitudes of a dominating metropolitan center ruling a distant territory," while colonialism is almost always a consequence of imperialism, "the implanting of settlements on distant territory."[11] In this study, colonialism refers not only to formal colonies established by the British in places like Australia and Canada, but also to the looser, semi-permanent British settlements in territories where the British were far outnumbered by indigenous peoples: settlements in India, in the South Pacific, in Asia, and in Africa. And the accumulation of colonies, formal or informal, makes up an empire. Britain's empire consisted not only of territories thousands of miles from Westminster, but was also made of annexed territory closer to home, in Ireland, Scotland, and Wales, which can be seen as England's first imperial possessions. And, finally, when I use *England* I mean to refer to England and English culture, excluding Scotland, Ireland and Wales; Britain and Great Britain refer to England with the addition of imperial possessions both close to home and far away, possessions that varied in number over the years. Therefore, the sentence, "The English have a long history of imperialism both within the British Isles and in overseas colonies, which by the nineteenth century led to a well-established British empire" is meant to be understood as "The ruling peoples of England, as opposed to Scotland, Ireland, and Wales, practiced imperial ideology both within the islands constituting present Great Britain and in overseas settlements in which they exercised great political, military, and/or economic control, leading eventually to the constitution of a British Empire."

There is no such thing as a concise history of the British Empire, and I will not attempt one here. That said, however, I would like to at least give a broad sketch of the rise of the British Empire, with particular emphasis on those elements that are especially important to the children's books I am examining here. Some imperial events—the Indian Mutiny, the Scramble for Africa, World War I—were especially influential upon children's texts. They will be discussed in greater detail in the context of the novels to which they are important. Here I would only like to give the broadest possible outline of the British Empire and of British nationalism, particularly from the mid-nineteenth century onwards.

The British Empire grew without a conscious plan, in a haphazard way, over many centuries. Early imperial expansion was commercial, not military or governmental in nature. The Hudson's Bay Company in North America and the British East India Company are two examples of commercial enterprises that wielded quite a lot of control over foreign territory. Colonial outposts were important sources of raw material for industrializing England, and as the years passed, they also became important markets for British manufactured goods. Various commercial enterprises had a series of agreements with the Crown regulating the power a company could exercise over indigenous peoples; the taxes it could or could not collect; the military forces (either mercenary or British) it had a right to deploy; and so on. The British government was not always an enthusiastic partner of colonial enterprise, fearing that expansion overseas could lead to either armed conflict with competing European powers (particularly the French and, later, the Germans) or to a drain on domestic capital. For a very long time the government preferred that the private sector take the economic gamble of investing overseas.

There was no single government office to oversee colonial outposts until 1801, when the Colonial Office was created as an appendage of the Home Office and the Board of Trade, reflecting the commercial beginnings of imperialism. By the 1850s, at which point Britain's empire was not only expanding, but was in increasing need of more centralized control and governance, the Colonial Office became a separate government department with the means to discipline and pressure colonial governments when necessary. No end of problems arose in the colonies, from appointed colonial governors who had private agendas and ignored Whitehall, to uprisings by indigenous peoples (the Indian Mutiny of 1857 and the Zulu War of 1879 among the most important of them), to conflicts with other European powers for control of foreign lands (struggles with the French over control of Egypt and with the Boer for control of the Transvaal).

Capitalism and political strategy were not the only impulses behind British imperial expansion: missionaries had a large role to play, and at times influenced government policy overseas, particularly in Africa. Pressure from missionaries and from abolitionists led to an 1807 prohibition of slave shipment in British ships or to the British colonies, and in 1833 slavery was abolished throughout the empire. Missionaries felt a Christian and humanitarian need to abolish human slavery, but they also felt they had a Christian duty to convert the "heathen." Missionaries often—necessarily—combined evangelism and exploration: they had to find the heathen before they could convert them. The most famous of these Christian missionary explorers was David Livingstone, who crossed Africa between 1852–56; who went back for a third time in 1866–73; and who was famously found by the American journalist Stanley in 1871. Livingstone's primary purpose was to Christianize and civilize African natives, but by traveling through the unmapped and dangerous African interior, he paved the way for commercial expansion and eventual British annexation of parts of Africa. The feats of Livingstone and other early explorers and missionaries in Africa cannot be overstated: the combination of tsetse flies and mosquitoes, sleeping sickness and malaria, not to mention daunting geography and antagonistic natives, made a nineteenth-century journey to the interior of Africa as dangerous as the first manned flight to the moon. Nonetheless, the chance of saving souls for Christ and the need for raw material proved irresistible to Europeans.

As the empire grew, it became increasingly difficult to control, which led to a number of conflicts with competing European powers. Russians had imperial intentions towards British-held India, and the British expended much energy in thwarting them (something Kipling explores in the Great Game in *Kim*). The Suez Canal opened in 1869, and, as the gateway to both India and East Africa, was of crucial importance to British trade. When there was an Arab uprising in northern Africa, Britain had to negotiate among British, Arab, and French interests. The British found themselves warring not only against African tribes, but against the independent Boer republics of South Africa. Germany, particularly under Kaiser William II at the end of the nineteenth century, set a course at making Germany's presence abroad commensurate with her industrial strength. Bismarck had seen colonies as an expensive luxury, but William II saw them as a means of gaining national prestige and of challenging British imperial domination—part of the complex of reasons leading to World War I.

World War I was the official beginning of the end of the British Empire, although there were signs of trouble decades earlier. Britain was on the winning side of the war, but at enormous cost: millions of European soldiers, many of them British, perished in the war, which was the first technological war, employing chemical weapons, artillery, and aircraft. At the end of it, national boundaries and national priorities had shifted. Britain's colonies had supplied both soldiers and raw materials for the war effort (a war that had colonial, as well as Western, fronts). By the time of the Paris Peace Conference, the dominion colonies had gained independent international recognition by becoming charter members in the League of Nations. In 1931 they achieved full equality with Britain in the Statute of Westminster, which gave full legislative authority to the dominions, although they could ally themselves with the Commonwealth of Nations, which most did. By the outbreak of World War II, the dominions made declarations of war independent of Britain's.

As the empire began to shrink, the language of nationalism and patriotism became more pronounced. It is no coincidence that at the end of the era of colonial expansionism we find the beginnings of the so-called Heroic Age of Exploration. This period really begins in Africa in the nineteenth century, with the search for the source of the Nile, but reaches its apex in polar exploration and in mountaineering, particularly in the years on either side of World War I. The race for the South Pole was couched in nationalistic terms similar to those that had been used to claim land in Africa at the end of the nineteenth century. The Antarctic landscape is the most forbidding landscape on earth, and whichever country could first lay claim to reaching the pole could have bragging rights to being the noblest and strongest nation in the world. There was absolutely nothing to gain at the pole except national pride and reputation: there were no resources or natives to exploit, no land to be developed and civilized.

But the national importance of the race for the South Pole can be seen in the reporting of such events as Robert Falcon Scott's failed 1912 expedition. Scott was bitterly disappointed that the Norwegian Roald Amundsen beat him to the pole by a mere month. Amundsen's expedition survived, but Scott and his men, poorly trained and supplied, froze to death on the eight-hundred-mile march back to camp. Nonetheless, Scott and his men became national heroes, and seemed to have some intimation that this was to be their fate, evidenced by letters written as they succumbed to Antarctic weather. Scott's final letter was addressed to the British public, and read in part, "[W]e are setting a good example to our countrymen, if not by getting into a tight place, by facing it like men when we were there."[12] The British lauded the amateur Scott for having failed "heroically" in the race to the South Pole, while dismissing Amundsen's successful team as mere foreigners. The British were still made of heroic, empire-building stuff, even if the boundaries of their post–World War I territory indicated otherwise, and even if the upstart Norwegians—who had had an independent country only since 1905—were first to the pole.

When the South Pole was no longer available as an emblem of national superiority, the British turned their sights to the mountains, and especially to the Himalayas. Britain had an advantage here over other Europeans because of her colonial holdings in India, and had been challenging the daunting eight-thousand-meter peaks of the Himalayas since at least 1848, when the great botanist J. D. Hooker (accompanied by the British Superintendent of Darjeeling) attempted Kanchenjunga, the third highest peak in the world after Everest and K2. Everest, named for Sir George Everest, for twenty years the Surveyor General of India, was not conquered until 1953. Even as late as this, exploratory feats were used to bolster national pride. The fact that Edmund Hillary (a New Zealander, and thus a product of empire) had summited Everest was announced to the British on Coronation Day, and the book by the *London Times* journalist who accompanied the mission was entitled *Coronation Everest*.[13] Unsworth, in his admirable book on the history of Everest mountaineering, writes:

> And so the British . . . had not only won the last battle but had timed victory in a masterly fashion. Even had it not been announced on Coronation Day it would have made world headlines, but in Britain at least the linking of the two events was regarded almost as an omen, ordained by the Almighty as a special blessing for the dawn of a New Elizabethan Age. It is doubtful whether any single adventure had ever before received such universal acclaim: Scott's epic last journey, perhaps, or Stanley's finding of Livingstone.[14]

Everest was important because it came at a time when other signs of imperial might were in short supply. The dominions had long since received full and equal status to Britain, but now colonies were agitating for independence. India, Pakistan, and Ceylon gain independence in 1947; the Gold Coast in Africa becomes the independent Ghana in 1957; Hong Kong reverts to Chinese sovereignty in 1997. At the height of the British empire, Britain controlled one quarter of the earth's landmass and one quarter of its population; today Britain has control over only thirteen small territories—the Falkland Islands, six territories in the Caribbean (including Monsterrat, rapidly becoming uninhabitable due to volcanic activity), and other small territories that would have difficulty surviving on their own, like Pitcairn Island. Closer to home, Scotland and Ireland are demanding more independence.

This imperial history plays out in children's novels from the end of the nineteenth century through to World War I and beyond. The future rulers of Britain learned imperial and cultural values from many venues, but among the most important is the literature provided them as children, the literature that is the focus of this study.

## NOTES

[1]William C. Dowling, *Jameson, Althusser, Marx: An Introduction to the Political Unconscious* (Ithaca: Cornell University Press, 1984), 115.

[2]Roderick McGillis, *The Nimble Reader: Literary Theory and Children's Literature* (New York: Twayne, 1996), 106.

[3]Ibid., 112.

[4]Patrick Brantlinger, *Rule of Darkness: Imperialism and British Literature 1830-1914* (Ithaca: Cornell University Press, 1988), 190.

[5]Ibid., x.

[6]Edward Said, *Culture and Imperialism* (New York: Knopf, 1993), xii.

[7]John M. Mackenzie's collection of essays, *Imperialism and Popular Culture* (Manchester: Manchester University Press, 1986) provides an excellent overview of imperial ideology of the period I am discussing here, and J. M. Magnan's *The Games Ethic and Imperialism* (New York: Viking, 1986) is an indispensable study of the relationship between imperialism and public schooling.

[8]Perry Nodelman, "The Other: Orientalism, Colonialism, and Children's Literature," *Children's Literature Association Quarterly* 17:1 (1992): 32.

[9]Jacqueline Rose, *The Case of Peter Pan: The Impossibility of Children's Fiction* (Philadelphia: University of Pennsylvania, 1984), xii.

[10]J. D. Stahl, "Introduction," Special Issue on Cross-Culturalism and Children's Literature, *Children's Literature Association Quarterly* 17:1 (1992), 50.

[11]Said, *Culture and Imperialism*, 9.

[12]Quoted in Marc Girouard, *The Return to Camelot* (New Haven: Yale University Press, 1981), 14.

[13]Jan Morris, *Coronation Everest* (London: Faber and Faber, 1958).

[14]Walt Unsworth, *Everest: A Mountaineering History* (Boston: Houghton Mifflin, 1981), 340.

# EMPIRE'S CHILDREN

# CHAPTER 1

# Setting Sail

The vast majority of literary references to empire refer to only two of Britain's imperial outposts: India and Africa. Although Britain's empire extended to the Caribbean, to South America, and to Southeast Asia, it was primarily India and Africa that captured the imaginations of writers for both children and adults. These countries, although real geographic places on the map, often functioned as fantasy lands and magical kingdoms in children's fiction. What Africa and India and other foreign territories hold out for children—and for adults as well—is the possibility of adventure. Because Britain had an empire, Britons had relatively easy access to exotic lands that promised adventure, romance, and riches beyond belief to those who chose to venture beyond England's shores. The story of empire is often presented as a kind of fairy tale, in which the valiant but unrecognized hero travels to strange realms, overcomes obstacles and villains, all in order to reach the pot of gold (or ivory, or spices, or oil, or rubber, or diamonds) at the end.

Children's stories of empire are common long before the appearance of the texts that are the focus of this book. A number of missionary tales for children have imperial plots—Mrs. Sherwood's "Little Henry and His Bearer" (1834), for example—and any number of evangelical tracts either encouraged child readers to work for the salvation of heathens or to consider emigration to one of the colonies as a means to a new beginning, both materially and spiritually. Frederick Marryat's *Mr. Midshipman Easy* (1836) combines evangelical fervor with the adventures of the Seagrave family, marooned on a desert island while emigrating to Australia. Charles Kingsley looks back in time for his historical adventure of Elizabethan expansionism in *Westward Ho!* (1855). In the mid-Victorian period there are dozens of novels (primarily meant for a juvenile male audience) that took empire as both setting and theme. There are several good histories of this kind of fiction available,[1] and rather than giving a summary of these texts, I would like to focus on probably the single most influential of these earlier novels, R. M. Ballantyne's *The Coral Island* (1858), which employs nearly all the images of empire that inform later children's fiction, even domestic fiction.

J. S. Bratton points out that *The Coral Island* has "an undoubted right to the status of children's classic" and "shows vividly the version of moral and social relations which an average Briton in the stirring world of the 1850s . . . wished to pass on to the rising generation."[2] Some of the virtues rewarded by both *The Coral Island* and other adventure fiction of the period include "dash, pluck, and lion-heartedness," qualities that tend to outweigh "obedience, duty, and piety."[3] The novel is not, on the surface, concerned with empire at all: three boys are shipwrecked on a Pacific island, where they live an idyllic and pastoral (if isolated) life until arcadia is invaded first by cannibals and then by pirates. Yet the underlying ideology of the novel is shot through with imperial values. The boys (and particularly the narrator, Ralph) want to rove "throughout the length and breadth of the wide, wide world." While this is a desire many young boys (and girls) may share, Ralph's status as Briton makes it possible for his wishes to come true. Because Britain is a nation heavily invested in foreign exploration and trade, activities supported by the strength of Britain's merchant marine and its naval forces, Ralph and his friends have a realistic route to fantasy adventure: they can join the merchant marine.

The swift movement of the story from coastal England to exotic Pacific island is similar to the swift movement from the real world to the fantastic in children's fantasy: Alice quickly abandons her domesticated sister to fall down the rabbit hole, and C. S. Lewis's children waste little time moving through the wardrobe to Narnia, for example. Fantasy novels want to move readers out of the realm of the ordinary as quickly as possible, and this holds true for adventure tales like *The Coral Island* as well. In adventure fiction, we appear still to be in the real world, but one that provides much more excitement and exoticism than can be found in dreary and domesticated England. The treatment of foreign lands as both realistic and fantastic is common in fiction of empire, as we shall see. In *The Coral Island,* as well as in Kipling's *Kim,* Ransome's *Missee Lee,* and other texts, much attention is paid to the details of local flora and fauna, of native customs, and so forth. There is a kind of ethnographic gloss to these books that suggests to the reader that foreign lands are not made-up fantasy lands, but real places that can provide real adventures, if only one can get to them.

If foreign lands and potential colonial holdings are perceived as realistic fantasy lands, if you will, one can only exploit them by importing some of the values of civilization, something made clear in *The Coral Island,* which stresses the importance of hierarchy and leadership. Ballantyne's boy heroes certainly understand this. Their leader is the oldest boy, Jack (as in Union Jack); second in command is the narrator, Ralph; and the third is the youngest and smallest, Peterkin. The hierarchy is clear: Jack is stronger and bigger, and has read enough books of foreign travel that he can recognize breadfruit trees and knows how to get life-sustaining liquid from coconuts; Ralph is full of both common sense and Christianity (he regrets losing his Bible and says his prayers every morning); Peterkin provides entertainment—his lesser status is indicated not only by his diminutive name and comic nature, but by the fact that he is the only boy who cannot swim, a serious drawback on an island paradise. But although Peterkin sometimes holds the other boys back, Jack and Ralph work together to make sure Peterkin survives. When threatened by pirates, for example, the two older boys help a frightened Peterkin to hold his breath and dive to an underwater grotto where they can hide. All three of the boys have a say in how to govern themselves and create their own society, although they also know when to defer to Jack's leadership. One of the novel's more exciting adventures concerns a shark attack. The three boys are floating on a log in deep water, fishing, when a shark begins to circle for the attack. When all appears lost, Jack says "Now obey my orders *quickly.* Our lives may depend upon it." He has a scheme for fending the shark off by jamming the oar down its throat at the last possible moment, but success depends upon the instant obedience of the other boys, who of course do as they are told and thus live to have further adventures.

The shark attack, as well as other incidents in *The Coral Island,* show the reader that adventures are possible, but are successful only if combined with some of the elements of civilized authority. Without such elements, one is left with William Golding's *Lord of the Flies* (1954), a novel which is among other things a retelling of *The Coral Island* . Golding's Ralph, Jack, and Piggy are caricatures of Ballantyne's Ralph, Jack, and Peterkin, and both *The Coral Island* and *The Lord of the Flies* share a "thematic concern with legitimate authority, leadership, and government."[4] Hierarchy, combined with democracy, leads the boys in *The Coral Island* to be successful in their adventures. The pirates they encounter have a strict hierarchy as well, but no democracy, and fail as a result. The natives have hierarchy but also savagery, and are the lowest of the low in the novel. One must have leaders, but leaders lead because they are respected and because followers have chosen them to lead, not because they wrest power for themselves. Of course, this holds true only within a racial and ethnic group: what is good for white Europeans may not necessarily apply to the "less advanced" natives Europeans encountered in their imperial conquests. Democracy can be understood and employed only by the civilized—the uncivilized benefit from the firm hand of a higher, nondemocratic authority.

These values of resourcefulness, hierarchy, and democracy can be found in fiction up to and beyond Kipling's *Stalky & Co.* (1899), and they are the values the British believed made them good imperial leaders. Resourcefulness is of primary importance, not only for boys stranded on Pacific islands, but also for boys destined to be imperial leaders. The boys in Ballantyne's novel start with even fewer resources than Crusoe: a broken and dull knife blade, the clothes on their backs, an oar with a bit of iron attached to it, a broken telescope, and—their most valuable possession—an ax. With these bits of flotsam and their own quick wits, the boys build shelter for themselves, make weapons, find food, and start fires with which to cook. This kind of resourcefulness was valued on the frontiers of empire, where civilized goods were hundreds if not thousands of miles away, and survival depended upon making the most of what one had at hand.

Even more important than physical resources, however, are the intellectual resources that allow the boys to know the value and potential use of what they have. After all, one could be sitting in the midst of endless bounty and not know how to make use of it—a complaint imperialists often made about the natives they encountered in Africa, India, and elsewhere, who seemed to Europeans to be wasting vast natural resources. The boys in *Stalky & Co.* make use of whatever is at hand—dead cats, leftover grease, a loophole in the rules—to win over their schoolmates, then take what they have learned off to India, where "stalky" behavior helps them subdue the natives. Ballantyne's boy heroes take the resourcefulness they have learned as underlings in the merchant marine and use it to survive on a deserted island, and ultimately to win over both cannibals and pirates: they conquer savagery, an underlying goal of imperialism.

The importance of both democracy and hierarchy will be seen again and again in children's novels that employ the imagery of empire. In Nesbit's tales of the Bastable children and Ransome's stories of the Walkers and Blacketts, children work in cohesive and democratic groups in order to arrange adventures for themselves, even if they must stay in England rather than sailing away to foreign ports. The children in these stories tend to defer to a leader—not always the same leader, but always a leader the children agree upon. When they do not agree upon who is to be leader, or some of the children disobey or ignore the orders of the leader, disaster follows: Roger is stranded on the mountain in *Swallowdale,* or the Indian uncle descends in wrath upon the Bastable children. Even tales that do not feature collective heroes, like Burnett's *A Little Princess,* still emphasize the importance of hierarchy and democracy. Miss Minchin has false authority and runs an empire with no democracy to it at all, and is punished for it in the end.

One reason resourcefulness and leadership matter is because they are the underpinnings of civilized domesticity. At first this appears paradoxical: how can adventure novels support the values of home and hearth?, particularly an adventure novel like *The Coral Island,* which has only one female character, Avatea, a native woman? Avatea is to be sacrificed by cannibals, and the word *sacrifice* provides the crucial link between adventure and domesticity. Whatever the actual reasons behind imperial conquests—be they mercenary, missionary, or military—there is a need to justify, if not idealize, one's often brutal actions in the pursuit of empire. One way of justifying one's actions is to demonize the native population (something Ballantyne does well) and another is to idealize the reasons underlying the conquest of foreign lands. Many writers suggest that monetary gain is only a pleasant side-effect of imperial intervention, and what the adventurers are really doing is both spreading civilization and upholding the values of dear and distant England, often personified as a female figure, either as Queen Victoria or other emblematic figures.

Victorian women were often perceived as figures of moral agency, perhaps most famously presented in the figure of the "angel in the house," the self-sacrificing woman responsible for the moral well-being of both husband and children, epitomized in Sarah Ellis's *Women of England* (1838) and Coventry Patmore's sequence of poems, *The Angel in the House* (1854–63). British imperial relations were often presented in familial terms, with England as the "mother country" and her colonial subjects as dependent children needing to be led to higher moral ground. The civilized values Britain wanted to bring to the colonies were often bound up with images and issues of family life. For example, one of the Indian customs much deplored by the British was that of suttee, the self-immolation of Hindu widows upon the funeral pyres of their husbands, and one of the most problematic (and also strangely exciting) problems in Africa was that of polygamy. Bringing civilization to the "savages" meant upholding the moral virtues epitomized by English womanhood, and thus, English womanhood often functioned as a convenient symbol for the virtues of civilization. Susan Meyer has suggested that "The domestic space of the home is at once an individual domicile and suggestive of the domestic space in a larger sense: the domestic space of England," and domestic space may not be separate from the concerns of imperialism.[5]

Although women and domestic space may function as useful symbols of English civilization, they are also problematic and tend to interfere with boyish adventure. *The Coral Island* presents the reader with a paradise uncomplicated by women. In the first half of the novel, women are only represented by Ralph's memory of his mother and his promise to her to pray daily. But by and large the boys provide domesticity for themselves and do not need women to show them how to make a comfortable "bower" or how to cook fish. We have an all-male paradise, a not-uncommon feature of adventure fiction: there is hardly a woman to be seen in Rider Haggard's *King Solomon's Mines* or John Buchan's *Prester John,* no sisters or mothers or wives to wring their hands and stand in the way of manly adventures. The lack of women reflects not only the limited possibilities for Victorian women and the wishful thinking of men, but also the reality of imperial enterprise, which was almost entirely a male endeavor. Most British contact with foreign lands came through commerce and through militarism, both of which excluded women. Women did have a place in missionary work, although they could not be missionaries without being attached to a husband or a brother (as St. John makes clear to Jane in *Jane Eyre*).

When a woman finally does make an appearance in *The Coral Island,* Ballantyne presents her in such a way as to allow his adventuresome boys to uphold virtuous womanhood without being in any danger of being trapped by domesticity themselves. Avatea, the native woman whom the cannibals wish to sacrifice, is interesting because, although she is not a white woman, she is lighter-skinned than the other natives. She is Samoan, and hence occupies a higher place on the racial ladder than do the darker-skinned cannibals. Ballantyne was influenced by Victorian theories of race and evolution, ideas that were in the air even before publication of Darwin's *The Origin of Species* (published just one year after *The Coral Island*). "Savages" were perceived as being childlike, remote ancestors of Europeans. Yes, they were human, and thus, distantly related to modern European humans, but they had not developed from savagery to civilization, and indeed were valued more for their "animal" qualities of physical strength than they were for their intellect. Morally and culturally, indigenous peoples occupied a much lower rung of the evolutionary ladder than did Europeans.

Avatea is worth saving because she is more European than the other natives, and provides an opportunity for the British Jack to prove his manhood by defending her. She is the stand-in for civilized values, since the reason she is being sacrificed is that she refuses to marry a native chief, her heart belonging to another Samoan. The chivalric ideal of true and monogamous love is grafted onto Avatea so that Jack may defend the ideal through her—and in doing so run no risk of being trapped in romance, marriage, and domesticity. She is not a threat as a potential wife not only because she is dark-skinned, but because she is already promised to another. Jack can act chivalrously and gallantly towards Avatea—and chivalry is one of the values important to the imperial mind, as we shall see.

As we have already seen in the scenes with the cannibals, the island that the boys once saw as their own is really a piece of contested territory, desired not only by the cannibals but also by a roving band of pirates. The boys realize early on, when they discover an abandoned hut and a desiccated skeleton, that they are not the first Western visitors to the island. They have also heard tales of native inhabitants of South Sea islands, and long before the cannibals show up, they—like Crusoe before them—fear their arrival. But until the boys actually confront the cannibals they, like imperial conquerors everywhere, reason that if they do not see any native inhabitants, such inhabitants must not exist, leaving the island free to be claimed by themselves. The battle for Avatea's life and honor is also a battle for control of the island: the forces of civilization versus the forces of cannibalism.

Without explicitly saying so, *The Coral Island* supports the boys' claim
to the island. Cannibals have a right to nothing except death, the novel suggests. They are presented in sensational language as being hardly human at
all. When they first appear they are described as being "almost entirely
naked," with "frizzed out" hair and bodies "black as coal," "tattooed" and
"besmeared with red paint," with "glittering eyes" that make them seem like
"terrible monsters" (173). When we see them in action, one of the cannibals
raises his club and fractures the skull of an enemy: "He must have died
instantly. . . . Scarcely had his limbs ceased to quiver when the monsters cut
slices of flesh from his body and, after roasting them slightly over the fire,
devoured them" (175). These are not the sort of beings who should be able to
lay claim to an island kingdom: they are anarchic and barbarous, and the
reader is meant to understand that they must either be Christianized and
hence humanized, or must be displaced or destroyed.

The cannibals are over-the-top stereotypes of the savage native, who
often shares fictional space with his opposite, the noble savage. One understands the savage native entirely after reading Ballantyne's description: savage natives are completely "Other," closer to animal than to human; they are
monsters; they are evil incarnate; they can—and must—be killed with
impunity. Their numbers are legion in popular fiction for boys, especially in
periodical fiction of the late nineteenth century, and they provide conveniently thrilling adversaries for boy heroes. Savage natives are unusual in the
children's classics I will be discussing here, largely because they are so identified with less worthy and less moral sensational fiction of the period.
Nonetheless, savage natives do show up to chase Doctor Dolittle through the
jungle and to threaten the lives of the Swallows and Amazons in *Missee Lee*.
In no serious writing for children, however, is the savage native described in
the vivid language of Ballantyne and other sensation writers.

More popular in classic children's books is the figure of the noble savage, more complex than the savage native, but still stereotypical. Noble savages tend to be more European in physiognomy than their fellow savage
natives; they struggle for the good of their people and sometimes even for a
more civilized (i.e., Western) life for them; they are strong and silent, but
respected by their fellow natives and, significantly, by Europeans; they are
willing to sacrifice themselves for the greater good. Avatea is clearly more
noble savage than savage native: she is proud, she is loyal to her own true
love, she is willing to die for that love rather than submit to a loveless marriage, and she does not fall into a quivering heap when facing death at the
hands of cannibals. Like other noble savages, Avatea has a number of admirable qualities that link her to the civilized, Western world, even though she
is clearly native and Other and not meant to be seen as an equal to Westerners.

Savages and natives in general are appealing characters to children.
Savages live outdoors rather than indoors; they don't pay much attention to

physical cleanliness; they wear few clothes or clothes that are more like costumes than like pinafores or trousers; they live closely with animals; they are crafty and have skills that allow them to win over competitors. The appeal of the noble savage is a romantic appeal: the noble savage escapes the constraints of civilization, but retains some of the essential moral characteristics of the civilized. This is the appeal of the noble savage to the adult reader, as well—a marriage of the best of the noble savage with the best of civilization is often the subtext beneath such novels as *King Solomon's Mines* and *Prester John,* not to mention *Robinson Crusoe.* The danger is that contact with the noble savage may corrupt one to the point that one "goes native." To some extent this happens to Jack in *The Coral Island:* he attacks the cannibals not after planning and organizing, but in a fit of blind rage as he goes "berserk," and in fact he is just as vicious as the cannibals, with the important exception that he is horrified by the idea of eating his enemies.

When a hero is not corrupted by native ways, he or she can benefit from them. In children's novels, one of the appeals of the noble savage is his skill in woodcraft, in living off the land. Through playing at Indian or savage, children in books are playacting the trials of growing up in their own world. Children expend a great deal of energy in trying to understand and navigate the world of adults; in fantasy play children can be successful at negotiating and understanding a world separate from adults. They become the subject, not the object, of the action. Kipling's Kim manages this play within the real world as he spies for the British and runs in disguise throughout India; the Bastables and Walkers (in the novels by Nesbit and Ransome) are more constrained by adults and are restricted to playing at building teepees, tracking animals, and battling enemies along the "Amazon" or at the head of the "Nile." Savages have a kind of freedom most children long for, but rarely achieve, and it is no surprise to find so many of them in the pages of children's novels.

Pirates are also common characters in children's fiction, and are appealing for many of the same reasons natives are: they live by their own rules, are seemingly free of authority, and have many more adventures than children restricted to nursery, garden, and school can have. They appear most famously in Stevenson's *Treasure Island* (1883), and his pirates influence every pirate to come after them. In Ransome's books, the Blacketts's Uncle Jim is more commonly known as "Captain Flint," the children fly a skull and crossbones for their flag and participate in pitched pirate battles and races upon their sailboats. But in *The Coral Island,* which predates Stevenson's influential novel, the pirates are not at all romanticized or even humanized: when they first appear, they kill a cat for sport, and Jack remarks "bitterly," "The man who will wantonly kill a poor brute for sport will think little of murdering a fellow-creature" (190), and when the boys decide they should flee to the protective underwater grotto, Ralph tells us that although they had always known the grotto would enable them to "take shelter from the savages," "little did we imagine that the first savages who would drive us into it would be white savages, perhaps our own countrymen" (193).

The pirates are condemned more thoroughly than the cannibals, because they have had the benefit of civilization and have turned their backs on it, "gone native." Before Stevenson romanticizes pirates for juvenile audiences, they tend to stand as warning signs for the reader. In Ballantyne's book, they are symbolic of at least two things. First, they symbolize what happens to humans when they "go native" and abandon their civilized ways. They become predators, as likely to turn on each other as on a common enemy. In this they are in direct contrast to the boys themselves, who as we have seen spend a great deal of time importing civilized values to their island, and who would never turn on themselves, but who would always band together to protect each other and vanquish the enemy, be it cannibal or pirate enemy. Second, the pirates can be seen as symbolic substitutes for foreign competition in imperial acquisition. Britain faced a great deal of competition from the French, the Portuguese, and others in their acquisition of colonial holdings, not to mention from indigenous peoples themselves. The struggle for control of Coral Island mirrors this imperial struggle: on the one hand are the undeserving cannibals and on the other, the undeserving pirates.

The pirates' actions can be seen as mirroring those of many imperial conquerors. They pass themselves off as sandalwood traders, but prefer piracy as an easier road to wealth, much as imperial invaders often claimed they were interested in opening up trade routes, when in fact they were mostly interested in taking what resources they could for as little as possible. Also like imperial invaders, the pirates are pragmatic and know that missionaries—although often tiresome—are also useful. As one of the pirates explains to Ralph, the pirate captain "knows, and everybody knows, that the only place among the southern islands where a ship can put in and get what she wants in comfort is where the Gospel has been sent to" (213), because "wherever the savages take up with Christianity they always give over their bloody ways, and are safe to be trusted" (221). The pirates exploit the missionaries in order to gain goods, just as imperialists exploited missionary work to help in the exploration and conquest of foreign lands. If Christianized natives will give up their "bloody ways," they are less likely to rise against foreign invaders; Christianized natives will want to emulate Westerners and become more civilized, which will have the effect of making European rule over them easier. Rulers can invoke the power of God as well as the power of the flag.

Significantly, the only pirate who is redeemed is Bill, who repents on his deathbed and is Christianized, and hence, his soul is saved—unlike those of the other pirates, who no doubt go straight to hell. Here Ballantyne combines the evangelical missionary tale with a tale of adventure and piracy on the high seas. The missionary zeal will largely disappear from children's books by century's end, and the pirates themselves will be tamed and domesticated within the boundaries of children's play, but the use of pirates and natives in the representation of empire will not disappear.

*The Coral Island,* then, presents the reader with a number of tropes that will appear again and again in children's books, tropes that suggest that empire and imperialism are good things: resourcefulness, leadership, pluck, moral virtue, and chivalry are qualities that make Ballantyne's boy heroes the rightful possessors of that island paradise: certainly the cannibalistic natives don't deserve it, nor do the marauding pirates. Neither group is Christian enough or civilized enough to know how to domesticate a foreign land and turn it to good use. The boys are more appropriate possessors of the island, and in the end of the novel aid a British missionary in Christianizing the natives, whom we last see building a church and giving a "loud cheer" to the departing boys. The boys themselves are homeward bound, leaving the island behind in the hands of the missionary and his converted natives, but significantly the ending of the novel is muted. The boys leave "with a thrill of joy, strangely mixed with sadness . . . for we were at length 'homeward bound', and were gradually leaving far behind us the beautiful, bright green coral islands of the Pacific Ocean" (339). We never see them arrive back in England, nor know what happens to them as adults, but their sadness in leaving the islands behind suggests not only their sadness at leaving childhood behind, but also at leaving the adventures of colonization behind. Even at the end of the novel, foreign lands beckon as potentially utopian shores—at least once they are Christianized and civilized.

The omnipresence of empire and its images in popular juvenile fiction is no surprise. Empire and exploration lend themselves to sensationalism, to exoticism, to ceremony, to jargon and lingo and secret societies, all of which have an appeal for children, and especially for boys of the period. But the omnipresence of empire in what are known as "classic" works for children is more surprising, and suggests how deeply the culture of empire was embedded in Britain, and how important adults thought empire was to the rising generation of children. The rise of imperialism is roughly contemporaneous with the golden age of children's literature (approximately 1860–1930), and the two grew up together. The books of this golden age, the classics under discussion here, were written by members of the ruling middle class and meant for a juvenile middle-class audience. We should not be surprised, therefore, to find prevailing middle-class attitudes about imperialism coloring the imaginative works written for children. Authors are not conscious of presenting empire in a positive light in their books, but they cannot help doing so: empire had as prominent and largely unquestioned a place in British society then as Disney does now. Empire and its effects were a part of everyday British life, and appear matter-of-factly in fiction for children. Like most imaginative literature, these classic children's texts do not set out consciously to propagandize for nation and empire, but they do so nonetheless.

Whether child readers were conscious of the imperial ideology in their books, and if conscious, whether they were swayed by it, is a moot point. The unconscious desire of the adult authors was to present the kind of adult world they wished children to grow up into and to rule themselves one day. Adult desires for children say more about the adults than they do about the children. Adult hopes and fears for children—for the future—are embodied in the hopes and fears they show children in texts meant for them. We can see this in the contemporary arguments and discussions over diversity and multiculturalism in children's books: there is a desire on the part of many (though perhaps not all, or even the majority) of adults to present children with a happily diverse and multicultural world, which is an adult vision of a utopian future, not a realistic vision of most children's lives today. There is a supersensitivity to derogatory language about race, ethnicity, and gender in children's books. For example, the Doctor Dolittle books have been edited to eliminate offensive words like "nigger" and offensive illustrations of large-lipped Africans. Ironically, the proponents of multiculturalism and gender equity rarely pursue the deeper ideological questions posed by children's books, either contemporary ones or those from earlier times. The majority of critics focus on listing and examining offensive stereotypes in books, not on looking at those stereotypes in a larger context. *The Little House on the Prairie* books contain offensive stereotypes of Indians, but few critics have looked at the novels from the perspective of the role of these stereotypes in the portrayal of Manifest Destiny, where believing Indians to be "savage" was necessary for settlers to justify their westward push. Those same "offensive" Doctor Dolittle books present a much more sympathetic picture of the woes of colonized people than, say, Burnett's *A Little Princess* does, but Burnett's novel has not suffered at the hands of censors, despite its problematic portrayal of Indians.

Children's fiction provides not only a glimpse of adult fears and desires, but also provides a way for cultural values to be transmitted over generations. While popular fiction, especially periodical fiction, has a short shelf life, classic works for children remain in print for generations: all of the classic works discussed here are readily available in paperback. One suspects that these books remain in print not because children are clamoring for them—my university students generally know only Burnett among these authors, although they are familiar with Dr. Dolittle through his film incarnations—but because adult teachers, parents, scholars, and historians deem them worthy. Because these books have remained in print and because they are still read, they have had an influence on the novels that followed them. Indeed, where attitudes towards empire are concerned, they have continued to be conveyed in British children's books well into the 1980s. The longing for empire, or at least for national importance, is reflected in children's books both of the golden age and our age. The next chapter will examine the writer most closely identified with empire and its literature: Rudyard Kipling.

**NOTES**

[1]See especially Martin B. Green, *Dreams of Adventure, Deeds of Empire* (New York: Basic Books, 1979) and J. S. Bratton, "Of England, Home, and Duty: The Image of England in Victorian and Edwardian Juvenile Fiction," in John M. Mackenzie, ed., *Imperialism and Popular Culture* (Manchester: Manchester University Press, 1986): 79–93.

[2]J. S. Bratton, Introduction to *The Coral Island* by R. M. Ballantyne (Oxford: Oxford University Press, 1990), vii.

[3]Martin B. Green, *Dreams of Adventure, Deeds of Empire* (New York: Basic Books, 1979), 214.

[4]Minnie Singh, "The Government of Boys: Golding's *Lord of the Flies* and Ballantyne's *Coral Island,"Children's Literature* 25 (1997), 208.

[5]Susan Meyer, *Imperialism at Home: Race and Victorian Women's Fiction* (Ithaca: Cornell University Press, 1996), 7.

# CHAPTER 2

# Kipling's Rules of the Game

Rudyard Kipling (1865–1936) is the logical beginning point for a study of empire and imperialism in children's books. His lifetime roughly coincides with the span of children's literature considered here and his writings consciously dealt with the anxieties and ambiguities of empire, anxieties and ambiguities reflected by other children's texts as well. Furthermore, Kipling's inspiration and obsession was India, the "jewel in the crown" of Britain's empire, and for many Englishmen synonymous with empire in a way that Africa, or Australia, or Jamaica was not. As V. G. Kiernan has pointed out, the "main patterns of all British colonial administration were formed [in India]; and to the public, empire with all its romantic associations meant chiefly India."[1]

Britain's—and Kipling's—connections with India were both romantic and complicated. British involvement in India began not with military or governmental intervention, but with the commercial interests of the British East India Trading Company, founded in 1600 in an attempt to break the Dutch monopoly of the spice trade. By 1657 the company was successful and powerful enough that the British government gave it the authority to coin money and to make war and peace with non-Christian powers in India, making the company the *de facto* governor of India, a role that was to expand over the years.

This uneasy mix of British commercial and quasi-governmental control prior to 1857 contributed to a number of internal problems in India (increasing unrest among certain native groups, growing gaps between the rich British and the increasingly poor Indians, internecine squabbling and plotting among the puppet princes) and ultimately to the Indian Mutiny of 1857. This Mutiny—which Kipling never wrote about as journalist or novelist, but which makes an appearance in the *Jungle Books,* of all unlikely places—was seen by the British as a savage and bestial attack on innocent men, women, and children; it caused hysterical street demonstrations in England; and ultimately brought horrible revenge upon the mutinous sepoys (native soldiers employed by the British Army), and civilian Indians who had supported the uprising. The Indians saw the Mutiny as the first battle in the Indian struggle for independence and referred to it as the Indian Rebellion, a more accurate term considering the numbers of civilian Indians involved in the revolt.[2] Ultimately, the Indian view turned out to be the correct one: by 1857 the sun still shone on the British Empire, but the sunset of Empire had already begun, in India and elsewhere.

Kipling was born in India, a complex and contradictory country of jungle and desert, mountain and plain, drought and monsoon; a country populated by a bewildering number of ethnicities and religions, languages and customs; a country with large numbers of native princes, but ultimately under the rule of white Europeans. That such a country spawned as contradictory and at times confounding a writer as Kipling is not surprising.

Kipling has posed difficulties for critics since he first began to publish. Elliot L. Gilbert begins the 1965 introduction to *Kipling and the Critics* by noting that "It would be difficult to think of another artist, dead thirty years, who continues to be at once so popular and so cordially hated as Rudyard Kipling is today."[3] Robert Buchanan, in 1900, asked "How, then, are we to account for the extraordinary popularity of works so contemptible in spirit and so barbarous in execution?"[4] In 1929 Bonamy Dobrée wrote that "The more one reads Kipling, the more complex and baffling he becomes."[5] This is as true today as it was seventy years ago. Zorah Sullivan has noted that Kipling's fiction "negotiates an uneasy series of truces between the resistance of the self to the authority of empire . . . and the antithetical longings for empire."[6] Others have pointed to Kipling's complexities and ambiguities as well. The difficulties certainly exist in the Indian fictions—*Kim* celebrates the life and variety of India, but also celebrates Kim's initiation into the British secret service that helps Britain rule India—but also pervade the non-Indian works. For example, *Puck of Pook's Hill* celebrates British history and "Britishness," but has as its heroes some of the invaders and colonizers of Britain. What is one to make of such a complex and contradictory writer? What, especially, is one to make of these complications when they appear in works for children?

The focus of this book is on the ways in which British children's literature incorporates and encourages British imperialism; therefore, the examination of the texts that follows looks at Kipling's work in this very narrow way—although with Kipling, what begins as narrow either broadens and muddies or constricts and becomes twisty and contradictory sooner than one can blink. Volumes have been written on Kipling and his portrayal of and attitudes toward British imperialism; *Kim* and *Stalky & Co.* in particular have been examined in this light. Less has been written on the impact of imperialism in the works Kipling meant more for children, especially *Puck of Pook's Hill, Rewards and Fairies,* and the *Jungle Books.* Kipling is both more straightforward and more pedagogical about empire and imperialism than later British writers could be, and in his stories of growing to maturity one can see, despite the complexities, some of the common themes that were to be reflected in many British children's books throughout the first third of the twentieth century.

Although Kipling's texts range from the fantastic to the realistic, they share a common concern with invasion, and invasion is clearly linked with issues of empire and imperialism. In *Kim,* for example, the eponymous hero is the son of a deceased Irish soldier. Kim belongs to a people colonized by the British, identifies with Indians colonized by the British, yet grows up to be the agent of the British invaders and colonizers of India. The *Jungle Books* give us Mowgli, an intruder first in the jungle, later in the village, where not only does he invade what should be his homeland, but with the help of outside animal allies, tramples the village to pieces. *Puck of Pook's Hill* ostensibly provides Dan and Una the opportunity to meet heroes of the British past, but a number of those "heroes" turn out to be foreigners who invaded England— Roman centurions and Normans among them. *Rewards and Fairies,* the sequel to *Puck of Pook's Hill,* gives us heroic French and Americans, both of whom have histories as enemies of England. *Stalky & Co.* is a series of tales of schoolboy invasions into enemy houses and into the studies of schoolmasters by boys who are being specifically trained to be colonial soldiers and leaders.

Another common theme in nearly all of Kipling's writing is a longing and search for a home. In *Kim* and the *Jungle Books,* especially, the heroes are caught between worlds, comfortable to different degrees in two or more cultures, but at home nowhere. The children in the two Puck books do have a home, in fact an ancestral home with a long history, but they, too, are caught between the worlds Puck invites them into and the childhood world they inhabit when not in his company. The boys in *Stalky & Co.* live in a school that is an intermediary home between their family homes and the wider adult home in the world they will find in colonial service.

Kipling's obsession with home and belonging is caused in part by his own homeless state: born in India, banished to England for schooling, he returned to India, but spent much of his adult life moving restlessly between Africa, Vermont, England, and points between. He was looking not so much for a domestic home as he was for a national home, a country and set of values he could claim. Kipling's lack of a sense of national origin and national home accounts, in large measure, for his obsession with empire and imperialism. Although he clearly suffered psychologically in his banishment from India to England, the effects of this banishment show up not in fictional dramas of family life, of psychological separations from and losses of family, but rather are reflected on the broader scale of dramas of *nations* as families, and of protagonists who struggle to belong to a national "family" either by masquerading as Other (as in *Kim*) or by marrying into or adopting a foreign culture as one's own (as in some of the short stories). Even when, as an adult, Kipling settles at last in Sussex and writes the *Puck* stories, he does not seem entirely at home. The Puck books are a search for the essential nature of Britons and Britain itself. Written for his own children, the stories seem to be an effort to provide them with the sense of national home that Kipling himself lacked.

Kipling's work also often concerns itself with the differences and the intersections between play and work. The metaphor for the British Secret Service in *Kim* is "The Great Game," and Kim sees much of his work for Creighton as being part of a vastly amusing game, albeit one with serious consequences in the adult world. Mowgli finds being schooled in the Law of the Jungle hard work, but the work often dissolves into a game with Bagheera, Baloo, or Kaa. For the children in the Puck books, their relationship with Puck is a playful one—they draw him forth through their fantasy play, and can often be seen playing in the books—but Puck, although he amuses Dan and Una with visitors from the past, also teaches the children British history. His goal is not to amuse, but to teach—to teach through amusement and play.

These themes of invasion, of a search for and definition of a national home, of intersections between work and play, adult world and child world, are linked to any interrogation of empire and literature. Obviously, invasion is necessary in the formation of empire, either mercantile or military invasion or a combination of the two. Definitions of *home,* in a nationalistic sense, are complicated by empire. Is "home" merely England, or is it also the further-flung empire? Are colonials like Kipling always looking towards the "home" of an England they perhaps have never seen, or does the colonized country become "home"? In what ways is England re-created in colonial lands as an echo of "home"? And (although the current study will not directly address this issue), what of the peoples whose "homelands" have been invaded by foreigners? In other words, how do "home" and "nation" shift their meanings in the context of imperialism? The idea of home is linked to another common metaphor for empire, that of family, with Queen Victoria and England as mother, and colonized peoples as children too immature and volatile to govern themselves, and thus, dependent upon an older and wiser nation (i.e. adult, parent). Children—both literal children and the metaphorical "child" subjects of the empire—often play at being adults, and through this play learn some of the lessons of empire.

The themes of home, family, and play are contextualized by empire in many works for children between about 1880 and World War II. Kipling was important not only as one of the first writers to embody these themes, but also as a writer who had a direct influence on many of the children's writers who followed him. *Kim* (1901)[7] is "particularly imperial . . . and depends upon an imperial framework."[8] Despite its adolescent hero, *Kim's* assignment to the category of children's text is problematic, given its complexities of language, structure, and history. Nonetheless, the novel is important to understanding both Kipling's vision of childhood and his vision of empire.

The first image we are presented with in *Kim* is of Kim himself, sitting "in defiance of municipal orders, astride the gun Zam-Zammah . . . Who hold Zam-Zammah, that 'fire-breathing dragon', hold the Punjab, for the great green-bronze piece is always first of the conqueror's loot" (49). To attain his perch upon the cannon, Kim has displaced a native boy. Here is Kim, who the second paragraph informs us is English, forcefully taking the place of a native boy upon the cannon, thus showing Kim (symbolically) to be ruler of all the Punjab. Kim is a member of the ruling, conquering, white race that does have control over India, even if he himself does not yet know this. He and the Indian boy may be equal as boys, but Kim's white heritage makes him the Indian boy's superior—even if Kim is masquerading as native at the moment.[9] Furthermore, Kim's whiteness will make him the superior to many of the Indian adults in the novel: his age is less important than his ethnicity. This is the same power of whiteness we saw at work in *The Coral Island,* where three British boys can rout a large force of dark-skinned adult natives, and will see again in Mary Lennox's treatment of her ayah (Indian nurse) and Dr. Dolittle's interactions with Africans.

Kim is superior to both adult and child natives, but his relationship to adult whites is more complex. Kim does seem superior to the rather dull-witted British soldiers who are not aware that Kim is spying upon them and who later fail to recognize his skills; superior to the whites who govern his school (whose rules and regulations Kim subverts); but he is inferior to Colonel Creighton, the British officer who recruits him for the Secret Service. Kim, in fact, respects and obeys only those white adults who see that he is an extraordinary boy, with extraordinary talents. No wonder *Kim* has appeal for adolescent readers: the hero is a special boy, marked by special talents, who lives largely free from adult supervision in an exotic and exciting land where he has adventures involving horse-stealing, spying, and masquerading in native costume. The child reader is enticed by these qualities of Kim. But Kim has other qualities as well, qualities that link him to the ruling adult whites of India, and the reader attracted to Kim and his adventures may also find him or herself attracted to some of the imperial underpinnings of the novel.

This opening scene presents military control of India as a central metaphor, and *Kim* takes place post-Mutiny, when England had taken control of the country and its government largely by military means, a military made up of both British troops and sepoy troops (officers, of course, always being British). Kim's uncertain status—Indian or English?—suggests that he is a

sort of civilian sepoy, native in looks and appearance (if not actually in ethnicity), yet ultimately loyal to the military and the government that keeps
India under colonial control. Sepoys, in fact, can never truly become members of the class to which they are loyal. The novel makes this clear in the figure of Hurree Babu, who is intelligent and well-educated, an ethnographer,
who has the unrealistic aspiration of being elected a fellow of the British
Royal Society, an ambition he ironically shares with Creighton. But Hurree
Babu is a comic character, overweight and prone to mangling British idiom,
an example of a common native type that we will meet in the works of other
writers as well: the humorous native whose humor is linked to his impossible
attempts to be a part of the colonizing class, not a part of the class of colonized Others to which he belongs.

Kim's Indian masquerade and his first appearance atop the cannon suggest both Indian complicity in British rule as well as the latent instability of
that rule. The cannon is "always first" of the conqueror's loot, suggesting that
there has been more than a single conqueror over the ages, and that just as
Kim has displaced one owner of the cannon, Kim (and by extension the
British) may also someday be displaced. India has a long history of invasion,
of internal conflict, of wars between moguls and princes, between various
ethnic and religious groups, and has not had many periods where it has
enjoyed a stable and far-reaching central government. Kipling, well-aware of
India's history, was also aware that Britain's power had been seriously challenged by the Indian Mutiny and continued to be challenged by competing
imperial powers, primarily the Russians, who aspired to overthrow British
imperial rule in India. Kipling knows that empires rise and fall, and that
Britain's time in India might be limited.

The instability of the imperial discourse in the novel continues in the
opening chapter, as the lama appears. Of this man, Kim says, "he is no man of
India that *I* have ever seen" and of course, he is not, he is a lama from Tibet,
another outsider like Kim, another potential invader. The lama asks about the
"Wonder House," the museum at Lahore in front of which the cannon stands,
and is shown inside by Kim to meet the British curator. The Wonder House is
filled with "friezes of figures in relief, fragments of statues and slabs crowded
with figures that had encrusted the brick walls of the Buddhist [temples] of
the North Country and now, dug up and labeled, made the pride of the
museum" (54). The artifacts are no longer the pride of India or of Buddhists,
but of European collectors, whose relationship to the artifacts is akin to the
relationship of colonizer to colonized: artifacts and colonized alike are
labeled, ordered, and controlled by Europeans and by European cultural values. Their country having been stripped of its culture, natives must now come
to the museum to see their culture out of context, to see in fact not their culture, but the European view of their culture and its meaning.

Sight is an important metaphor both here at the beginning of the novel
and throughout. The curator of the museum, noticing that the lama squints

through his glasses, gives him his own crystal lenses in trade. Thus, the lama will see India partly through English and partly through his own Tibetan eyes, and the curator will have gained yet another artifact and another perspective, Tibetan, through which to view India. Kipling's inclusion of the lama ensures that his novel will provide—or at least seem to provide—a multiple set of outsider eyes with which to view the bewildering complexity of India. The lama also allows Kipling to comment further upon Kim's nature. Kim becomes the lama's "chela" or apprentice, technically his subordinate. Yet the reader never believes in Kim's inferior status, not only because he genuinely loves the aged man, but because he is, ironically, the lama's protector and provider. It is Kim who takes the begging bowl to beg for food, Kim who knows the roads through India, and Kim who can arrange rail transport when necessary. At the end, it is Kim who physically defends the old man from foreign attackers.

The relationship of Kim and the lama is complicated in a way typical of Kipling. The adult/child relationship at first seems reversed, with Kim taking on the role of protector. But when Kim is discovered to be British and must go to school, it is the lama who provides his school fees, thus putting Kim back in the role of child and making the lama a kind of father figure. Kim is genuinely fond of the lama, but part of his attraction to the old man is based on the colonial urge for possession and appropriation. Tellingly, it is outside the Lahore museum that Kim first makes the acquaintance of the lama: "This man was entirely new to all his experience, and he meant to investigate further, precisely as he would have investigated a new building or a strange festival in Lahore city. The lama was his trove, and he proposed to take possession" (60). Yet, once again, Kipling complicates the matter by telling the reader that "Kim's mother had been Irish," reminding us of Kim's status as colonized, rather than colonizer, and also implying a genetic or ethnic basis for his curiosity and inquisitiveness, from a nineteenth-century point of view.

Kim's relationship to the lama is linked to another of the novel's themes, that of transformation. Both Kim and the lama are outsiders in India, free of caste and of family attachments, and thus free to transform themselves in ways not open to caste-bound Indians. The lama is on a quest to escape the Wheel of Life, to transform himself into a higher spiritual being. Kim, too, is attracted to transformation. He consciously disguises himself and switches from language to language in order to blend in with the local population (going so far as to dye his skin at one point), and he is an unconscious participant in his own transformation from child to adult. Significantly, it is only when Kim can resist seeing the vision of the transformed jar that Lurgan Sahib wants him to see that he is ready to take his place as an adult player in the Great Game: he must learn to separate truth from illusion, stability from instability. And of course, the transformation that underlies all the others is the transformation of India from a collection of independently ruled states to a single country ruled not by Indians, but by Englishmen. Kipling appears to be suggesting that just as Kim's transformation, though it may involve losses for him, is both inevitable and largely for the good, so too is India's transformation.

The theme of transformation, however, is at times undercut, or at least complicated, by Kipling's adherence to racial typing, which would seem to preclude transformation. When Kim is teased by older boys, we are told that "Where a native would have lain down, Kim's white blood set him upon his feet" (94). Elsewhere we are told that Kim "was Irish enough by birth to reckon silver the least part of any game" (84). The racial typing of Kim as Irish, and hence as outsider within English society, is compatible with contemporary English views of the Irish. The Irish were frequently characterized as animalistic and alien in the press of Kipling's time. The nineteenth-century ethnographer Robert Knox wrote that "human character, individual and national, is traceable solely to the nature of that race to which the individual or nation belongs,"[10] and Kipling's Kim has a number of traits Victorians would have seen as quintessentially Irish: he is acquisitive, crafty, quick and witty with his tongue, and "Friend to All the World," a charmer.

If Kipling is prone to describe his hero Kim in ethnographically stereotypical ways, he is even more inclined to do so with the Indian characters in the novel. For one thing, the Indians are often lumped together in a group as "Orientals," their otherness obscuring for the British the many cultural variations within Indian society. The English Bennet says that "My experience is that one can never fathom the Oriental mind" (136), and Colonel Creighton (himself an ethnographer) says, "The more one knows about natives the less one can say what they will or won't do" (159). When we meet individual Indian characters, they tend to fall into stereotypical categories. Hurree Babu is the comic native who apes British behavior and values[11]; Mahbub Ali is the shifty horse dealer who will help only when helping is to his own benefit; and when Lurgan Sahib (born in India, not in England) "goes native," he falls into the category of "mysterious and magical oriental." Even the lama is treated in a fairly stereotypical way, as the wise sage who cannot find his own way in our physical world.

But in a sense the racial typing does not undercut the theme of transformation. Both Kim and the lama end up as their true selves, back where they belong in the world: Kim as a member of the ruling British class, the lama back in his beloved northern mountains, wiser if not successful through his attempts to escape the Wheel of Life. What both Kim and the lama discover is the true self, not the disguised self. Kim can use disguise most successfully when he knows who it is he is disguising: he finds the answer to his frequent question, "Who is Kim?" The lama discovers that, as a living and breathing human being, he can never escape the Wheel of Life, but his greater understanding of that wheel permits him to be true to his self and his being, to be a better lama. And if this is true for Kim and the lama, what is true for India? Is she finding her true self through the transformations wrought by British intervention into her affairs? Or is she being transformed and disguised? In other words, is the empire a good or a bad thing for India? Kipling seems uncertain in *Kim,* but by and large the body of his writing suggests that he is in favor of British control of India.

Edward Said has written that it is at "the moment when a coincidence occurs between real control and power, the idea of what a given space was (could be, might become), and an actual place—at that moment the struggle for empire is launched."[12] This is the relationship that exists in Kim's India: there is an idea of control and power, represented by that cannon and those spectacles and, later, by the mapping and naming and control of Indian geography; there is the reality of India as it *is* next to India as it *could be* (India as complex, disordered, disunified versus India transformed and ordered by British law and railroad timetables). There is a similar correspondence between what Kim is or appears to be (Hindustani orphan) and what he can become (important player in British imperial policy); between what the fantasy friendship of boy/adult, colonizer/colonized, Christian/Buddhist is and what the reality would be. Imperial spaces, in other words, are spaces of possibility, spaces where the empowered can see their power reflected, spaces in which various fantasies can be played out by the colonizers.

And, of course, children themselves are spaces of possibility, territory upon which we can project our wishes, desires, and fears. Parents do this all the time with children, but a society can do it as well, projecting its hopes and fears for its future upon its children. Children, like colonial territory, provide a means by which adults can see their own power reflected: children provide an "other" by which we may define ourselves. The crucial difference, of course, is that children grow into adults, leave their colonized status to become the colonizers. Unlike Hurree Babu, they can expect someday to be permitted into the equivalent of the Royal Society. And if these children will someday be empowered adults, the current adults have a vested interest in seeing that these children grow up internalizing the values the adults hold dear. In Kipling's time—and, as I will argue, for far longer than has been realized—those values include the idea that empire is good and valuable and must be maintained, both by current adults and the adults of the future, including the child readers of *Kim* and their descendants.

Kipling's novel is not only a fantasy about idealized relationships between colonizer and colonized, but also about idealized relationships between adults and children, and, in fact, between adulthood and childhood. The adult Indians in the book—especially Mahbub Ali and Hurree Babu— exist in a childlike, subservient relationship to Creighton and many of the other colonizers. Mahbub Ali, for example, is also known as "C251B," who provides the British rulers with information about "explorers of nationalities other than English" and with "a small portion of that vast mass of 'information received' on which the Indian Government acts" (69). His Indian name is obscured and his identity obliterated by his official number, and he is valuable to the English only because he provides them with information that will help them to maintain colonial power. In other words, he is valuable because he participates in maintaining his own colonized and childlike state, because he participates in the Great Game of espionage, which benefits not his country, but his colonizers. And he is happy about this state of affairs, because he stands to benefit individually, if not communally.

Zorah Sullivan, in writing about the fantasy nature of friendships in this novel, refers specifically to the relationship between the lama and Kim when she writes "What appears to be a boy's adventure story is also a complex fantasy of idealized imperialism and colonialism, and the friendship between Kim and his lama is Kipling's fable of the ideal relationship between the Englishman (ever a boy at heart) and the Indian—eternally passive, unworldly, and childlike."[13] The fable that she refers to is that interracial friendships are not only possible, but may indeed be truly loving and, to some extent, equal. Her argument is complicated, however, by the fact that the lama is Tibetan, not Indian, and the British never had colonial control over Tibet (which has its own complicated colonial history with China). Kim does not have any comparable relationships with Indians in the novel: he jokes with Mahbub Ali, suggesting a shared status; but he also does Mahbub's bidding, and at the same time undercuts his orders with his own actions. In the end he is Mahbub Ali's "boss" in some senses, having risen in the ranks of the Secret Service. In fact, his subservient status to Mahbub Ali suggests an apprentice stage that he will outgrow, and his cleverness suggests he will outdo all his mentors in the end. And even the lama, who appears to be Kim's mentor on the Grand Trunk Road, is, in fact, dependent upon Kim's worldly knowledge. By the end of the novel Kim uses his relationship with the lama as cover in order to complete a spy mission in the north of India, thus subverting Eastern spirituality to the causes of Western colonialism.

What does a child reader take away from such a story? While it is impossible to say what every child takes away from a book, there are certainly ideas and ideologies that a child could and probably does take from this book, especially considering that its ideology was by no means isolated in this particular novel, but could be found in everything from boys' periodical fiction to Baden-Powell's Boy Scout movement to music hall songs. *Kim* does suggest that British rule over India is a good thing. As one small and concrete example, trains—brought by the British—are seen as beneficial by the Indians. The lama is told by a Sikh passenger on the train not to be afraid, for "This thing is the work of the Government" (75), and the following pages treat the reader to conversations among the passengers in which the train is praised as being both a money-saver and a time-saver, as being a means for democratizing Indian society by making various castes sit shoulder to shoulder, and as an aid in quelling an uprising of a border tribe against British construction of a road in 1877. Even the Indians see the British road as superseding Indian factionality.

Another idea a reader might take from the novel is the sense that childhood, or at least adolescence, is preferable to adulthood, unless adulthood can be played as an adolescent game. Kim's childhood on Indian streets is romanticized: he does not seem to suffer from hunger, or disease, or maltreatment, or any of the other woes a solitary child in the crowded streets of Lahore or Amritsar might endure. His is a childhood filled with exotic and delicious-sounding food, with adults to be outwitted, with games and spying and playing and unfettered movement across the country. Who would not want such a childhood, free of adult concerns and constraints, in a country forever warm and fragrant? But Kim's heritage as a British subject, as well as his impending manhood, condemn him to school, an institution that with its physical and mental constraints, bland, Westernized foods, and emphasis on learning adult skills and rules stands in direct, and not kind, comparison to the ideal childhood Kim has had up to this point. Kim wants to go to the bazaar to buy sweets, but is told that it is "out o' bounds" to the schoolboys, even though "Kim did not know what bounds meant" (148). At school, the "strong loneliness among white men preyed on him" (151).

But of course Kim ultimately has his way, and strikes a deal whereby he will stay in school, but will be free on holidays to pursue his travels with the lama, and when he grows up, although he ostensibly has been trained as a surveyor—a measurer of colonial holdings—his real work is to play at the Great Game of spying. If Kim must grow up and must work, as all white men must, at least he can have a life like that of Colonel Creighton's, "a man after his own heart—a tortuous and indirect person playing a hidden game" (165). He has his cake and eats it too.

But the Indian setting of the novel is crucial, because India provides opportunities that England does not. England, Kipling's novel obliquely suggests, is full of rules and dullness and stodginess and known quantities. Setting Kim's story in India gives Kim opportunities he could not possibly have in civilized England. The exotic setting is essential to the story of a boy who grows to be a man but still somehow manages to stay a boy. This is one of the great attractions of colonial spaces: they provide a landscape of opportunity, of escape not only from home, but from adult responsibilities and from adulthood itself. Yet at the same time, being alone (or nearly alone) in a colonial landscape means one is self-sufficient. It is no wonder that stories of empire, adventure, and colonization were so appealing to boy readers of the time period, who could move on from adolescents playing at adulthood in *The Coral Island* to adults playing at adolescence in the novels of Kipling, Haggard, and others.

Kim, of course, escapes his author's fate, and is never exiled to damp and gloomy England—school is as close as he comes. In that sense, *Kim* is

Kipling's fantasy alter-ego, the boy who never had to leave India or give up Indian ways, who found a way to stay in the first and best home, one that Kipling longed for most of his life, even though he knew he could never recapture what India had been to him in his childhood.

Kipling's other major Indian work for young readers is the *Jungle Books*.[14] There are two major categories within these tales, the tales featuring Mowgli and those from which he is absent (among the latter are two tales of the Arctic, which fit only very loosely with the other tales). Mowgli's story, as critics have noted, can be seen as a story of initiation into manhood; a story of an Edenic paradise from which Mowgli must eventually be excluded; as a story of the importance of order and the Law of the Jungle, which is not "eat and be eaten," but rather a pragmatic moral code that rules all the animals of the jungle. The Mowgli stories—the ones best known and best-loved by child readers and best-remembered by adults—are not overtly concerned with imperialism, although John McBratney has argued that the *Jungle Books* broaden "the terms of imperial identity" through a "subtle handling of imperial space,"[15] and Don Randall has argued that the *Jungle Books* provide a kind of post-Mutiny allegory.[16] Randall asserts that "Post-Mutiny allegories—that is, narrative sequences organized upon allusive evocations of Mutiny scenes, situations, and events—occur most notably in the Mowgli tales of *The Jungle Books*" (98), and "at the same time, the story of British India [is presented] as allegorized form, as imperial fable" (100). While Randall's assertion that *The Jungle Books* are specifically post-Mutiny tales is not entirely persuasive (with the exception of the tale "The Undertakers," discussed below) his broader assertion that the tales are informed by imperialism is valid, and has not been noted much by critics.

My own focus is on the non-Mowgli *Jungle Book* tales set in India, but to put these tales in context it is useful to consider the imperial framework of all the *Jungle Book* tales. Randall asserts that "Kipling's Indian jungle is not simply a culturally unmarked 'world'; it is India as jungle,"[17] a seemingly confusing and confused space, which nonetheless has an internal code or law that Mowgli masters and, to some degree, he has the power to shape and change by the end of his story. Mowgli can be seen as invader or colonizer of the jungle, one who is changed by the jungle as he himself changes it. The native animal inhabitants of the jungle tell him again and again that "man must return to man," and that the colonizing man-cub can never be a natural part of the jungle (256).

Reading Mowgli as an allegorical imperial colonizer of the jungle is problematic, however. Mowgli must abide by the animals' rules and Law, even if he can dominate them with his human gaze. He does not exploit the resources of the jungle, but lives in harmony with them, and even fights on the side of the animals in his battle with Shere Khan. He is ultimately exiled from the jungle. Most importantly, Mowgli is no Tarzan, no European boy raised by jungle animals, but an Indian boy. This alone would problematize his status as imperial proxy, but his situation is further complicated by the fact that when he returns to the village to rescue his parents, his human mother and father must flee for aid to British order and law in a cantonment some miles away. The British surround and contain the village and jungle, Mowgli and the animals: Mowgli, although he does not realize it, is as much colonized as colonizer.

However, the non-Mowgli stories set in India often specifically mention the British Empire, or use episodes in British imperial history as plot devices for the animal tales. The first of these stories is perhaps the best-known and best-beloved, "Rikki-tikki-tavi." The hero is an endearing young mongoose, described as being catlike, yet somehow foreign and exotic: "His eyes and end of his restless nose were pink; he could scratch himself anywhere he pleased with any leg, front or back, that he chose to use; he could fluff up his tail till it looked like a bottle-brush, and his war-cry as he scuttled through the long grass was: Rikk-tikk-tikki-tikki-tchk!" (117). Although Kipling could have given us an allegorical initiation tale of the mongoose without including humans at all, he instead gives us Rikki-tikki facing adulthood rites in the garden and bungalow of a British colonial officer, his wife, and young son. Yet unlike many animal fantasies where authors include human characters as a kind of bridge into the fantasy of talking animals (one thinks of *Charlotte's Web,* for example), the humans in this story are apparently secondary to the central plot of snake-killing. However, their very presence gives the story an imperial subtext, one that is apparent in every one of the non-Mowgli Indian stories.

Rikki-tikki, when swept away from his family's burrow in a flood, ends up bedraggled in the garden of the British family, whose son Teddy first thinks the small animal is dead. The father, however—who, it becomes clear, is much more conversant with India and its wildlife than his wife or child—suggests they dry it off and see if it is alive, and he also patiently tells his wife that the mongoose will not hurt their son, that indeed the mongoose may be useful to them. The animal is allowed to sleep with the son because, as the father says, "Teddy's safer with that little beast than if he had a bloodhound to watch him. If a snake came into the nursery now—" (119). The mother will take some convincing, however.

Rikki is pleased to be living with the family, and especially with their young son, because "every well-brought-up mongoose always hopes to be a house-mongoose someday" (119). Rikki earns his keep by killing first a small (but dangerous) snake in the garden, and then the larger and more deadly cobras who are intent on killing both the family and Rikki-tikki himself. After his first kill, he denies himself the pleasure of eating it, because "he remembered that a full meal makes a slow mongoose," (122) and he has other snakes to kill. His self-denial is emphasized a paragraph later, when that night at the family's dinner table "he might have stuffed himself three times over with nice things," but he remembers the two cobras in the garden, and as he is petted by Teddy and his mother, his eyes go red and he repeats his war-cry.

Although this is an animal fable, the presence of the humans gives the story a peculiar British twist. Rikki-tikki is between domesticated and wild, both catlike and weasel-like, as the narrator tells us. He finds himself between the worlds of the domesticated and the wild in the family garden, which is only "half-cultivated," and contains hybrid roses as well as bamboo, a garden containing poisonous snakes that threaten the idyllic life of the colonizers. The "half-wild" garden the British family has invaded and colonized is a metaphor for India itself, a garden-paradise harboring dangerous "natives" in the form of the snakes who resent the intrusion of humans into their kingdom. The colonizers—the British family—are incapable of fully taming the garden of India without help from cooperative natives. Rikki-tikki, in fact, can be seen as one of these helpful natives. The bungalow is conspicuously free of native servants—there is not a cook, nurse, butler, gardener, or housemaid to be seen—leaving the role of servant to the mongoose. Rikki exists, in the context of the tale, in order to make life safe and tidy for the European settlers.

That the natural enemy of the mongoose is the snake strengthens this reading of the tale. The cobra villains of the tale are highly emblematic of India itself.[18] Not only are they a kind of visual shorthand for "the Orient" in everything from nineteenth-century cartoons in *Punch* to Disney's *Aladdin,* they also are representative of that element of Orientalism that considers Orientals to be duplicitous and untruthful. The cobra couple in "Rikki-tikki-tavi" plot, lie, scheme, hide, and otherwise behave in ways that link them with stereotypical portrayals of exotic Orientals in much Western writing. The snakes are also representative of another aspect of Orientalism that Said discusses at length in his book: the seductive, dangerous qualities of the Orient. When a garden bird is threatened by the cobra, who says, "Little fool, look at me!", we are told that the bird "knew better than to do *that* [sic], for a bird who looks at a snake's eyes gets so frightened that she cannot move" (127). This hypnotic fascination is repeated when the same cobra threatens Teddy and his father, who says to his son "Sit still, Teddy. You mustn't move" (128). Looking too closely at the cobras, the face of India, makes one vulnerable to the dangerous qualities of the land and its natives.

The cobras are threatened first by the white family who threaten to domesticate the snakes' garden habitat, and second by Rikki-tikki, who refers to the human family as *his* family whose "honour" he is fighting for by fighting the cobras. Fighting for the honor of a white family effectively undercuts the natural animosity between the snakes and the mongoose, putting Rikki-tikki—an indigenous Indian animal, like the snakes—clearly on the side of European humans. Like many domestic Indian servants, he is willing to further the interests of the white ruling class because some of that privilege and power will transfer to the individual servant, if not to the entire class of native servants. Like Hurree Babu, Rikki-Tikki helps the colonizers at least in part from desire for individual gain.

As in the Anglo-Indian world of colonizer and native, the colonizer depends upon native protection and interpretation in order to keep control of the country. The unnamed Englishman in "Rikki-tikki-tavi" has learned enough of native life and custom (unlike his wife, the Mem Sahib) to know that the mongoose can be helpful, just as he no doubt knows a certain kind of native can be useful as sepoy or servant. But despite his colonial powers, the Englishman is incapable of protecting wife and child from native dangers— he only clubs or shoots snakes after they have been killed by Rikki-tikki, and, in fact, seems incapable of telling whether the snakes are dead or alive.

The native snakes in this story are threatened by the Europeans because only so long "as the bungalow is empty we are king and queen of the garden" and their yet-to-be-born children will need "room and quiet" in order to grow up well and strong (124). Their primary motive is to remove the white owners of the bungalow and to provide a proper, wild, and Indian environment for their growing children, thus to perpetuate the race of cobra, that is to perpetuate the native population. This Darwinian struggle is framed not so much in animal terms, but in human ones: the cobras are fighting humans for habitat, not mongooses. Kipling emphasizes this for us by having the boy child threatened with death by the cobra, thus symbolically threatening the continued life of the British in India—just as Rikki-tikki, faithful native servant, destroys not only the parent snakes, but their eggs as well, effectively ridding colonial space of troublesome natives.

The British Empire itself is never overtly mentioned in "Rikki-tikki-tavi," and is only suggested by the presence of the sahib and his family in the bungalow. But elsewhere in *The Jungle Books* imperialism plays an overt role. "Toomai of the Elephants" is told from the perspective of the young elephant handler or *mahout,* not of the animals, but his story is filtered through a European narrator, who mentions the "Afghan war of 1842" in the first paragraph of the story, in order to tell us that Kala Nag, the central elephant of the tale, pre-dates this event. Kala Nag is in the service of the British and has been used to "carry a mortar upon his back" and to carry "twelve hundred pounds' weight of tents" (133), and since he is in the employ of the British army, he has also seen "Emperor Theodore lying dead in Magdala" and has performed so nobly in wartime conditions that the soldiers think him "entitled to the Absynnian War medal" (134). The war referred to here is the First Afghan War, during which the British invaded Afghanistan and placed a puppet-figure of the East India Company as shah. The British were eventually undone by a native uprising, and after briefly recouping their losses, withdrew from Afghanistan altogether. During the course of the story, Toomai's status rises partly because Kala Nag makes it possible for him to witness the elephants' wild dance, and partly because this event so impresses the resident sahib and elephant-hunter Peterson. As in "Rikki-Tikki-Tavi," the status and importance of native figures is linked to their association with and usefulness to the colonizers: both Toomai and Kala Nag are important only because of their associations with the colonizers. Empire is also an important part of the last story of the first *Jungle Book*, "Servants of the Queen," which will be discussed in greater detail below. But the story that combines the animal-fable qualities of "Rikki-tikki-tavi" with explicit uses of empire is "The Undertakers," in which a crane, a crocodile, and a jackal trade stories, the crocodile having center stage for most of the tale.

The crocodile is old, huge (twenty-four feet), and venerable. For obvious reasons, he is feared and respected by both the other animals and by the natives in the village. In fact, he has been the "godling" of the village ever since the villagers perceived him to be sending back floodwaters within their banks. The crocodile tells the listening crane and jackal that "You do not know the English as I do" (246), and proceeds to tell a long story about some of the best eating he ever had, the eating of "white-faces." The story concerns a time in his youth when first white, then Indian, bodies came floating in multitudes down the river. From the geographic and temporal clues given us by the crocodile, it is clear that the "rich waters above the Benares" (246) are rich with the dead from the Indian Mutiny of 1857.

At least fifty novels about the Mutiny appeared before 1900,[19] but Kipling himself, often considered the most jingoistic of British writers, wrote nothing about this crucial event except what appears in "The Undertakers." The Mutiny itself had a number of causes, the underlying one being Indian discontent with colonial rule. More specifically, ammunition for a new kind of rifle was suspected by sepoy soldiers of being greased with cow and pork fat. This was bad enough for observant Hindi and Muslims, but the ends of the cartridges needed to be bitten before they could be used, forcing both Hindu and Muslim, from their point of view, into sacrilege. On 10 May 1857 the sepoy forces at Meerut mutinied, killing British officers and other Europeans. They then marched to Delhi, where more killing occurred and where they named the aging Mogul emperor as emperor of all India. By July the mutiny had spread to Cawnpore where, notoriously, a number of British were slain, including women and children. The mutiny was finally put down in 1858, but not before England had become nearly riotous over atrocities committed against the British. The net result was that the British government took sole control of the government in India, Victoria was crowned Empress of India in 1876, and the British empire had received an early warning signal that the glory days of its empire were beginning to wane.

There is a wonderful, sly irony at work in "The Undertakers," whose central trope has to do with eating and being eaten—ostensibly the issue behind the beginning of the Mutiny. But Kipling sidesteps the troubling questions raised by the Mutiny by putting his story in the mouth of the crocodile, a good opportunist who finds that the Mutiny serves his appetites quite well: ". . . the dead English came down, touching each other. I got my girth in that season" (248). When the dead English stop floating down the river and into the jaws of the crocodile, they are replaced by "one or two dead, in red coats, not English, but of one kind all—Hindu and Purbeeahs—then five and six abreast, and at last, from Arrah to the North beyond Agra, it was as though whole villages had walked into the water" (250), and during the night the crocodile hears guns and cartwheels and shod feet marching. Later, he hears the people of his village say "that all the English were dead; but those that came, face down, with the current were *not* English, as my people saw. Then my people said that it was best to say nothing at all, but to pay the tax and plough the land" (251). Without becoming explicit, Kipling takes note of the huge number of Indian victims of British retaliation for the Mutiny.

Here, in a nutshell, is a crocodile-eye-view of the Indian Mutiny of 1857, complete with a proper imperial ending, as the natives learn to say nothing, to pay tribute (taxes) to their imperial lords, and to go back to ploughing the land so they have the money for the taxes and can avoid further retribution. The crocodile is an equal-opportunity scavenger, preying on the British as well as the Indians, but he ultimately gets his comeuppance from the British, and in quite an interesting way. At the same time the crocodile is feasting on victims of the Mutiny, a boat filled with women and children sails by him in the river. He is not hungry so much as interested in practicing his hunting skills, and he rises in the water to try "for sport" to grab the trailing hands of a small white child. Miraculously, the child's hands slip through the crocodile's teeth and he is saved, aided by pistol shots from his brave mother. After the crocodile has told his story to the jackal and the crane, he goes to sleep and is spied by two white men upon the bridge. One is warned by the other not to shoot the crocodile, since he is revered by the villagers. But the rifleman says, "I don't care a rap. He took about fifteen of my best coolies while the bridge was building" (253). The crocodile is shot, killed, and decapitated by the soldier, who then says that the last time his hand was in a crocodile's mouth he was going downriver by boat: "I was a Mutiny baby, as they call it. Poor mother was in the boat, too, and she often told me how she fired dad's old pistol at the beast's head" (254). The crocodile—a dangerous indigenous Indian crocodile—is killed by the grown-up white child he once tried to eat. Just as the British successfully put down the Mutiny, they successfully put down another emblem of dark and dangerous India, the crocodile. Just as Teddy, at the end of "Rikki-tikki-tavi," lives on to continue the British race and rule, so the white boy in this story lives on into adulthood and soldierhood, conquering animal and human life along the way.

Don Randall, in his argument for the *Jungle Books* as post-Mutiny allegory, says that the death of the crocodile "seems almost to be a necessary effect of the triumphant manifestation of British technological and

administrative know-how," and that the "British-Indian colonial confronta-
tion resolves itself once again in favor of the imperialist and by means of
extreme violence."[20] I would take Randall's argument a step further: "The
Undertakers" is a story of cultural obliteration. The crocodile has been both
revered and feared by the native population: he is a god to them, responsible
for the behavior of the life-sustaining river. His death suggests the death of
native Indian culture and religious belief, subsumed by British rationality and
engineering. The Indians have dealt with the changeable river by worshipping
its *genus loci;* the British simply override the river by building a bridge. Of
course, bridges may be washed out by floods, which from an Indian perspective become more possible now that the crocodile is dead: both the Indians
and the British may suffer from the absence of the river "godling."

The last story in the *First Jungle Book,* "Servants of the Queen," signals
with its title its central concern with hierarchy and imperial duty. This story,
alone among the tales in the *Jungle Books,* concerns domesticated animals
that serve humankind and who lack independent lives of their own. All of the
animals, whether indigenous to India or to the West, are in a lower "caste"
than all of the humans in the story, because they are in servitude to humans.
And this story, among all of the *Jungle Book* stories, spells out a moral concerning imperialism most clearly and unambiguously. In this story, thirty
thousand men and many thousands of animals have come together in order
"to be reviewed by the Viceroy of India" (152). The adult narrator of the story,
routed from his tent in the middle of a rainy night by escaped camels who
have gone on a rampage, overhears a conversation among loose bullocks,
camels, mules and horses, a conversation that sheds light upon how the
British have maintained their empire.

The camels—animals indigenous to the East and not to the West—are
the instigators of the animal rampage. The Eastern camels are presented as
being inferior to Western mules and horses. When he meets some horses who
have broken loose, the camel says, "humbly," "My lords . . . we dreamed bad
dreams in the night, and we were very much afraid. I am only a baggage-
camel of the 39th Native Infantry, and I am not as brave as you are, my lords"
(154). The camel's humble speech, his identity as a member of the native
infantry, and the faintly foreign cadence of his speech mark him as Other to
the English horses. His susceptibility to superstition and dream also mark
him as Oriental. The loose bullocks are also Indian, and they tend to speak (as
they pull) in tandem. They have a certain dullness of mind, and whereas the
camels are linked with the dark and mysterious aspects of the Orient, the bullocks are associated with another Oriental "otherness"—dullness of mind and
a lack of individuality. One bullock is the same as another, just as one native
often appeared no different from the next to the European eye. They also have
an Oriental fatalism about fellow bullocks killed in battle: "This is Fate—
nothing but Fate. . . . There is all the more grazing for those who are left"

(159). The only native animal who escapes being treated as a stereotypical Indian is Two Tails, the elephant, who is superior because he is self-conscious and understands the nature of battle and what his fate might be as a participant in that battle. The elephant sees himself as "betwixt and between," and hence, not always able to obey, because he is too aware of the nature of the link between human and animal. He is, in many ways, analogous to the sepoy soldiers: aware of the links between colonizer and colonized, on the side of the colonizer for the moment, but harboring the ability to disobey and revolt.

Among the British animals, the mules rank slightly lower than the troop horses, since the mules are used as beasts of burden and the horses are partners, of a sort, with their human masters. Interestingly, the mules and horses—whom we might see as the animal equivalent of British infantry soldiers—are bred in Australia, one of the so-called white or settler colonies, and in fact, much of the colonial infantry in India was made up of regiments from white colonial holdings, such as Australia and Ireland. All of these animals, in the night, share conversation about their roles in the human world, about why they have to fight at all ("Because we're told to" is the troophorse's response), and then they all go back to their proper places, in order to be ready for the mustering of troops in the morning.

When the reader is finally given a description of this mustering of all thirty thousand troops, the English (adult) narrator tells of a Central Asian chief who asks how such an event was organized. A sepoy officer answers, "An order was given, and they obeyed" (166). The chief responds by saying "Would it were so in Afghanistan! for there we obey only our own wills." The officer responds, "And for that reason, your Amir whom you do not obey must come here and take orders from our Viceroy" (167), providing the closing words and moral of this brief tale. The sepoy officer has completely allied himself with "our Viceroy," with the colonial power, seemingly unaware that he is participating in his own colonization.

The story is appealing for its brief, evocative sketching of the personalities of the various animals and their relationships with one another, and appealing especially to children because of the conceit that animals can talk among themselves, and occasionally humans are lucky enough to overhear and understand them—a conceit quite common in writing for children. But the story also functions as an allegory of imperialism. Kipling quite carefully orders his animals in a hierarchy that is dependent upon birth and upon caste, and emphasizes that convincing others to obey orders is at the heart of successful governments. Obeying orders—obeying the Law—is at the heart of Mowgli's jungle, too, but that Law has explicit imperial overtones.

Kipling's interest in empire was not limited to the British role in India. He was also interested in the reasons behind Britain's rise to imperial power, in the essential nature of the Briton that underlay British world supremacy. And, like many Victorians, he was keenly aware of the parallels between the Roman and British empires and their intersections in the past, when Rome ruled Britain for a time and left a mark not only in the ruins of Hadrian's Wall but also on the British character. The two books of Puck stories, *Puck of Pook's Hill* (1906) and *Rewards and Fairies* (1910), are his explorations of this intersection, and it is the first of these volumes that is my interest here.

The stories in *Puck of Pook's Hill*[21] take empires and empire building as their explicit subject matter. Alfred Noyes's 1906 review of the book says that here "Kipling has for the first time dug through the silt of modern Imperialism" to go back to the "groundworks" to give "the pageant of our history with breadth and nobility."[22] Kipling approaches these subjects through fantasy and adventure narrative. The stories are doubly-mediated for the reader, first by the magical figure of Puck (the kind of fairy figure common in children's texts of the period, although Puck goes out of his way to distance himself from winged fairies who "flit"), and then through the responses of Dan and Una as they meet a number of figures from Britain's past. The characters Puck introduces to the children are chosen carefully by Kipling. They are not imposing historical figures brought to life from the children's schoolbooks— not Henry VIII and Nelson, for example—but ordinary people who had extraordinary adventures in Britain's past and played an important (though unheralded) role in the shaping of Britain's history. Puck conjures these figures up in their adult form, but their tales are ones of youthful exploits, ensuring that Dan and Una (and the reader) will be interested in what they have to say about outwitting pirates and keeping Hadrian's wall intact. History is taught along the way, but it is adventure and exploit that are emphasized. Furthermore, these historical figures never condescend or pontificate to the children—they simply tell their stories, from which certain morals may be drawn, but these morals are not often drawn by the historical personages themselves, or by Puck.

The children who receive Puck's magical visitations are not just any children. Their names are Dan and Una, and they live in an old Sussex house whose history goes back hundreds of years. Corinne McCutcheon has observed, "Kipling gives the children names strongly suggestive of *The Faerie Queene:* Una, the name of the first book's heroine, and Dan, which by association with Daniel of the Bible recalls the lion that befriends and defends Una in the forest."[23] McCutcheon is arguing that *Puck* and *Rewards and Fairies* together form a romance, and thus is interested in *The Faerie Queene's* romance elements and their influence upon Kipling's work. But *The Faerie Queene* is not only romance; it is an allegorical romance, combining spiritual growth with British history. The Recross Knight, for example, can be read both as allegorical mankind and allegorical England; Una is truth, but also the English church, and she defends both faith and England. Kipling for the most part ignores the spiritual elements of Spenser's allegory, but the names of the children suggest that they—like all the British—will have to fight to maintain the truth and integrity of British history and culture. They will carry these truths into the future and into the next generation. Kipling, in naming the children, signals to the reader (at least a reader who knows Spenser) that the stories the children hear through Puck's conjurings are not simply fairy stories, but stories with serious cultural import.

Yet part of the genius of these tales is that, with one exception, they are calculated to appeal to the popular taste of children of the time. Puck himself narrates two of the tales, including the first, and fairy figures like Puck were omnipresent in children's books of the late nineteenth century: one thinks of Mrs. Ewing's *The Brownies and Other Tales* (1870) and Lang's series of Fairy Books, beginning in 1889, or the incarnations of Puck and Pan-like figures in *Wind in the Willows* (1908) and *The Secret Garden* (1911). The figures Puck introduces to the children also have parallels in juvenile popular fiction of the time. The first important narrator is Sir Richard, a twelfth-century knight who plays a role in the assimilation of Norman and Saxon into one people. Tales of knights and of medieval life in general were extremely popular at the end of the nineteenth century, for both adults and children. William Morris and Tennyson both give poetic renderings of medieval lives and loves, and Howard Pyle's illustrations for *The Merry Adventures of Robin Hood* (1883) and *Otto of the Silver Hand* (1888) were enormously popular among young readers. Although Sir Richard has an important tale to tell about Britain's history, it is framed by tales of battles and hidden treasure, the same kind of tales that (without the same historical and cultural overlay) were mainstays of late Victorian juvenile sensation fiction.

The second important narrator is Parnesius, a young centurion posted to Hadrian's Wall in the fourth century. Parnesius, like Richard, has parallels in other popular works of the period. Not only was Rome and its empire a popular subject with nineteenth-century historians, but there were any number of historical fictions based on ancient Rome, works like Walter Pater's *Marius the Epicurean* (1885) and Macaulay's series of poems, *Lays of Ancient Rome* (1842). Parnesius's tale comes at the point when the Roman empire is beginning to dissolve and the seeds of the British empire have already been sown, but again the history is framed by stories of marches, battles, and of boyhood friendship. The third narrator, Hal o' the Draft, at first seems utterly unlike the other narrators: he is an artisan, not a soldier, and he doesn't go to battle, he is engaged in repairing a church. But his difficulties in repairing the church, it transpires, have to do with a plot to supply pirates with cannon that rightly belong to the king, so that once again Kipling mediates a story of empire building (this time a fifteenth-century tale) through adventure stories. The last of the narrators is a Jewish physician named Kadmiel who plays a role in the drafting of the Magna Carta, who is unlike the other narrators in many ways, and who will be discussed at length.

All of these narrators, despite the fact that they span some thousand years of British history, share qualities that, in Kipling's mind, were qualities from which empires were born. The tales in *Puck of Pook's Hill* emphasize not the political or military skills necessary to build and maintain empire, but rather the human qualities or the qualities of what late Victorians would term "character" necessary in empire builders. This accounts for, among other things, the masculinity of the stories. Una, Dan's sister, may listen to the stories and admire Richard and the others, but there is not a single important female figure in any of the stories, nor is there a female narrator. The women who are mentioned in passing—a Saxon maiden, a Roman mother—have importance only in their relationship to men. They are not the movers and shakers of empires, although, of course, emperors are born of mothers and marry wives in order to leave (male) heirs.[24]

The first of the qualities Kipling emphasizes is the importance of male friendship and camaraderie. Of the ten stories in the volume, six have double heroes. The tales of twelfth-century England are narrated by the Norman invader Richard, but Saxon Hugh turns out to be his best friend and the figure with whom he shares not only friendship and adventure, but also the beginnings of what we now recognize as Britain. Parnesius narrates the stories of Roman centurions at Hadrian's Wall, but he would not have been successful without his best friend and ally Pertinax. Even the stories that do not have such pairings still emphasize the importance of male friendship and bonding: in "Hal o' the Draft," the alliance of the local justice of the peace is important; in "Weland's Sword," it is friendship that finally frees Weland; and even in "The Treasure and the Law," brotherhood is important.

This emphasis on male alliances and friendships was nothing new: it was a virtue lauded by British public schools, Baden-Powell's Boy Scouts, the culture of muscular Christianity, the British military, and other institutions of Kipling's time. Kipling, however, has a twist on the theme, a twist that he would refer to as "stalkiness," the term used by the schoolboys in *Stalky & Co.* to describe behavior that is clever and cunning, behavior that leads to the comeuppance of the enemy, behavior that is exuberant and energetic and fun. "Stalky" behavior may not be moral, but it is often, in Kipling's view, the most efficient means to a desired end. *Stalky & Co.* will be discussed at length, but it is significant that the boys in those tales not only succeed at juvenile pranks through cunning, deception, disguise, and occasional untruthfulness, but that it is precisely these qualities that make the boys successful adult leaders on the frontiers of empire. The same ethos is often at work in *Puck of Pook's Hill.*

For example, Richard tells the story of helping De Acquila (a Norman lord who has the vision to see a future unified England) outfox an underling who is betraying him to the king of England, the upshot of which is that they first "encourage" the traitor to tell his tale by putting him at the bottom of a tide-well while the tide is rising (a more sophisticated version of flushing schoolboy heads down toilets, perhaps); and second, they outfox the traitor who has been playing both sides by using his own tool—the written word—against him. The entire tale is told as if by schoolboys enjoying high jinks, not by knights who stand in danger of losing their own lives and England to boot. De Aquila, in a more serious moment, stops the jesting to say, "Be still. I think for England" (112), but the serious moments are overshadowed by the exuberant actions of Norman and Saxon together. In "Hal o' the Draft," Sebastian Cabot discovers that the cannon he is charged with delivering to the King have been redirected to pirates. He rides off to report to Sir John, who comes up with a scheme for Cabot to get both the cannon he had consigned and two he had not commissioned, which "are not in the King's Order" (176). Sir John says to explain that the malefactors are acting from "Kindness—loving-kindness" and that in his "zeal for the King and his love for you, John adds those two cannon as a gift" (176). This, obviously, makes it impossible for the cannon-thieves to refuse the king the cannon. In "Dymchurch Flit," the fleeing fairies convince a deaf and dumb man and a blind one to take them across the channel to England—thus making it impossible for anyone to discover what the two of them saw or heard. The Old Things of England are, perhaps, the originators of British "stalkiness."

Indeed, the inclusion of fairy-like beings—Puck and the Old Things of "Dymchurch Flit"—in a collection of stories about historical figures may at first seem odd, as if Kipling is either elevating mythological figures to the level of historical figures or mythologizing historical figures. Neither is the case—the Old Ones, and particularly Puck himself, function in an important metaphoric way for Kipling. Puck, the mediator of all the stories in the collection, is as old as Britain itself, if not older. He tells the children that he was around "when Stonehenge was new" (47), and he is still around, "long lived," when all the other People of the Hills, "giants, trolls, kelpies, brownies," have left (47). He was witness to the arrival of all the mythological "People of the Hills," thus predating them and outliving them. They left little by little, over the centuries, and "Most were foreigners who couldn't stand our climate" (50).

The diction here is important. Puck is one of the "People of the Hills", thus suggesting that he, and they, are intimately connected with the land, that they are in some senses *genii loci,* spirits of place, spirits of England and Britain itself. The *our* in "our climate" further emphasizes this: the People of the Hills are allied, are part of the same group, as contemporary British children. Third, although the remark about climate may seem on the surface to be just another amusing remark about England's notoriously damp and chilly weather, in the context of the stories in this collection, the "climate" is the social and historical climate of Britain, as well as the climate of its character. Puck stays first because he is older than the People of the Hills and perhaps is not a foreigner, as they are, and second because his character—which is "stalky" at core—is well-suited to Britain's climate. He is both Shakespeare's Puck and the older Puck upon whom Shakespeare built. Not only is he, by definition, a crafty sort of figure who can conjure up persons from the past, but some of the specifics of the stories he tells posit him as a "stalky" character. Kipling seems to be suggesting that craft and cunning, "stalkiness," is an inherent part of British nature or character, as personified by Puck. Puck appears in "Dymchurch Flit," impersonating an old friend of Hobden (a factotum on the children's estate), and in "Weland's Sword" bewitches a character and makes possible Weland's release from England.

That Puck stays in England, rather than leaving with the other foreigners, is suggestive of another lesson of empire Kipling is presenting in these stories: when invaders arrive in England, they are either forced to leave because the "climate" doesn't suit them, or they are assimilated into English (and ultimately British) national culture and character. This is clearest perhaps in the stories narrated by Richard, the Norman knight. The Normans invade Saxon England, ostensibly to take it over and impose Norman culture and language upon the Saxons. But of course, the Normans themselves are assimilated into Saxon England, leading to one British people in the end, and leading to a Britain whose language and culture owe at least as much to the Saxons as to the Normans.

Puck sets up this story in "Weland's Sword," the story of the making of the sword that plays an important role in the Norman Richard's tale. The sword is made as a reward by Weland, a foreign god who comes into the country "telling me [Puck] how he was going to rule England. . . . *I* didn't care! I'd seen too many Gods charging into Old England to be upset about it" (51). Weland is unsuccessful, but leaves a sword behind, a sword that is ultimately given to the Saxon Hugh, who loses it in battle to the Norman Richard, who came to England thinking he would be a conqueror, but who ultimately is conquered by the Saxons, remaining in England as lord of a manor and marrying a Saxon girl. Hugh, the Saxon girl's brother, says to the Norman military leader De Aquila, "I am a Saxon . . . I have not sworn fealty to any Norman," to which De Aquila replies, "In God's good time . . . there will be neither Saxon nor Norman in England" (73). The sword becomes a symbol not only of authority, but of the very nature of Englishness. It originates with a foreign god, but has been so long in England that its foreign associations are largely lost. The sword changes hands as the ruling power in England shifts—but it never leaves England and plays a crucial role not in the partitioning of England among competing forces, but in the unification of warring factions into a cohesive and powerful whole, a whole that will ultimately expand its powers overseas, as the Romans had before them.

The Roman tales of Parnesius and Pertinax take us back to Britain before the Norman invasion, and in fact show us the waning days of the Roman

Empire in Britain. There is an implicit message here for nineteenth- and early twentieth-century readers, who were well-used to the comparisons made between the Roman Empire and their own British Empire. The unraveling of the Roman Empire is localized for us through the stories of the young centurions upon the wall, who have the unwelcome task of trying to hold fast the edges of empire against both the native Picts and the invading Saxon Winged Hats—the same Saxons who will give us the character Hugh and who will be triumphant over Norman invaders, just as they were over Roman ones, suggesting that Saxon blood may be the root of British national strength. That Parnesius and Pertinax are ultimately unsuccessful, Kipling makes clear, is through no fault of their own. They are loyal, hardworking, intelligent, compassionate: they have all the makings of good leaders. But they are under the command of Maximus, who makes the mistake of trying to "drive three mules," of trying to rule Britain, Rome, and Gaul, which proves too much for one man. Kipling implies that at least one of the reasons the Roman empire failed is that it tried to govern too much territory with too few resources. This has further implications for the British Empire of his own time, which was straining the resources of the government and was visibly unraveling, both in increasing demands from the white settler colonies for greater autonomy and from increasing unrest and rebellion among colonized peoples, epitomized for the British by the Indian Mutiny of 1857, the nearly disastrous Zulu War of 1879, and other uprisings within the empire. Kipling is giving the children of England an implicit warning that the British Empire itself may fall—although England itself, as exemplified by Puck, will live on.

Dan and Una are the inheritors of England, its rightful owners, as Puck emphasizes when he gives them "seizin" of the land, explaining that land did not properly belong to someone until its owner had literally cut out a piece of land and given it to the new owner. Puck does this for the children, telling them, "Now are you two lawfully seized and possessed of all Old England" (48). Their names—especially Una's—further link them to England, her past and future. Una's name, through Spenser, links her to Queen Elizabeth, and Dan's name is linked to the biblical story of the lion's den. The biblical Daniel stood alone against all enemies and won, much as England has done throughout her history. But Dan's name comes from the Book of Daniel, an apocalyptic book of the Old Testament, which was intended to encourage Jews in the face of persecution. While at first linking Dan to Jewish persecution may seem odd, in fact it is not odd, on at least two counts. First, Daniel is a member of a persecuted people, and while the British have never been persecuted the same way the Jews have, in the course of history the British have been persecuted by a number of invaders: attempts to quash British language and culture go back as far as British history does, and have continued into the twentieth century, if one looks at the history of the Irish, Welsh, and Scots. Second, Daniel's link to Jewish history provides a link to the last, and puzzling, narrator of these stories, Kadmiel, a thirteenth-century Jewish physician, born among the Moors in Spain, who plays a central role in the drafting of the Magna Carta.

What is a Jewish figure doing in a collection of stories about the history of Britain, let alone in the last, culminating tale? Is this a reference to Disraeli, conservative prime minister from 1874–1880, the prime minister who named Victoria Empress of India? Among other oddities, Kadmiel is the only narrator who does not emphasize stories of his youth, but instead concentrates on a major story of his adulthood. He is more foreign than the other foreigners in the stories, his very language having a foreign cadence to it. He awes the children more than the other characters do. But he does have a place in these stories, although I believe his tale speaks more to the adult readers of *Puck of Pook's Hill* than do the other tales. His inclusion grows out of Kipling's interests in secret societies, and particularly in the Freemasons, of which he had been a member since his youth in Lahore.

The Freemasons had a philosophy that emphasized human brotherhood regardless of race, creed, or nation. A Freemason lodge in India at the time Kipling was a member might include Anglo-Indians, Muslims, Jews, Hindus, and others, all of whom shared a kind of fraternal equality within the lodge walls, although this equality did not necessarily extend outside the walls. It seems surprising that a writer often considered the most jingoistic and imperialistic of British writers would be a lifelong member of such a society. But Kipling had felt estranged from family, from India, from home of any sort his entire adult life, and the Freemasons gave him a means of going back to that caste-less state of childhood, where he could freely mingle with all sorts of Indian inhabitants, including the Hindus who had been such an important part of his life. For a man who lacked a sense of home, both in the sense of family home and in the sense of a national home, the Freemasons could provide a reasonable substitute—importantly, a substitute family that existed around the globe, in whose lodges Kipling would always be welcome, regardless of where he was geographically. It should not surprise us that one of Kipling's poems about the Freemasons is entitled "The Mother-Lodge."

The kind of fraternalism that existed within the Freemason lodge did not extend to the outside world. A white Anglo-Indian might treat a Hindu or a Jew as an equal within the lodge walls, but without the walls, the Hindu would be the Anglo-Indian's servant and the Jew would be ghettoized. This may strike the contemporary reader as either schizophrenic or hypocritical, but it is fairly typical of Kipling's complex and ambiguous feelings about the nature of imperialism and colonialism. He grew up more a Hindu child than an English one, yet as an adult was a socially superior white Anglo-Indian, who counted Hindus and others among his friends, but who could not acknowledge them as truly equal friends given the prevailing notions of imperialism and racism. Kipling supported much of the British empire, but also refused to attend Victoria's jubilee, and wrote "Recessional," a dire warning of the imminent collapse of the British empire.

Kipling wanted fairness, if not equality, for people. The difference between fairness and equality, of course, is that it might be fair for certain people to be relegated to lesser positions in society and to not be treated identically (equally) with people in superior positions; but the law ought to apply fairly to everyone. This, I think, is the key to understanding "The Treasure and the Law." This is the tale that brings together Weland's sword and the gold hidden by De Aquila in the Norman stories, and suggests that Britain is on the road to becoming an imperial power that would outstrip Rome. Kipling saw Britain as a country that believed in fair play and fairness. His Indian stories focus more frequently on ordinary soldiers rather than on officers, and those soldiers are often from marginalized British groups, from the Irish in particular. *Stalky & Co.*, set in a school whose purpose is to train boys for colonial service, praises the cunning and craft of the schoolboys, but they use that cunning and craft only to level the playing field, as it were: they scheme in order to return fairness to the school world, not to rise above it.

Keeping these things in mind, Kadmiel becomes more understandable as a choice for final narrator. He says, among other things, that "You Christians always forget that gold does more than the sword" (199). Not only has this been proven throughout the stories, and particularly in the Norman stories that precede "The Treasure and the Law," but it is also an important tenet in colonial rule. War is expensive, and it sometimes makes better sense to strike political and financial alliances than to go to war. This, of course, is the major way Britain gained so much of her empire, through commerce rather than through warfare. As a Jew and a moneylender, Kadmiel has access to the gold that King John needs to keep warring with his barons, rather than negotiating with them over rules of law. Also as a Jew and moneylender, he knows that peace is better for his own private fortunes and the fortunes of his people. He knows that if King John is kept to the laws outlined in the Magna Carta, "the land will have peace, and our trade will grow. If we lend he will fight again" (203). Kadmiel, therefore, does two things. First, he convinces those drafting the Magna Carta that the fortieth of the new laws should read, "To none will we sell, refuse, or deny right or justice," rather than the original *"To no free man"* [sic]. This sets the stage for equal treatment of Jews under the law (although Kipling conveniently does not mention that plenty of laws restricting Jews existed in Britain well into his own time). Second, Kadmiel knows King John will not sign if he has enough gold to keep fighting, so Kadmiel comes up with a crafty scheme to disable the keepers of Pevensey, to get his hands on the gold hidden there by De Aquila, and to sink that gold in the sea, so that moneylenders cannot lend it to King John.

That Kipling has fairness on his mind, rather than equality, is suggested by the contemporary framing of the story. Dan and Una are playing outside during pheasant season, and keep hearing the sound of guns across the fields as hunting parties go about their business. One of the hunters is the Jewish Mr. Meyer. On the one hand, Jews seem to have become recognized members of the British upper class, welcome on pheasant hunts. On the other hand, Mr. Meyer is not a very good shot. He is excitable and shoots at rabbits, mistaking them for pheasants, which is inexcusable, first because it shows him not to be steady of hand and mind, but second because his shots at the rabbits will spook the pheasants and make them harder for everyone to kill. But Mr. Meyer goes further: he has mistakenly "peppered" one of the beaters, a Gentile, and pays for his indiscretion by giving the victim a sovereign, making the victim very happy indeed.

Mr. Meyer is fairly included in the pheasant hunt, but he is not equal to the British gentlemen on whose land he is hunting, just as Hindus are fairly included in Masonic lodges but are not equal to British gentlemen on the streets of Lahore. This is a crucial distinction, one that underlies the idea of the "white man's burden:" others may not be equal to us, but they must be treated fairly. Although it is overly simplistic to say that this is the philosophy that underlies the British abolition of slavery in 1833 but allows them to keep Africans and Indians in subservient positions, it is certainly part of the philosophy, a philosophy Kipling believed in and that runs through all his writings.

In his autobiography, Kipling said the tales in *Puck of Pook's Hill* "had to be a sort of balance to, as well a seal upon, some aspects of my 'Imperialistic' output in the past."[25] They are a balance in the sense that they provide a historical perspective to the British Empire and that they show Britain's own experiences as colonized nation, as well as her rise to imperial power. They are a seal in that they present his imperial beliefs more overtly than in many other works, and in that they are stories meant for children, and in fact for Dan and Una, children busy playing at empire themselves in their "colonizing" of the territory surrounding their home; in their fantasy play at being explorers, having given up playing at pirates. In fact, one can see the progression from pirate to explorer as being emblematic of European conquest as a whole. The British begin by pirating wealth from the New World, from India, from Africa, but when wealth and territory is no longer as readily available they turn to exploration, heading to the South Pole or Everest with no expectation of monetary or territorial reward, but with expectations of glory instead.

The juvenile work that most clearly outlines Kipling's overall sense of what it takes to rule an empire and how to train future imperial leaders is *Stalky & Co.* (1899).[26] The book is a series of stories covering several years in the lives of the boys of Number Five Study at "the Coll.," a school based on United Services College in Devon, where Kipling had been a student. The book raised the ire of early critics: A. C. Benson described the boy characters as "little beasts," Somerset Maugham wrote that "a more odious picture of school life can seldom have been drawn," and the famously virulent Robert

Buchanan condemned it thoroughly by stating that "Only the spoiled child of an utterly brutalised public could possibly have written *Stalky & Co* . . . only a perusal of the whole work would convey to the reader its truly repulsive character. . . . The vulgarity, the brutality, the savagery . . . reeks on every page."[27] The irony is that these same beastly and brutal boys are sons of gentlemen and, as adults, will be responsible for maintaining the boundaries of empire.

Part of the negative reaction to *Stalky & Co.* was caused by its stark contrast to other boys' boarding school stories of the period, which emphasized fair play, honor, perseverance, and competition, virtues taught as much (or more) on the playing fields as in the classroom. J. A. Magnan notes that the "games ethic" provided the means by which the schoolboy learned "the basic tools of imperial command: courage, endurance, assertion, control, and self-control . . . It was widely believed that its [the games' ethic] inculcation promoted not simply initiative and self-reliance but also loyalty and obedience. It was, therefore, a useful instrument of colonial purpose. At one and the same time it helped create the confidence to lead and the compulsion to follow."[28] This ethic reached its apotheosis in the verse of Sir Henry Newbolt, who "gave public expression to the absolute belief that Anglo-Saxon training for conquest took place on the football pitches and the cricket squares of the English public schools,"[29] and was voiced by many a headmaster at chapel. It was also further idealized in boys' school stories that appeared both in papers like *Boys' Own Weekly* and in volume after volume of novels by popular writers.

Kipling's view towards this games ethic is jaundiced, to say the least, as expressed through the language of his boy pupils. The leader of Number Five Study is Corkran, alias Stalky, whose aunt has sent him off to school with what she considers to be edifying reading: a copy of Dean Farrar's enormously popular *Eric, or Little By Little* (1858), one of the most popular and influential boarding school novels of the Victorian era. The reaction of the boys to this novel of saintly boyhood is to declare, more than once, that they "won't tolerate any beastly Ericin'" at their school. Farrar's novel is inappropriate not only because by 1899 it was dated and had been superseded by novels less overtly moralistic, but also because it portrays a boarding school built on the Eton model, not the specialized and rather pragmatic boarding school Kipling both went to at United Services College and fictionalizes in *Stalky & Co.* All of the students at Stalky's "Coll." are sons of soldiers or colonial administrators, in training for the Army examination and for eventual posting out into the empire.[30] They study Latin, not because it is part of a gentleman's classical education, but because it is part of the preliminary exam for admittance into the army. Games playing strikes these future soldiers as a waste of time and energy. Number Five Study scorn any and all games playing, finding what to their minds are more useful and amusing ways to expend their energy. Patrick Scott calls the boys' actions "a guerrilla campaign of disruption, not a programme of sterling leadership in manly sports."[31] Much energy is expended on finding ways to avoid detection while the boys smoke, go out of bounds, booby-trap rival boys' studies, and otherwise engage in high jinks.

The opening story sets up the general pattern of this guerrilla campaign, and also suggests Kipling's theory of imperial education. The narrative voice is not overtly pedagogical, but by the time we reach the last of the tales, in which the adult boys share stories of their various exploits on the frontiers of empire, it is clear that Kipling approves of the way his school trains future imperial leaders. In "Stalky," Stalky and his friends M'Turk and Beetle watch as another group of boys fails in its attempts to harry a local farmer's cows into an inconvenient spot. The boys are caught and locked in a barn while the farmer goes off to find a school official to whom he can complain. Stalky and his companions manage not only to free their fellow schoolmates, but to lock up the farmer and his friends in their stead, then to appear to "rescue" the farmers, and are finally rewarded with praise and, more importantly, a full tea provided by the farmer's wife. Stalky demonstrates for us the origin of his name in his "stalky" behavior, behavior that is devious, clever, resourceful, and in general turns the tables on his opponents.

The opening story also shows us the indirect ways in which the boys are educated in the ways of empire. Throughout *Stalky & Co.*, Kipling is interested in showing how these "beastly" boys are actually receiving an entirely appropriate education for future imperial leaders, and that such education occurs more often out of class than in it. Stalky and his friends are already familiar with the language of empire. They refer to the local farmers as "natives" (a term Ransome will borrow in *Swallows and Amazons*) and to masters of whom they approve as "sahibs." They have relatives who have been in service, and their rooms are filled with West African war drums and other souvenirs of empire. They frame their pranks in military language, referring to "pickets" and "skirmishes" among "armies" of enemies, for example—not unusual in descriptions of childhood play-fights, but significant at a school whose entire purpose is to train boys for the armed services. But the boys know they are still boys and not yet soldiers, and that they are subordinate to the power of masters. As children, bound by school rules and authority, they share much in common with colonized people in India and elsewhere, with the crucial distinction that the boys' masters are dedicated to raising the boys out of their subordinate status. Stalky and his friends can hope to rise to the status of the "old boys" who return to school and tell tales of life in India. Like all children, they will grow out of childhood; unlike most children, they are being trained specifically to assume imperial authority in India or elsewhere in the empire.

Kipling understands that most of what the boys learn in the classroom will be learned by rote, and that within the classroom the master must be obeyed without question or a caning will ensue. The classroom may teach the boys discipline and order, but it does not teach them leadership. Whereas traditional boys' school stories presented competitive sports as a way to teach leadership and cooperation, Kipling apparently did not believe traditional sports gave boys enough opportunity to practice initiative. The boys of Number Five Study invent their own games, games usually involving harassment of a master or of boys who annoy them. They do not depend upon a rule book or a referee: they play by their own rules (which have a moral base, as we shall see), and their exploits provide them with more chance to think on their feet, to plan and execute mischief than a game of cricket ever could. In "An Unsavoury Interlude," Number Five Study torments another house by planting a dead cat under its eaves to rot. The narrator informs us that "Outside his own immediate interests the boy is as ignorant as the savage he so admires; but he has also the savage's resource" (80). This is an important observation on Kipling's part. Kipling recognizes that children are, to some extent, little savages, but that a little savagery is necessary on the frontiers of empire—not physical savagery, but a kind of native cunning and an ability to put limited resources to their best possible use. If one is going to go out to India as either an army officer or a colonial administrator, one is going to find rules of "fair play" less useful than certain guerrilla techniques, and one will often have to make up the game as one goes. Kipling implies that the guerrilla tactics the boys practice on their own will be at least as useful to them as Latin.

The masters themselves seem aware of the importance of guerrilla tactics as a part of the boys' education and tacitly support or at least ignore some of their actions. In "The Moral Reformers," the school parson delicately suggests that the boys themselves might like to take care of some school bullies, a task that Stalky and his friends are eager to undertake. They do so by first tricking, and then methodically roughing up, the two bullies in question in a scene that goes on for pages, which outraged contemporaries for its cheerful approval of violence and vigilantism. But the violence the boys perpetrate is not gratuitous: the bullies not only deserve punishment, they need a taste of their own medicine, given in such a way that they will not be tempted to turn around and vent their anger on younger and more vulnerable boys. Such punishment is better meted out by peers than by headmasters. Stalky and his friends are interested in fairness of treatment, and they only treat the bullies as the bullies have treated victims. Bullies in traditional school stories are always punished as well, but in Kipling's version the bullies are not found out by masters, or repent of their sins, or lose the football match: they are given an eye for an eye by boys who will no doubt deal with other bullies, both native and British, out on the frontier.

As in *Puck of Pook's Hill* and indeed in all of Kipling's writing, the emphasis here is on fairness, not on fair play in the cricket sense of the word. Fair treatment for bullies—or for troublesome Indian natives—may indeed violate the rules of fair play and require some out-of-bounds behavior. The implied message is that ends justify means, but the ends must be dealt out by people who know what they are doing. One of the ironies of *Stalky & Co.* is that Kipling apparently approves of rebellion and insurrection, but only when tempered with obedience to authority. Number Five Study breaks more rules than it obeys, but the reason they succeed and other boys fail is that they take the time to plan, they always act on accurate information, and they obey Stalky's command: they never rebel against each other, only against whomever is the enemy of the moment. This is the key to leadership on the frontiers of empire: use any guile or ruse you have to against troublesome natives, so long as you obey your leader and have no dissent within the ranks.

The final story in the collection, "Slaves of the Lamp II," shows the outcome of the boys' education. We have had hints of the kind of future in store for them when the "old boys" return to school, subjects of hero worship on the part of the boys for their experiences in battle in India. The final story reunites many of the characters at a country house some years after they have left school and been posted to foreign lands. Not all the boys return: some have been killed, some are still on active duty. Stalky is not present—he is still in India—but the telling of his exploits forms the centerpiece of the story. We learn that out in India, "your asses of Politicals reported the country as pacified, and the Government, being a fool, as usual, began road-makin'" (282). The country is not pacified, and natives are sniping at the British road-crews, and the crew led by Stalky has been besieged for five days. Stalky explains to Dick Four (who narrates this tale) that "'The whole country's up' . . . He grinned, but I [couldn't] see where the deuce the fun was"(284). Stalky saves the day by leaving their cover at night, covering his passageway with the body of one of his soldiers, sneaking off down a gorge, killing a native guard at the enemy camp in such a way that the natives will think a rival group has done the deed, comes back (climbing over the body again), and thus ensures that the natives will fight each other and not his besieged British and Sikh troops. Stalky is a daring, inventive, and cool commander, and what he does under pressure in India is not materially different than what he learned to do at school: keep trust with your allies, sow dissension among the enemy, and leave no tracks. Better yet, arrange things so that an innocent party is blamed and not oneself. And why does Stalky have to go to such lengths? Because of the "Politicals," men in offices far away who know nothing of the realities of life in the interior. Going against their orders is fair, because the orders are not fair or wise in the first place. These are precisely the ethics Stalky and his peers learned at school, and they turn out to be much more useful than Latin declensions or the rules of cricket.

Kipling wrote of empire both more forthrightly and less simplistically than many other writers for children. He was writing when the British empire was still strong enough that any ambiguities or anxieties he felt about its rule tend to be undercut by his belief that empire is, in the long run, a good thing while it lasts, even if it doesn't last forever. He is not so much optimistic about empire as he is matter-of-fact about its existence: empire is here, we are in charge, how do we do the best job possible? The themes that pervade all of his fiction, themes of invasion, of the importance of hierarchy and fairness both, of the dangers and necessities of empire, of the interplay between colonizer and colonized, of the need for creative insubordination, are themes that are woven throughout much of the writing for children in the early years of the twentieth century. They become more muted, but no less present, in children's fiction well into the twentieth century.

## NOTES

[1]V. G. Kiernan, *Lords of Human Kind: Black Man, Yellow Man, and White Man in an Age of Empire* (Boston: Little, Brown & Co., 1969), 32.

[2]I will be referring to this incident as the "Mutiny" rather than the "Rebellion" in accordance with the point of view of Kipling and colonial authorities of the time.

[3]Elliott L. Gilbert, *Kipling and the Critics* (New York: New York University Press, 1965), v.

[4]Robert Buchanan, "Voice of the Hooligan," in Gilbert, 26.

[5]Bonamy Dobrée, "Rudyard Kipling," in Gilbert, 51.

[6]Zorah T. Sullivan, *Narratives of Empire: The Fictions of Rudyard Kipling* (Cambridge: Cambridge University Press, 1993), 1.

[7]Rudyard Kipling, *Kim* (1901; London: Penguin, 1987).

[8]Judith Plotz, "The Empire of Youth: Crossing and Double-Crossing Cultural Barriers in Kipling's Kim," *Children's Literature* 20 (1992): 123

[9]In fact, Kim's ability to masquerade, to pass among all classes and castes of Indians, shows his superiority to native Indians: he can go where he pleases and do what he wants, marks of imperial power as well as of the caste-less position of children in India.

[10]Robert Knox, *The Races of Men: A Fragment* (Philadelphia: Lea and Blanchard, 1850), 27.

[11]*Babu* is a Hindu word, a title of respect the British used to refer to a native clerk who wrote in English. A babu is "a subaltern figure trained in the practices of cultural translation who is produced by the empire for its maintenance and reproduction." Deirdre David, *Rule Britannia: Women, Empire, and Victorian Writing* (Ithaca: Cornell University Press, 1995), 3.

[12]Edward W. Said, *Culture and Imperialism* (New York: Vintage, 1994), 78.

[13]Sullivan, 150.

[14]Rudyard Kipling, *The Jungle Books* (1894,1895; London: Penguin, 1987).

[15]John McBratney, "Imperial Subjects, Imperial Space in Kipling's *Jungle Book*," *Victorian Studies* 35:3 (1992), 278.

[16]Don Randall, "Post-Mutiny Allegories of Empire in Kipling's *Jungle Books*," *Texas Studies in Literature and Language* 40:1 (1998): 97-120.

[17]Ibid., 107.

[18]Snakes and gardens also suggest the Book of Genesis from the Christian Bible, but Kipling purposefully obscures this reference beneath an orientalist veneer.

[19]Patrick Brantlinger, *Rule of Darkness: British Literature and Imperialism, 1830–1914* (Ithaca: Cornell University Press, 1988), 199.

[20]Randall, 117.

[21]Rudyard Kipling, *Puck of Pook's Hill* (1906; London: Penguin, 1987).

[22]Quoted in Roger Lancelyn Green, *Kipling: The Critical Heritage* (New York: Barnes and Noble, 1971), 300.

[23]Corinne McCutchan, "Puck & Co.: Reading *Puck of Pook's Hill* and *Rewards and Fairies* as a Romance," *Children's Literature* 20 (1992), 73.

[24]*Rewards and Fairies* does provide some female narrators—a tubercular girl and Queen Elizabeth—but neither has the power of the male narrators.

[25]Rudyard Kipling, *Something of Myself* (Garden City, NJ: Doubleday, 1937), 190.

[26]Rudyard Kipling, *The Complete Stalky & Co.* (1899; Oxford: Oxford University Press, 1987).

[27]Green, 306–307; 318; 244–245.

[28]J. A. Magnan, *The Games Ethic and Imperialism* (New York: Viking, 1986), 18.

[29]Ibid., 45.

[30]Beetle, Kipling's fictionalized self, is the exception. He is physically unsuited for soldiery, so the Head finds him a posting as a journalist of empire.

[31]Patrick Scott, "The Schooling of John Bull: Form and Moral in Talbot Baines Reed's Boys' Stories and in Kipling's *Stalky & Co.*," *Victorian Newsletter* 60 (1981), 7.

# CHAPTER 3

# The Empire at Home: Burnett and Nesbit

Juvenile domestic fiction of the nineteenth century and the early twentieth century, aimed primarily at girl readers, differed significantly from the adventure tales of Ballantyne and Marryat and their peers, tales primarily intended for boys. Foster and Simons provide a convenient brief description of domestic fiction, a fiction that "emphasized feeling and emotional or psychological development in the private sphere of home and family, and portrayed the heroine's growth to ideal womanhood."[1] Such domestic fiction grew out of evangelical writing earlier in the nineteenth century, writing that emphasized the moral and spiritual growth of characters in didactic ways. The most famous of these is probably Mrs. Sherwood's *The Fairchild Family* (1818) in which the sections have titles like "The All-Seeing God" and the children are taken off to view a public hanging in order to impress upon them their probable end if they do not redeem themselves morally for various mild childhood transgressions. As was true for juvenile fiction as a whole, domestic fiction becomes less overtly didactic and evangelical over the course of the century, at the same time that sharper distinctions are being drawn between fiction for boys and fiction for girls. Girl heroines must still learn lessons, but the lessons become more social than theological. Ethel May, in Charlotte Yonge's influential *The Daisy Chain, or Aspirations* (1856) must give up her scholarly ambitions in order to help support her orphaned siblings, which she does cheerfully. In most domestic fiction for girls, the heroines must give up aspirations for a more public life, or give up "madcap" or tomboy ways, or give up hopes for further education, in favor of the challenges and joys of domestic life. For girls, family life is not something to run away from (as it often is in adventure tales for boys) but rather is "as eventful and exciting as a voyage into the unknown."[2]

Although girls' fiction might be "best described as what got left behind" in boys' fiction,[3] and we might, therefore, expect that the imperial desires we find in boys' fiction would not appear in girls' fiction, this is not the case. The treatment of empire differs significantly and is largely based on assumptions made by writers about the gender of both character and reader, but empire and imperialism are as omnipresent in domestic fiction as they are in adventure fiction and other genres aimed more specifically at boys. We can see the ways empire is domesticated in the fiction of both Frances Hodgson Burnett (1849–1924) and E. Nesbit (1858–1924). Unlike Kipling, neither of these writers had direct experience with empire, and neither sends her characters off to India for adventures, although both Mary Lennox and Sara Crewe begin their lives in India. Yet the novels of both women are shaped by empire just as significantly as are the works of Kipling, and for Burnett especially, India is the focal point of empire.

The mere fact that two of Burnett's most famous novels, *A Little Princess* (1905) and *The Secret Garden* (1911), begin in India suggests how omnipresent the empire, and especially India, was at the time. At first the appearance of India seems only gratuitous, a plot device to open the action. *A Little Princess* hinges on Sara's lost and found diamond wealth, restored to her partly through the agency of the Indian servant Ram Dass. Both Sara Crewe and Mary Lennox are born in India and are transplanted to an England that at first seems as foreign to them as India was to most of Burnett's readers. *The Secret Garden,* unlike *A Little Princess,* has no major Indian character, but there are constant references to *rajahs* and to other signs of empire. A closer look at both novels indicates that empire and its values are not merely superficial gloss to the stories, but have a profound effect on how the stories are shaped, and on what values they project to the reader.

Burnett, despite her years in America, maintained close ties to England, and even while living in the United States would have been aware of English empire-building and women's role within it. As we have already seen, women are important in the imagery of empire insofar as empire was often presented in metaphoric guise as a family, with Queen Victoria the head of the "mother country," and colonial subjects as immature children in need of discipline and order given by the "mother" imperial power. But beyond metaphor, women had a real and important role in the building of the British empire. They went to the colonies as missionaries and educators; as wives; and occasionally as servants. Even women who stayed at home in England were involved in domestic imperial endeavors. There has been much excellent recent work on the role of English women in British colonialism and empire, including Jenny Sharpe's *Allegories of Empire,* Susan Meyer's *Imperialism at Home,* and Julia Bush's *Edwardian Ladies and Imperial Power.*[4] There were at least 250,000 Englishwomen involved in a variety of domestic groups and societies whose purpose was to encourage emigration to the colonies, or to improve the lot of women (both native and English) in the colonies, and in general to propagate imperialism at home and abroad—societies like the

Girls Friendly Society, the Primrose League, the British Women's Emigration Association, and the Victoria League.[5] The last was founded under the direct influence of Viscount Alfred Milner, high commissioner of South Africa (1897–1905) and the British official most directly responsible for the Boer War: an intransigent imperialist. His patronage of the Victoria League—as well as patronage by the Queen, the Archbishop of Canterbury, the headmasters of Eton, Harrow, and Westminster, and by Kipling—points to the prestige and potential influence of the league and its women members in areas ranging from education to foreign policy.

The imperial influences in *A Little Princess* have not gone unnoticed by critics of the novel, including Roderick McGillis in *A Little Princess: Gender and Empire*.[6] McGillis recognizes that Ram Dass is presented as a stereotypical "Oriental" and is representative of "the Other." McGillis also provides a perceptive reading of many of the early covers of the book and their imperial content, but his reading of the novel focuses more on gender than it does on empire or on the intersections of gender and empire. Other critics of *A Little Princess* focus on the fairy tale, Cinderella qualities of the story, or on its various incarnations as story, play, novel, and film, and deal only glancingly with the story's imperial content. But the imperial content of the novel goes far beyond the inclusion of Ram Dass as minor character and, I would argue, provides the reader not only with Sara as a late-nineteenth-century Cinderella, but also with a fairy tale for England about the role of India in its empire.

Keeping in mind that *A Little Princess*[7] is entirely framed by empire—empire gives Sara wealth, removes that wealth, and then restores it—the novel presents the reader with two other domestic, as opposed to foreign, imperial colonies. Both the school and the Large Family function as metaphors of colonization. Each has a leader who rules without question; each has a territory with specific boundaries that exists within a wider world of people not bound by the colony's rule (the indigenous Londoners); each has control over a set of colonized subjects, the children who exist within the colonial boundaries of school or home. The first of these domestic colonies, Miss Minchin's school, is malevolent and ill-run because its governor, Miss Minchin, has her own interests at heart, not the interests of her subjects. The second empire is the benevolent one of the Large Family, about whom Sara fantasizes. The Large Family, unlike the school, has a kind colonial governor in the father and, in combination with Sara's restored imperial fortune, forms the ideal domestic empire in which Sara finds her rightful place.

There are several things wrong with Miss Minchin's empire, not least of which is that the empress of this schoolroom kingdom is unmotherly. Motherliness was not a quality necessary to boys' schools (it is utterly lacking in *Stalky & Co.* and other school stories of the period); it is necessary for girls' schools. Girls will grow up to be ladies and mothers and need appropriate models if they are to grow well. Miss Minchin is an unsuitable model because she presents her pupils with a dark mirror of domesticity, not with the ideal. She is unmarried and rules, with her weaker sister, in a kind of parody-marriage in which the weaker "wife" is incapable of ruling either herself or the children, and even more significantly, cannot influence the moral development of the tyrannical "husband." This poorly run empire brings out the worst, not the best, in its subjects, in contradiction of the goals of both families and the empire.

Miss Minchin is first described as being like her house, "respectable and well-furnished" but "ugly," with "hard bones" and a "severe varnished look" (6). None of these descriptors suggest warmth, love, or care, important qualities not only of motherhood, but, by the end of the nineteenth century, increasingly thought to be important for educators as well. The real-life Brocklehursts and Squeers were gradually supplanted by the gentler followers of Pestalozzi and Froëbel. Miss Minchin is decried by Burnett not because she is a spinster, but because she is unmotherly and values money over the moral well-being of her child subjects. These are not only educational flaws, but are potential imperial flaws as well. The British saw the saving of souls and the raising of moral standards among natives as one of the compelling reasons behind imperialism. Britain was to provide a model of moral and Christian behavior to colonial subjects, just as teachers were expected to provide similar models for students. In the case of schooling for girls, such modeling was especially important because girls would grow into women, considered to be the keepers and transmitters of moral values in Victorian society. Miss Minchin rules a very small empire indeed, but in her petty way she reflects some of the shortcomings of colonial governors who did not provide a moral compass for their subjects.

Like a corrupt colonial administrator, Miss Minchin wants to strip the resources of her subjects by belittling them. She values Sara not because she is intelligent (indeed, the fact that Sara speaks better French than Miss Minchin is held against her), but because she is wealthy and is the kind of star pupil who might attract other wealthy pupils to the school. When Sara loses her wealth, she is not cast into the streets, but kept to work as a sort of indentured servant. Miss Minchin has paid for many of Sara's goods in the belief that she will be reimbursed by Captain Crewe. When the Captain is reported both dead and bankrupt, she tries to recoup her losses by making Sara work for little food, a cold attic, and no salary at all. Again like a colonial administrator, she does not see her subject as a human being, but only as a means of production. This is not only inhuman, but it is un-Christian, and thus inexcusable. Sara resists in ways that would be recognizable to a native Indian resisting colonial rule: she resists by silent opposition, by refusal to do anything beyond what she is absolutely required to do—and by keeping her own childhood language and culture alive, in secret.

Sara, after Miss Minchin tells her she has been orphaned and demoted to servant, "kept her big, strange eyes fixed on [Miss Minchin], and said not a word" (100). When Sara misses dinner while performing errands, the cook asks, "Did you expect me to keep it hot for you?" and "Sara stood silent for a second" (205). When Miss Minchin metes out unfair punishment, "Sara stood in the middle of the room in the darkness. She was clenching her little teeth and opening and shutting fiercely her outstretched hands. She could scarcely stand still, but she dared not move until Miss Minchin had gone down the stairs and all was still" (216). Sara is struck into both powerlessness and voicelessness once she is impoverished. But Sara knows the power of interior thought, and recognizes that her freedom is not entirely gone when she says to Miss Minchin, "I will beg your pardon for laughing . . . but I won't beg your pardon for thinking" (166).

Sara maintains her silence and what freedom of thought she can when confronted with Miss Minchin and the culture of the school, but when on her own turf in the poor attic space to which she has been shifted, she can maintain vestiges of her prior life through the agency of language and of play-acting stories that assuage her loneliness and hunger. Significantly, this is not a solitary act: Sara shares her fantasy life with both the servant girl Becky, the rather dim-witted pupil Ermengarde, and with the motherless Lottie, all of whom are also persecuted to one degree of another by Miss Minchin. Although all these girls are subject to the edicts of the schoolmistress' empire, within the attic world their own childhood culture is what both rules and sustains them. Sara remains a princess within the attic and within her own thoughts, even when dethroned by Miss Minchin. Like a deposed native leader, she bides her time and waits for restoration to her rightful place.

Miss Minchin fails as mother and as moral instructor of both Sara and her other subject/pupils. She can neither understand nor nurture little orphan Lottie and—even more significantly—she tolerates the spitefulness and meanness of Lavinia and her friends as long as their spite is directed at other subject/children and not at the administrators of the colony/school. Leadership is important, but despotic leadership will backfire. Miss Minchin's lack of moral leadership and her dependence upon despotism has as its end the creation of ill-educated and spiteful young women like Lavinia—hardly an example of ideal womanhood.

Sara outshines Miss Minchin in all respects. Unlike Miss Minchin, Sara knows how to nurture and love and how to provide moral leadership. She undertakes the mothering of Lottie, who calls her "mother." She finds a way to teach Ermengarde her lessons. Most importantly, she recognizes the servant Becky as a fellow human being, telling her more than once that they are both "just girls" and equal in their humanity, and she also recognizes the humanity of the urchin girl for whom she sacrifices her buns outside a bakery. Sara—unlike Miss Minchin—sees the spiritual equality of all human beings, regardless of class or ethnicity, and in this she is like many of the missionaries who went to the colonies to save native souls, seeing them as equally valuable in the eyes of God, if not in the eyes of society. Sara is treated like an indentured native by Miss Minchin, but the reader is meant to see in Sara all the virtues of Christian womanhood in embryo. Unlike a real native, she can expect to grow into her rightful place as a member of the adult ruling class. She is unfairly treated as an equal of Becky, who will not be able to rise above her class.

The empire of the seminary is unhealthy because it is not moral and does not foster in its pupils the values and morals necessary for the ideal girl to grow into an ideal woman who will rule an ideal domestic empire. That ideal domestic empire is seen in the Large Family so admired by Sara, a family with "a stout, rosy mother, and a stout, rosy father, and a stout, rosy grandmother" (140), with eight children who are "always doing something enjoyable and suited to the tastes of a large family" (141). Their family feeling extends to Sara when one of them gives her a sixpence, mistaking Sara for a beggar, after which the entire Large Family becomes interested in Sara and her life. This alternate empire, one based on love and family ties and domestic morality, is the empire Sara yearns to enter. It is the empire she is destined for by her very nature and birth, a nature that cannot be corrupted by her unfortunate experiences at school, much as Oliver Twist cannot be corrupted by exposure to Fagin and his gang. A servant girl like Becky may also be unfairly treated, but although Sara recognizes her as an equal in the eyes of God, Becky is destined to always be a member of the working class, although one hopes she finds a better domestic empire in which to serve.

Neither the Large Family nor Miss Minchin's Select Academy might strike the reader as being tropes for empire if it were not for the fact that Sara is at Miss Minchin's as a direct result of British involvement in India and because she escapes Miss Minchin's empire through the agency of the larger British empire. Sara comes to the seminary because all Anglo-Indian children were sent "home" to England for schooling. The concept of home was a complicated one for Anglo-Indians and for other white English colonial subjects. Home was a place they had never known, yet had always known: never known because they had never seen England before being sent "home," and always known because the cultural values and even the architecture of their colonial homes were English, not native. Teatime was still sacrosanct, even if one took it on a verandah beneath tropical foliage in India, and public school values were played out in colonial administrative offices. "Home" was further complicated because the mere fact that British subjects were living in a heathen land threatened British moral values and in fact threatened the very Britishness of the colonial officials. There was a real fear that Britons isolated in colonial outposts, surrounded by native Others, might themselves "go native" and be seduced by the temptations of native life: by exotic food, lush surroundings, and, most importantly, by sex. Many of the cultures Britons came in contact with through imperialism endorsed polygamy, or eschewed much clothing, or clothed women in a way that—to Westerners—was more sexually revealing and enticing than the crinolines worn by English women. Indians might see the sari as a modest garment, but to an Englishman used to Victorian modes of female dress, the sari must have been both shocking and exciting. The British were fearful of, and attracted to, native life at the same time. Those who returned to England from the colonies were suspect because they might carry with them some of the taint of nativeness, of Otherness, and did not always fit easily back into English society.

When Sara comes home to England and to Miss Minchin's school, she is suspect not for having gone native nor for any sexual transgression (real or perceived), but for another reason colonials were often resented: wealth. She is not the only literary character whose colonial wealth causes problems. Jos Sedley in *Vanity Fair* is despised and distrusted for his ostentatious display of wealth when he returns from India, and Magwitch's Australian wealth causes difficulties for Pip in *Great Expectations*. Unlike Jos or Pip, Sara is seemingly unaware of how her clothing sets her apart from her English peers. Her ermine cloaks and valenciennes lace are not only inappropriate for a child, but unattainable by any of the other girls who have not had Sara's colonial advantages. Her wealth makes her special and suspect, even as it makes her exotic and intriguing. The ambivalence of feeling towards Sara is suggested by the fact that even the shopkeepers to whom her father takes her think she "must be at least some foreign princess—perhaps the little daughter of an Indian rajah" (11), and by the fact that although some of the schoolgirls resent her, all of them want to hear her stories of India. Yes, Sara is an English schoolgirl, but no, she is not: she is too wealthy, too "foreign-looking" with her large eyes and dark hair. She has about her a touch of the orientalized Other.

The source of Captain Crewe's wealth, the wealth that makes possible Sara's attendance at Miss Minchin's, is never made entirely clear in the novel. He is described as a soldier with the rank of captain, but he seems to have wealth far and above what would be usual for a British military captain of the period. Yet his wealth is not inherited wealth: he appears to have no family whatsoever, leaving Sara orphaned with even fewer options than Mary Lennox. Some of the wealth apparently comes from his investments in diamond mines, investments that fail and indirectly contribute to his death and to Sara's fall from grace at Miss Minchin's.

While the diamond mines can be read as a convenient modern equivalent of the merchant-father's wealth in traditional Cinderella stories, the diamonds have a specific imperial context. Burnett seems to be alluding to the fact that the first, and for a time nearly the only, source of diamonds in the world was India. But starting in the 1860s, huge diamond deposits were discovered in

South Africa, setting off a diamond rush and ultimately ending in the formation of the DeBeers diamond cartel. England may have had access to Indian
diamonds early in its colonization of India, but the Boer had control of the
diamond mines in South Africa, and one of the underlying causes of the Boer
War in South Africa was the struggle for the immense natural resources of the
area. Thus it is perfectly possible that Captain Crewe may have had interests
in diamond mines either in India or in Africa, that he was a temporary victim
of the wild fluctuations in the diamond market of the time, and that ultimately
he (or Sara, after his death) is enormously wealthy, having finally mastered
the intricacies of the market or benefited from English success in the Boer
War. Sara's wealth is not magical fairy-tale wealth: it has its source in British
imperialism and in the exploitation of native workers in African and in India.
Sara is, specifically, an imperial heiress.

The importance of imperial wealth is underlined by the first appearance
of the "Indian gentleman" next door, who turns out to be Captain Crewe's
Anglo-Indian business partner. The "Indian gentleman" is introduced, appro-
priately enough, through his possessions as they are moved into his new
abode, possessions that include a teakwood table, a screen with "rich Oriental
embroidery," and a "superb god Buddha in a splendid shrine" (152). Before
we know anything about the gentleman, his name, his provenance, his purpose in London, we know that he is wealthy and that his wealth is connected
with imperial enterprise. This provides not only a foreshadowing of his future
role as Sara's surrogate father, but is also a signifier of both Captain Crewe's
and Mr. Carrisford's imperial character and their right to rule empire, domestic as well as colonial. Both Captain Crewe and Carrisford have earned their
wealth through colonial enterprise and military intervention, neither of which
is ever questioned in the novel. The irony is that exploitation of native workers is not only never questioned but never even raised in the novel, whereas
the exploitation of Sara is Miss Minchin's greatest sin and causes of her eventual downfall. Exploitation of the Other by men in the colonies goes unmen-
tioned and has tacit authorial approval; exploitation of a British girl by an
adult British woman is condemned.

Sara escapes Miss Minchin's empire through the double agency of a
colonial subject, Ram Dass, and his master, Mr. Carrisford. We meet Ram
Dass before we meet his employer, and as McGillis notes, Burnett makes a
point of the similarities between Ram Dass and Sara: both are strangers in a
strange land, both are in the position of servants, both are lonely. Yet McGillis
also points out that the similarities are undercut by Ram Dass's subservient
language and behavior towards Sara, to whom he speaks "as if he were speaking to the little daughter of a rajah," and whom he reminds of her own Indian
servants "whose foreheads almost touched the ground when she spoke to
them, who were her servants and her slaves" (162). Ram Dass both recognizes and accepts his lower social status, whereas Sara knows she has been

exiled from her proper place in the world, and although she tolerates her circumstances, she never fully accepts them.

Ram Dass is the "agile, soft-footed Oriental" (264) who makes possible the transformation of Sara's attic and who provides the link between Sara and Mr. Carrisford. Burnett is relying upon Ram Dass to be the magician of the story, and thus is relying upon the exotic qualities of India—a country of fakirs and palm readers and snake charmers—to provide a realistic magic in this tale, just as the diamonds provide realistic fairy-tale wealth. He is also the link between domestic empire and imperial empire. Throughout the novel Sara yearns not for her lost wealth, not for the physical environment of India (the only home she has known), but rather for her lost father and his love and protection. She yearns, in other words, for the restoration of her domestic empire, not for restoration to her place in the British empire. But in *A Little Princess* as well as in *The Secret Garden*—not to mention *Vanity Fair, Jane Eyre, Mansfield Park,* and a number of other Victorian novels—the domestic empire is inseparable from the foreign empire ruled by Britain, and Ram Dass is the embodiment of this intersection. Britain's empire, in concrete ways, provided much of the wealth that made middle- and upper-class domestic empires possible. It would not be womanly of Sara to return to India, not even as a missionary or teacher or charity worker, if she were not connected to a domestic empire, through husband or father or brother, first.

Sara's charitable impulses are, therefore, not directed towards converting Ram Dass or making his life materially easier, but are redirected towards domestic charity. She not only shares the warmth and food Ram Dass provides with the other poor girls in her attic, but deprives herself of much needed nourishment when she gives up her hot buns to a ragged girl in the street. The episode is meant to show Sara as a true princess, someone who understands *noblesse oblige,* even though at the time she looks more like a street urchin than a princess. The scene is also meant to show her moral connections to the Large Family, one of whose children has shown similar charity to Sara by giving her a sixpence, mistaking her for a beggar child. The charity of both the Large Family and especially of Sara underlines her moral superiority to Miss Minchin.

When Sara is restored to her rightful place and becomes an honorary member of the Large Family, she is happy for two reasons: she can "give buns and bread to the populace" (292) and she can be a loving daughter/wife to Mr. Carrisford, to whom she wants to kneel down "just as she used to kneel by her father when they were the dearest friends and lovers in the world" (272). The ending of the novel is brilliant in the way it fuses imperial and domestic desires. Sara gains imperial wealth, but only by domestic means. She is both female and child, and thus, can have no direct involvement in amassing wealth by exploiting the resources and labor of foreign lands. But she benefits from commercial imperial enterprise nonetheless, through inheritance of her father's wealth. Even better, she gains not only his half of the diamond wealth, but also Mr. Carrisford's, since she is his surrogate daughter and/or wife.

The portrayal of Sara as both daughter and wife/companion to Mr. Carrisford is not atypical of Burnett: the same sort of confused parent/child relationship exists between Little Lord Fauntleroy and his mother, whom he calls "Dearest." Although there are obvious psychological ramifications here, in terms of the conventions of domestic fiction, Burnett is having her cake and eating it too. Sara is removed from her unsuitable servant status at Miss Minchin's and given dutiful daughter status with Mr. Carrisford, on whom she will be able to practice the domestic skills of nurturing and nursing, practice that is suitable training for her future role as dutiful wife—one suspects as the wife of either Mr. Carrisford himself or one of the sons of the Large Family. Sara's desire to do good in the world and to behave like a real princess is fulfilled both within the home and through the extension of her domestic virtues into the wide world as she aids the poor and unfortunate. Foreign empire gives Sara an entrée into domestic empire, which further allows her to influence the domestic version of natives, the poor working classes. This is the ideal of empire: that the imperialists gain more than the natives in terms of material goods, but the natives have their standard of living raised somewhat, and their moral natures raised quite a lot, if the colonial governorship is a worthy one. What Burnett has done in *A Little Princess* is to deliver this lesson in domestic terms, framed in an imperial context. The fairy tale of the novel is not only Sara's Cinderella-like restoration to princess status, but the portrayal of empire (or at least well-run empire) as an agent of good for all.

*The Secret Garden* has received more critical attention than *A Little Princess,* not only because of the power of its central metaphor, but also because it succeeds at being many things at once: a pastoral; a story of Mary's psychological development, and Colin's as well; a commentary on Gothic narrative conventions; a romance. In recent years the novel has been analyzed by feminist critics, who tend to disagree about whether or not Mary is disenfranchised at the end of the novel so that Colin may take center stage.[8] Other recent critics have taken note of some of the imperial aspects of the novel. Mike Cadden, for example, notes that when Mary thinks about and reacts to the idea of home, "we see how the home is linked to racial essentialism . . . [H]ome is connected to issues of blood"[9] and thus, Mary's proper home is in a land inhabited by blood relatives, fellow Anglo-Saxons, and not in India with native Others. Jerry Phillips, in a sustained and persuasive argument concerning class politics in *The Secret Garden,* argues that one question the novel presents is "how does the mother country cope when the colonies have to return home?" and notes that India "is signified in the text by at least two modes of discourse, both Orientalist at root: on the one hand, the rhetoric of despotism (values and images of servants and potentates, minions, and rajahs) and, on the other, the rhetoric of mysticism (the discourse of 'fakirs,' 'animal charmers,' storytelling and priests)."[10] These are the same modes of discourse we saw in *A Little Princess* and, like that novel, *The Secret Garden* joins these with a third discourse, that of the domestic empire. The novel is bifurcated: the first half gives us Mary as explorer and colonizer of a strange new world, and the second half shows that this same world already has an emperor, Colin, who emerges as the imperial head of Mary's domestic empire.

India is Mary's first imperial home, as it was Sara's, but India is an important setting in *The Secret Garden,* whereas in *A Little Princess,* India is only memory and metaphor. Unlike Sara's father, Mary's father is not a soldier, but holds a "position under the English Government" in India,[11] and Mary's mother is referred to as the "mem sahib." The "mem sahibs" in India were "expected to bring with them to the imperial territories those same qualities of domestic virtue that were required of them in the home country . . . They were to be the velvet glove on the iron fist of colonial aggrandizement."[12] Sir George Trevelyan in his 1865 history of the Indian Mutiny or Rebellion, *Cawnpore,* notes that these mem sahibs had spent their youths in "the pleasant watering places and country homes of our island, surrounded by all of English comfort and refinement that eastern wealth could buy" and that their domestic virtues were often dulled by the tedium, the insularity, and the hardships of a posting in India."[13] This description certainly fits Mrs. Lennox, who is "tall, slim, and pretty" (4) in her lacy dresses, but who is so lacking in domestic virtues that she ignores her daughter, leaving her in the hands of a native ayah, and in the end sacrifices her family's health on the altar of superficial social engagements, postponing seasonal travel to the hills in order to attend a party.

India has brought out the worst in Mrs. Lennox, not the best. Instead of focusing on raising her daughter to be a proper English lady, she abandons the child to the care of natives, while she herself is seduced by the ease and luxury that the colonial class could afford in India. Mrs. Lennox makes no attempt to train or to uplift her native servants, but leaves them to their own devices, allowing a child to rule them. Mrs. Lennox has not gone native the way Kurtz does in *Heart of Darkness,* but she is demoralized by her life in India: she loses her moral and spiritual footing and neglects her proper place in the domestic empire of house and home. Her abandonment of her domestic responsibilities is the primary reason for her daughter's unhappiness: both mother and daughter are made the worse by their Indian experiences. We are told that Mary's "face was yellow because she had been born in India and had always been ill in one way or another" (1). Mary's yellow face is referred to more than once,[14] and like Sara Crewe, she is confused with the ethnic Other.

The servant Martha tells her, "When I heard you was comin' from India I thought you was a black too" (32), and when she pulls back the sleeping Mary's covers to see the "black," she discovers Mary is "no more black than me—for all you're so yeller" (32). The yellowness here is associated with physical illness and perhaps also moral illness, but it also links Mary to the exotic East, to India, and marks her as an outsider not only to Misselthwaite, but to England as a whole. As Mike Cadden puts it, she is "sick with the contagion of India."[15]

Colin is also sick, not with the contagion of India, but with despotism, which Burnett links to India. Colin is a boy who believes he is both center and ruler of his universe, and Burnett often refers to him as a "rajah," since he expects his every command, no matter how unreasonable, to be obeyed. That he is referred to as a "rajah" and never as "sahib," as Jerry Phillips has noted, suggests that Colin is a despot and rules his kingdom unfairly, just as Miss Minchin did in *A Little Princess*. Good rulers, imperial or otherwise, rule through respect and not by fear. The boys in Kipling's *Stalky & Co.* always obey the Head, whom they respect, and disobey the masters, whose punishment they may fear, but whose authority they do not respect. Miss Minchin's rule also relies more on fear than on respect, and in *The Secret Garden* Colin certainly rules through fear. When he throws one of his tantrums, the servants come for help to Mary who thought "it was funny that all the grown-up people were so frightened that they came to a little girl just because they guessed she was almost as bad as Colin himself" (210).

Mary has also ruled by fear, never hesitating to slap her Indian ayah when displeased. At Misselthwaite, however, she begins to learn the limits of her own authority, that the racial authority she had in India vanishes in England: she thinks the servant Martha might slap back if slapped first. Uncertain of how to deal with this new kind of servant and as yet unaware of Colin's presence, Mary spends the majority of her time out of doors, where there are fewer rules and fewer adults to challenge her authority. She feels free enough to pursue the secret of the garden, even though she knows it is forbidden territory.

The combined setting of house and garden allows Mary to replay the story of imperialism, but to replay it in a domestic setting that is healthier than India and will provide Mary with a framework for her adult life. Whereas the imperial British went off to India and tried to transplant English culture while exploiting Indian resources, Mary must leave India, return to England, and try to root out the inappropriate behaviors and beliefs she acquired in India. Explorers and colonists come to new lands assuming they are unclaimed or uninhabited and thus, free to be claimed by foreigners, just as Mary comes to the new land of the Misselthwaite garden and claims it for her own. Like colonial explorers, she does have some sense that the garden is not free to be taken, but she chooses to ignore the fact for her own convenience. Like colonial explorers, Mary must learn a new language (the Yorkshire dialect) and must learn the names of strange new plants and animals. She must accommodate herself to odd local customs (dressing herself); she must depend upon friendly local guides (Ben Weatherstaff, Martha, Dickon) to help her navigate the strange new land. And the new land seems mysterious, hidden, forbidden, and wrapped in myth—something like the interior of Africa or the mountains of northern India.

Mary's behavior in the garden echoes that of colonial explorers in India and elsewhere. The irony, of course, is that the garden is no strange new land, but Mary's natural home. Mary must play at colonizing and domesticating the wild garden in order that she may recolonize herself into English ways. When she comes to Misselthwaite, she might as well be an Indian native for all she knows of the proper ways of English girlhood. In attempting to resurrect the garden, she resurrects her English self. For Mary, colonial experience in India has been destructive; to heal herself she must repeat the experience of colonization, but in a positive way. She plays at being emperor in the garden, but in truth it is the garden and what it stands for—sacrificial womanhood—that colonizes her.

Mary understands the importance of the garden and has both a psychological and an imperial need to keep the garden for herself. The garden is central to her physical and moral well-being, but until she is further along the road to being an angel in the house, she does not want to share her garden: she has, if you will, an imperial desire to keep her garden kingdom to herself. When she slips and tells Colin, early in their friendship, of the garden, she panics, thinking that "Everything would be spoiled—everything!" if Colin makes the servants take him to the garden, as he says he will. Mary "would never again feel like a missel thrush with a safe-hidden nest" (158). Her need here is mostly an emotional need for safety and a place she can think of as her own, but Burnett puts her desire into an imperial context through Colin, who says he doesn't care that the servants have been forbidden to speak of the secret garden: "I would make them" answer questions (156), and he says "I will make [the servants] take me there and I will let you go, too" (158). His language here is significant: he will "make" servants do things and "let" Mary go where she has already felt free to go. He is threatening because of his ability to wield control over access to the garden, a control that up to now only Mary has had. He threatens her garden rule, as well as her emotional security and safety. Only gradually does Mary become willing to let Colin join her in the secret garden, once he promises to keep the secret with her. At that point they become co-conspirators and, in a sense, co-monarchs of the garden kingdom, although Mary will soon be displaced in favor of Colin.

Mary explores not only the garden, but also the house, becoming increasingly interested in its hundred rooms and their contents. Jerry Phillips has suggested that the house represents the "dead weight" of history,[16] but it also represents, more than the garden, the domestic sphere that Mary must some-day rule—if not Misselthwaite Manor itself, then some other substantial English house. Mary's first exploration of the rooms of the house comes in the chapter before the robin shows her the key to the garden, with the effect that the house is presented as being equally as important as the garden, although the house is never as compelling a setting as the organic, lively garden.

The house, like the garden, suggests empire, but it is Colin's empire and not Mary's. She feels like an interloper even before she discovers Colin. When she first explores the house, she thinks the portraits of men and women in "queer, grand costumes" must be wondering "what a little girl from India was doing in their house" (66), and she is particularly struck by a portrait of a young girl who holds "a green parrot on her finger" (67). Mary instinctively knows that the house is not hers and that her place in it is suspect: she is Indian and not English, an unwelcome foreign presence. But we also learn that past inhabitants of the house have had imperial connections just as Mary has had: hence, the tropical parrot on the English child's finger. Later she discovers a room with "inlaid furniture such as she had seen in India" (67), and finally she discovers a cabinet filled with "about a hundred little elephants made of ivory. They were of different sizes, and some had their mahouts or palanquins on their back" (68). Mary plays with the elephants for awhile— they are familiar creatures to her—and then carefully places them back in order, not taking a single one with her to her underfurnished nursery, whose only toy is a skipping rope provided by Mrs. Sowerby.

Jerry Phillips argues that the Indian room at Misselthwaite is "the beau idéal of assimilation," a "model of otherness displayed, framed, and under control . . . a quotation of national prowess and a tribute to the British imperial spirit."[17] He is right about this, but the room gains even more significance if we consider it in context with the garden, with Mary's situation in the household, and with the masters of Misselthwaite, Mr. Craven and Master Colin. Whereas Mary feels almost no compunction at appropriating the garden for her own uses, she does feel compunction about disturbing the Indian curios. Not only is she an outsider to the house, but she has heard from the moment of her arrival that Mr. Craven is the powerful and unseen uncle who has control of her destiny. It is he who has decreed which room shall be her nursery, where she can and cannot go.

Mary is an outsider not only because of her foreignness, but because of her femaleness. She feels more entitled to a place in the garden, which is con-nected to but not part of the masculine house, which has no mistress beyond Mrs. Medlock, whose primary role in Mary's life is to relay Mr. Craven's wishes. Further, gardens are traditionally associated with women, the secret garden especially so, linked as it is with Colin's dead mother. Mary has explored the grounds just as she has explored the house, but she feels much more freedom in the gardens. The house, unlike the secret garden, carries with it the burden of having to understand people whose ways and often whose language is utterly unfamiliar to her. If Mary's colonization of the garden is relatively easy, that is because it is largely forgotten and unclaimed territory. The house is neither, yet must also be claimed by Mary if she is going to truly blossom into ideal womanhood. A woman without a house to rule in Edwardian England is hardly a woman at all, and certainly not a lady.

Mary can only appropriate the house and its values by combining forces with its despotic ruler, Colin, who is hidden in the "heart of darkness" of his curtained and secret bedroom, access to which is through a curtained doorway, just as entrance to the garden is through a curtain of leaves and vines. When Mary penetrates Colin's curtains, she finds a mysterious boy who "could have anything he asked for and was never made to do anything he did not like to do," who says he will "let" Mary do things, and who "mak[es] her tell him a great deal about India" (155). He is a male version of Mary's earlier Indian incarnation, a point Burnett underlines by repeatedly referring to Colin as a "rajah." He is the ruler of the empire of the house, yet he is no sahib. Indian rajahs ruled their own people, but ultimately answer to the British, just as Colin rules over the servants of the house, but must ultimately answer to his father, who is the sahib of the manor. Yet Mr. Craven is a poor sahib, since he has abandoned his responsibilities and thus left the way open for his despotic rajah of a son to rule the kingdom of the house.

There is an inherent critique of empire suggested here. When the legitimate ruler, be it Mr. Craven or a colonial administrator like Mr. Lennox, relinquishes authority, the rule that arises in his place may well be despotic and without limits, a rule breeding fear rather than loyalty among its subjects. This is precisely what happens in *The Secret Garden*. Mr. Craven should stay in England to run his estate and to help raise his son into proper British manhood, and when he abandons his responsibilities, he leaves his son to govern without limits and without guidance.

Mr. Craven's behavior mirrors that of Mrs. Lennox, and perhaps of her husband as well. Mrs. Lennox abandons her daughter as thoroughly as Mr. Craven abandons his son. That she can spend her time and energies in social pursuits rather than on mothering implies that her husband, whatever his skills as colonial administrator, is not a very good administrator of his own family. He, too, ignores his daughter and allows his wife free rein, with the result that both parents die and Mary is left as an unwanted and unpleasant child. If failure of imperial rule leads to unruly behavior among native subjects, failure of parental rule leads to upstart and bossy children. Family life mirrors, in miniature, some of the larger issues of empire.

Burnett's primary purpose in the early stages of the Mary/Colin relationship is to show Colin as a parallel figure to Mary, to show Mary's growth and change through the garden, and to provide a means to get Colin out of the house and into the garden and a state of health. This shift to an emphasis on

Colin has been problematic for critics, leading to a variety of arguments about whether the novel keeps Mary at its core or capitulates to male authority and to patriarchal forces. If we put the novel in an imperial context, the arguments for Mary's capitulation and the lessening of her importance in the novel gain strength. In the world of the British empire, Mary can participate in empire not as direct colonial ruler, but only as an adjunct to male political power. Her rescue of the garden has been preparatory play in the proper use of imperial power, but in order for Mary to become an ideal woman she must give up direct control of any empire or land she thinks she has discovered for her own. It is not for her to have direct rule of a kingdom, not even a garden kingdom or a domestic kingdom. Men hold the true power, and Mary can rule only indirectly through Colin, and Colin only indirectly through his father, at least until he comes into his inheritance. Colin's imperial behavior is based on his status as landed gentleman; Mary's has no basis at all.

As soon as Mary meets Colin, as soon as empire, gender, and class intersect in the novel, Mary diminishes in importance and begins to concentrate not on nurturing herself, but on nurturing Colin. Burnett means the reader to understand that nurturing Colin helps Mary nurture herself, helps her become less self-involved, but this is a lesson not so much in self-fulfillment as in self-denial. Mary becomes Colin's substitute mother, singing hymns to him in Hindustani and giving him a good talking-to when he needs it. She is learning, through Colin, to subordinate her own desires (for garden, for power) in order to benefit others. She is, in fact, learning some of the essential lessons in being an "angel in the house," rather than in being an individual. She shares the garden with Colin, but in doing so loses the garden completely. The last paragraph of the novel presents Mr. Craven, for the first time, as "Master of Misselthwaite," and the last words of the novel describe Colin as "Master Colin." Mary has become invisible, not even the "Mistress Mary quite contrary" she was at the beginning of the novel. The men have mastered themselves and their domain—and Mary.

In the arc of character development in this novel, Mary goes from being the equivalent of a female rajah (if women could have been rajahs in India) to companion and guide to a male rajah, to the invisible woman whose place in the household is totally dependent upon male acceptance and approval. Colin, on the other hand, goes from tyrannical rajah to competent, athletic, ideal British boyhood, and is ready at the end to be joined by his reformed father and to be educated as befits a worthy heir to British imperial history and wealth, exemplified by Misselthwaite Manor itself.

Jerry Phillips has argued that the spiritual egalitarianism of the novel—its inclusion of working-class characters like Dickon, Martha, and Ben Weatherstaff in the resurrection of the garden—is undermined by class-bound elitism: Dickon and Ben are also invisible in the last scene of the novel. Phillips is right, I think, but I would take his argument even further.

Just as *The Secret Garden* suggests that spiritual egalitarianism does not equal social egalitarianism, imperialism—and particularly imperial missionary work—also suggested that although we may all be one in the eyes of God, we are not all one in the eyes of the British Empire. Becky will remain a servant in *A Little Princess* and Sara will not; Mary may regain physical and moral health in England, but she loses her status as colonial ruler and is subjugated to the masculine rule of primogeniture. Her best hope is to grow up to be a spouse to Colin or someone like him, and thus gain indirect power through running a domestic empire, not an imperial one.

In many ways Burnett's novels are more closely associated with the nineteenth century than with the twentieth: they look back to romance, to fairytale, to the pastoral, to the image of children (or at least middle-class children) as innocents. But as Marcus Crouch has noted, "E. Nesbit is the key figure" of the Edwardian age[18] and "stands squarely in the doorway between the nineteenth and twentieth centuries,"[19] and Suzanne Rahn writes that "E. Nesbit, if anyone, could be called the children's writer's children's writer of our century."[20] Her works influenced C. S. Lewis, Arthur Ransome, Noël Streatfield, and other twentieth-century writers for children.

Yet at the same time, the nineteenth century, including the tropes of imperialism and empire, is omnipresent in her works, as are references to Rudyard Kipling (whom Nesbit knew and admired, as Kipling admired her). At first this may seem odd, since Nesbit was one of the founding members of the Fabian Society, affected the aesthetic clothing of forward-thinking women, cut her hair short, and smoked in public. Yet despite her socialism and her daring public persona, Nesbit did not support women's suffrage, and at times her political views seem as contrary and contradictory as Kipling's.

There is no doubt that the fictional children she invented, particularly the Bastables, had profound effects upon children's books that followed. Nesbit was not the first writer to present mischief-making children—Catherine Sinclair's *Holiday House* (1839) and Yonge's *The Daisy Chain* had trouble-prone protagonists—but Nesbit is very nearly the first to tell her stories in the voice of a child, not an adult. As Oswald Bastable narrates his adventures with his siblings, no adult narrative voice steps in to comment upon the action or to moralize. Everything comes to us filtered through the consciousness of a (precocious) child. His narration "functions to alleviate a difficulty often present in children's books—the split between the adult writer and the child reader, as well as the split between the adult narrator and the child character.[21] Oswald is both "dramatized narrator and dramatized author," who endorses the childhood values of "honesty, courage, and imagination," while disapproving of "excessive piety, sneakiness, lying and lack of imagination."[22] These are the same values espoused by Stalky and his friends in Kipling's novel, published the same year as *The Story of the Treasure Seekers*. Nesbit

writes "*against* Maria Edgeworth and *for* Rudyard Kipling,"[23]against didacti-
cism and authorial intrusion and for a more realistic portrayal of childhood
and the voice of children. In this she is certainly writing against the didacti-
cism of nineteenth-century evangelical writing. But in writing "for Kipling"
Nesbit is also espousing the values of imperialism.

*The Story of the Treasure Seekers*[24] is the story of a middle-class, motherless family of five children who have fallen on hard financial times, and
who determine to restore the "fallen fortune" of the House of Bastable (11).
This they attempt through a variety of schemes suggested to them by fiction
they have read, and all of which backfire in comic ways. The novel ends with
the appearance of a fairy godfather in the person of the "Indian uncle," who,
indeed, does help restore the fortunes of the House of Bastable (and perhaps
influenced the creation of Mr. Carrisford in Burnett's *A Little Princess,* published just five years later).

Oswald, the narrator of the Bastable books, introduces us to his siblings,
who at first appear to be industrious and obedient: Dora, for example, is
mending a hole in some stockings. But seriousness and industry, those solid
Victorian virtues, are undermined by child's play, which is where the children
prefer to direct their energies. Alice, we are told, once tried to knit a scarf for
her brother, but when he refused to wear it, "we used it as a pennon" (11) in
imaginative play. Their play is almost always informed by books they have
read, books that range from popular tales of Dick Turpin to Charlotte Yonge's
*The Daisy Chain* and, most significantly and most often, to Kipling's books,
particularly the *Jungle Books,* which play a large role in the second volume of
the series. The only adult who is privy to their play is Albert-next-door's-
uncle, himself a writer who has spent time in India (and is a precursor to
Arthur Ransome's Captain Flint).

Although the Bastable family has fallen on hard times—Mr. Bastable
can no longer afford the school fees for his children—the children are rich in
both imagination and in literary background. Just as romantic literature
helped sustain Sara Crewe in her attic, adventure fiction sustains the Bastables. Oswald may admit that *The Daisy Chain* is more "ripping" than one
might think, but stories of pirates, highwaymen, and explorers are what really
attract the children and color their view of the possibilities of their world,
even if they are for the moment hard-up bourgeois children.

The bourgeois values of the Bastables are apparent in their concern about
keeping up appearances. No one in the family ever talks directly about the
increasing poverty of the Bastables, nor do any of the neighbors, many of
whom are also living in genteel middle-class poverty. Oswald also frequently
reminds the reader of the "honorable" way of doing things; the children may
get into mischief, but they never intend to; they always apologize for mistakes, never sneak, and never tell lies. All of these suggest solid middle-class,
even public school values in these children, despite the fact that (like Ransome's children), the Bastables are on perpetual holiday.

The Bastable children are sensible and aware of the adult world around them, and the adult world at the turn of the century was often preoccupied with matters of empire, especially after the outbreak of the first Boer War (1880–81) and the second in 1899. Matters of empire are woven into Nesbit's books with a naturalness suggestive of the omnipresence of imperial matters in British domestic life. We hear that the children have a cousin in the Navy; that Oswald likes Albert-next-door's-uncle because "his hair is light and his face is brown. He has been to sea, but now he writes books" (27) and refers to the children's play-tent as "the Turkish Bath" (33); Oswald himself plays at being "an Arab physician" with a turban (115); the children become bored when they hear adults discussing "Native Races and Imperial something" (216). As these brief examples indicate, much of what the children find intriguing lies not within the borders of England, but overseas in Britain's imperial possessions. Albert-next-door's-uncle, we later learn, is brown not only from sailing, but from his years spent in India; naval officers were often posted to the colonies to keep order or to protect trade routes; and the children have perhaps learned of Turkish baths and Arab physicians not only from novels, but also from overheard discussions about Egypt and the Suez Canal. Talk of empire is common among the adults, and it inspires the children's play as much as detective novels and tales of pirates do.

The writer most often referred to by Oswald and his siblings is Rudyard Kipling, who is mentioned by name five times in *The Story of the Treasure Seekers* and six times in *The Wouldbegoods*. The Bastables in *The Wouldbegoods* play a game based on the *Jungle Books,* which opens the novel and lands the children into serious trouble with the Indian uncle. Oswald credits Kipling with teaching him elements of the craft of narrative, and when the children meet Mrs. Leslie (a fictional portrait of Nesbit) she gains their immediate liking and admiration because she asks if they are going to the zoo "to look for Bagheera."

What attracts the children to Kipling is the energy and excitement of his tales, and the promise he holds out of adventure. These are the same qualities that attract the children to detective novels, stories of pirates, and stories of arctic exploration (the latter an increasingly important image in children's fiction as the empire began to wane). The children do not question that adults can take off for foreign lands, meet exotic foreigners, and have adventures involving treasure and tigers. Going off to soldier, or to administer to colonial subjects, or to explore and appropriate new lands, struck children as being delightful prospects, promising action, power over others, and status as discoverers of a new world, all things guaranteed to appeal to children. Adults, too, were susceptible to the call of adventure. Heading out to India or Africa offered adult men, at any rate, the chance to escape responsibilities at home, to play out in real life what they could only play act as children: fighting "savages," discovering new lands, taming (or slaying) wild animals. Going out to the colonies provided adult men the possibility of remaining adolescent forever, free of women and family, free to roam the world in the company of like-minded, competent, courageous, sun-burned men like themselves. A dynamic tension existed between adventure fiction and actual imperial adventure: imperial exploration often inspired adventure stories, which in turn inspired young men to go off on real adventures of their own. Martin Green has argued that the kinds of adventure stories influencing the Bastable children's play comprised "the energizing myth of English imperialism. They were, collectively, the story England told itself as it went to sleep at night; and, in the form of dreams, they charged England's will with the energy to go out into the world and explore, conquer, and rule."[25]

In the first volume of the Bastable stories, empire is a constant hum beneath the narrative of the children's adventures in London, and empire is linked to adventure. The children want both to amuse themselves and to restore the family fortunes of "the ancestral home" (10), and decide that digging for treasure in the backyard might restore them to fortune. But the girls "wouldn't dig with spades that had cobwebs on them. Girls would never do for African explorers or anything like that" (22). They try to sell some of their poetry, and on the way to see an editor, stop at St. Paul's to look at the monument to Charles George Gordon, imperial hero in the Crimea, in China (where he directed the burning of the Chinese emperor's summer palace and gained the popular sobriquet of "Chinese Gordon"), and in Africa, where he was governor of Equatoria in the Sudan and where, in 1885, he was killed by Sudanese rebels and made a martyred warrior-saint by the British public. The children consider his monument to be "very flat, considering what a man he was" (59). When they try to produce a newspaper, they write a serial story about "Sam Redfern the Bushranger" (104). When a "robber" gets into the house, he tells the children he has been "a war-correspondent . . . and a colonel of dragoons" (191). This undercurrent of imperial references is often linked to more romantic sorts of adventure stories: digging for treasure prompts Oswald to mention not only African explorers, but pirates; and when the children hear of their mother's Indian uncle, they think not only of India but of North American Indians and the novels of James Fenimore Cooper. Imperialism is everywhere, and it is nearly always linked with romantic adventure tales.

The inclusion of the Indian uncle brings the combination of empire and romantic adventure from the background and into the foreground. Early in the novel the children wish "a fairy would come down the chimney and drop a jewel on the table—a jewel worth just a hundred pounds" (113) and the Indian uncle becomes such a fairy, although he arrives by carriage and not by chimney flue. We first hear of the uncle late in the novel, when Mr. Bastable announces, "Your dear Mother's Indian Uncle is coming to dinner tomorrow night . . . and he is coming to talk business with me" (211). Hearing of the uncle naturally makes Oswald think of Kipling, and he ends the chapter announcing the imminent arrival of the Indian uncle by saying, "The next day was the most memorable day in all our lives, but we didn't know that then. But that is another story. I think that is such a useful way to know when you can't think how to end up a chapter. I learnt it from another writer named Kipling" (212–13). The Indian uncle provides a combination of seemingly magical riches and their very realistic imperial provenance.

When the children first glimpse the Indian uncle, "He didn't look like an Indian but just like a kind of brown, big Englishman" (214). Like Mary Lennox, his color links him to his foreign origin. He may not be yellow but a healthier brown, but he still complains of his "liver" when asked to partake of pudding by the children (222). The children have asked him to dinner in their nursery under the misapprehension that he is a "poor" Indian, mistaking the meanings of "unfortunate" and "poverty-stricken." They apparently have three contexts for Indians: Kipling's Indians, North American Indians, and Alexander Pope's "Lo, the poor Indian!" which Oswald quotes twice. The lines is from the first epistle of Pope's *Essay on Man* and the lines read: "Lo! the poor Indian! Whose untutor'd mind/Sees God in clouds, or hears him in the wind," suggesting the pagan nature of Indians rather than their economic status. The children overhear the uncle say he is a "poor broken-down man," which further confirms their idea that the uncle must be impoverished. And of course, North American and subcontinental Indians would also be poor from the children's point of view, and all of them would be "untutor'd" in Western ways. The children's confusion about the nature of Indians continues despite the uncle's talk of elephants and tigers. The children ask him about "wigwams, and wampum, and moccasins, and beavers, but he did not seem to know, or else he was shy about talking of the wonders of his native land" (224).

The children do not differentiate between natives in North America and natives in India, and why should they? All natives are Other, and what matter is that they *are* different, not in *how* they are different, either from each other or from Englishmen. Nesbit uses the children's haziness about what "Indian" means to comic effect in her novel, but what underlies the comedy are several assumptions about imperialism and imperial thought. The first assumption is that generic Otherness matters more than cultural or national or individual identity. Second, native Others are exotic creatures with strange clothes who provide entertainment for Westerners. This is the assumption underlying everything from turn-of-the-century America Wild West Shows, to traveling exhibits of Hottentots and "native villages" in England. Third, native Others can provide Westerners not only with entertainment, but with wealth, as the Indian Uncle's later actions demonstrate.

The Indian Uncle indulges the children in their desire for exotic narrative and romantic stories. The children's dinner party incorporates elements of fantasy, as the uncle joins them in pretending the rabbit is really a deer they slew in the forest and the pudding "a wild boar at bay, and very hard indeed to kill, even with forks" (222). Dinner is followed by stories "about tiger shooting and about elephants" (224). The next day the uncle transforms himself into a fairy godfather. The day is gloomy and rainy, but Oswald spies a carriage coming down the street and says, "Here comes the coach of the Fairy Godmother" (229), reiterating the children's hope that somehow the family fortunes can be restored. In a scene Burnett seems to have borrowed from wholesale, the Indian Uncle is announced, like Mr. Carrisford, first by his possessions. The carriage has "boxes on the top and knobby parcels sticking out of the window . . . The cabman got down, and some one inside handed out ever so many parcels of different shapes and sizes" (229) until finally the Indian Uncle appears from inside the carriage and announces that all the parcels are for the children, including "model engines . . . and some ivory chess men for Dicky: the castles of the chessmen are elephant-and-castles. There is a railway station called that; I never knew what it meant before" (231–32).

The list of presents the Indian Uncle gives to the children suggests that India is both a source of British wealth and a shaper of British culture. The uncle brings exotic and foreign goods to the Bastables, goods that reflect not only imperialism in general, but specific British forays into Asia, particularly Japan. Even the single object that is not foreign in origin—the model engines—suggests imperialism. The railway is a marker of industrialized and "advanced" nations, and the thousands of miles of rail the British laid in India and Africa helped them consolidate their imperial role. The silks and silver bangles and brass objects and carved fans the Indian uncle brings to the Bastable family represent the appropriation of foreign wealth for domestic purposes. The uncle not only brings presents for his nieces and nephews, but also delivers Mr. Bastable from his business troubles and moves the entire Bastable family into his substantial mansion. India and other imperial holdings bring wealth to the Bastables as they did for Britain as a whole.

Imperialism impacted Britain not only economically, but also culturally. Oswald's realization that the name of the tube stop The Elephant and Castle has its origins in India shows that elements of Indian culture have crept into the fabric of England itself, have been domesticated and tamed and industrialized: we have tube stops, not elephant stops, but the tube stops refer to India under the raj. The interweaving of foreign imperial matters into everyday life has already been suggested in the undercurrent of imperial references in the novel, but in the climax of the story is foregrounded. The fates of India and Britain, by 1899, were inextricably entwined, on levels both cultural and political. Indian words had become English words: jodphurs, verandahs, pukka, and so forth. Curry was beginning to appear on English dinner tables at the same time English was becoming *lingua franca* in multilingual India.

There is an unspoken assumption in *The Story of the Treasure Seekers* that treasure, for Britain, is to be found not at home, but in the colonies, and that removing treasure from the colonies and bringing it home to England is both good and natural. India has not only made the Indian uncle wealthy as an individual, but India also restores the fortunes of the British bourgeoisie. The only "treasure" the children find on British soil are the sovereigns planted by Albert-next-door's-uncle, whose money comes from the stories he writes about his experiences in India. India is the source of a wealth of toys and gifts for the children, the source of rescued finances for the father and, by extension, for the health of the British economy.

The theme of imperial bounty continues in *The Wouldbegoods* (1901),[26] which begins with the Bastables living with the Indian uncle in a house "with vineries and pineries, and gas and water, and shrubberies and stabling, and replete with every modern convenience, like it says in Dyer & Hilton's list of Eligible House Property" (11). The Bastables have two other children visiting them, and on a day the adults are absent, the children go out to the large garden to play at Kipling's *Jungle Book*. They have the great advantage of being able to borrow—without asking—a number of the uncle's Indian souvenirs, with which they can make their play more realistic. The two visiting children, Denny and Daisy, have neither read Kipling, nor had much experience at the boisterous fantasy play the Bastables enjoy. The Bastables borrow the uncle's animal trophies and drape them over sofa bolsters to serve as wild beasts, and Oswald unlocks a glass curio cabinet to borrow a stuffed fox holding a duck in its mouth, to which they add a variety of stuffed birds, and finally, they drape two tiger skins over beer stands and bolsters. To make all as realistic as possible, they turn on the garden hose to create a river and cataracts.

But everything falls to pieces when the visiting Daisy, who has not been playing but has been inside reading, comes outside "just as Dody and Noël had got under the tigers and were shoving them along to fright each other" (22). Poor Daisy utters "a shriek like a railway whistle" and falls "flat to the ground" (23), and before she can revive, the adults appear on the scene. As Oswald tells us, "We had no clothes on to speak of . . . Daisy was in a faint or a fit or dead, none of us then knew which. And all the stuffed animals were there staring the uncle in the face. Most of them had got a sprinkling, and the otter and the duck-bill brute were simply soaked. And three of us were dark brown [from dye applied to the skin]. Concealment, as so often happens, was impossible" (24).

The scene is a comic *tour de force* not only because the children behave so realistically, but because Nesbit manages to capture both their intense pleasure and pride in their inventiveness, as well as their sudden realization that they have crossed the line and are in serious trouble with their uncle. In fact, their father will send them off to the country in the next chapter, to get them out of the bachelor uncle's hair. But part of the humor also has to do with the ways Nesbit is playing with imperial imagery. To begin with, Kipling is at the heart of the scene, and not only because the adult Nesbit admired his writing: his books, and especially the *Jungle Books,* were enormously popular with children. In fact, Kipling provided many children with their first literary experiences of empire. Second, there is a marvelous irony in the way civilized English children take the dead and domesticated emblems of empire, and in trying to enliven them end up as half-naked "savages" themselves. Nesbit depends upon the contrast between "civilized" English child and child-playing-at-"savage" for her comic effect, because of course the children are savages, at least in the eyes of the horrified uncle. The children have managed to go native within the confines of a manicured English garden. Third, the children, in the guise of natives, have disobeyed the spirit of the law of the adults, here stand-ins for the civilized British colonizers. The children have not specifically been forbidden to take souvenirs to the garden and give them a good hosing, but they ought to have known better.

The core of the humor of this scene is the clash of child culture and adult culture, which in the context of the fantasy play of the children is given an imperial twist by Nesbit: the clothed and civilized ladies and gentlemen are aghast at the unclothed and "savage" children, who are then banished to the countryside until they learn to be good. Their poor uncle wants to enjoy his imperial wealth and imperial souvenirs in peace: he does not want to replay imperial conquest in his garden.

*The Story of the Treasure Seekers* ends with the Indian uncle as fairy godfather raising the Bastables back into middle-class solvency, and *The Wouldbegoods* and *The New Treasure Seekers* (1904) are, at least in part, stories of how the Bastable children are acculturated into middle-class values: class status rests not only upon one's finances, but also upon one's values. W. W. Robson points out that despite Nesbit's socialism, "it cannot be denied that [her] stories are about middle-class children and imply middle-class values."[27] Like Kipling, Nesbit would use fantasy and time travel in later fantasies like *The Story of the Amulet* (1906) to convey Britain's past to children, although for Nesbit "history was a source of romantic adventure; for Kipling, it was a key to the problems of the present."[28] But in the Bastable stories, history in the generalized sense of the ancient roots of the British present, as well as the ways the British present might be leading to the future, are Nesbit's concerns—and since British history was imperial in past Roman times and imperial in Nesbit's time, the history the children encounter is shot through with imperial issues and events.

The first indication that *The Wouldbegoods* is not only a parody of earlier moral tales for children, but also a kind of introduction to British culture and nationalism, is the setting of the country Moat House, to which the children are banished by their father and the Indian uncle. The Moat House is set where "There has been a house since Saxon times. It is a manor, and a manor goes on having a house on it whatever happens" (26–27). The house, much like Dan and Una's house in the Puck books, suggests the longevity and stability of Britain. Nesbit implies here that Britain begins with the Saxons and that there is a continuity to the British people and their history, symbolized by the house. Times may change and Romans and Normans may invade, but what matters is that the land persists, and even if the current owner of the Moat House rents it out because he prefers a home with more modern conveniences, the House remains, along with its lands and its faithful retainers. As Anita Moss has noted, Nesbit's "desire for social justice and a humane order" did not always coalesce with "her sometimes conservative idealization of the past."[29]

The idealization of the past can be seen in "The Sale of Antiquities" chapter of *The Wouldbegoods,* where the children, trying to be helpful, plant some "antiquities" in a field they know is to be searched by a group of amateur archeologists. The would-be-archeologists want not only to dig up a barrow, but also to view the Moat House which, as the president of the society writes in a note, is not only beautiful but, "as you are doubtless aware, of great historic interest, having been for some years the residence of the celebrated Sir Thomas Wyatt" (185). The land and the house, then, have a history going back to the Romans, up through the Renaissance, and into the present, and that history is both cultural and political: Roman antiquities are both historical and cultural artifacts, and Wyatt was both poet and diplomat at the court of Henry VIII. Furthermore, in the children's expedition to bury household objects for the antiquarians to discover, they rely upon recent events in British national history for aid.

As the children set off from the house with their relics, two of them are "sent on ahead as scouts to see if the coast was clear. We have learned the true usefulness of scouts from reading about the Transvaal War" (192). Nesbit does not specifically refer to Baden-Powell's Boy Scout movement, but the Bastable books are contemporaneous with the founding of the Scouts. The first edition of Baden-Powell's *Scouting for Boys* was published in 1908, after its author discovered that boys like Oswald had been reading and using his adult works on scouting and tracking. Furthermore, the founding of the Scouts came hard on the heels of the Defense of Mafeking (1899–1900), in which Baden-Powell became a national hero by holding off a much larger Boer force until the siege could be relieved.

Scouting had explicit imperial roots and connections. The full title of the Girl Guide book Baden-Powell cowrote with his sister Agnes in 1912 is *The Handbook for Girl Guides, or How Girls Can Help Build the Empire,* and he wrote in *Empire Book: Your Empire* (another Scouting text), "Empire is not a jingo-term meaning that we want to spread ourselves aggressively over vast territories in rivalry with others—it stands for team work of free young British nations growing up in different parts of the world in friendly comradeship of goodwill and co-operation."[30] Although the Bastables do not belong to the Scouting movement, they are clearly influenced by it and by the Boer War campaign in South Africa, which makes more than one appearance in *The Wouldbegoods.*

The antiquarians are searching for Roman relics, for reminders of Britain's past as part of imperial Rome, a past that both Kipling and Nesbit suggest paved the way for Britain's own Anglo-Saxon empire. The children unknowingly manage to bury a real piece of Roman pottery for the antiquarians to discover, and which they must later reclaim and return to its proper owner, the owner of the Saxon Moat House. The entire incident suggests links between the Saxon and Roman pasts and the imperial presence. Furthermore, the importance of the antiquarians suggests the importance of history for all British, the influence of history upon the present and upon the future imperial status of Britain.

The Boer War makes another appearance in *The Wouldbegoods* when the children encounter a regiment of soldiers in the neighborhood, practicing drill. The first time they see the soldiers the children salute, and then go home to make a Union Jack from scraps so that the next day they can wave it at the soldiers and cry out, "Three cheers for the Queen and the British Army!" (47). On the third day, the children dress as much like soldiers as they can, and finally the soldiers stop to talk to them. A friendly officer explains guns to them, showing them artillery that can throw fifteen-pound shells and explaining how the guns are taken apart and put together again. He then says, "You won't see us many more times. We're ordered to the front" (51). Later references to the Transvaal make clear that these soldiers are off to fight in the Boer War, probably the second Boer War (1899–1902) begun when the Boer attacked the British Cape Colony and Natal. The children, although they have only the foggiest idea of where these soldiers might be headed, or what the nature of war really is, or why the British would be fighting in far-off Africa, are nonetheless attracted to the romance of war, and it is the children's emotional responses to the soldiers that are most important to an understanding of the underlying imperial and patriotic spirit of the book.

Oswald wants to go off to Africa as a bugler and tells us that seeing the soldiers with their artillery was "glorious. It made you tremble all over . . . and Oswald felt differently to what he ever did before" (49). Both the girls and the boys are stirred by the regimental regalia of the soldiers, and they ask their father for money to provide keepsakes of tobacco and pipes for the soldiers to take with them to Africa. Nesbit here is using the same tactics—even if she is using them more subtly—as the boys' papers and popular novels of the period, which emphasized the adventure and glory of war, the pageantry of flying pennons and blaring bugles, and the overall superiority of British forces to others. The romanticizing of both empire and imperial martial conflict was omnipresent in British children's culture of the period. We have already seen Kipling's comments on boyhood education and militarism in *Stalky & Co.*, and J. A. Magnan, in tracing the idealization of empire in British public schools of the Edwardian era, says that "The English public schoolboy ran the British Empire,"[31] and those children (like the Bastables) who could not attend public schools could, and did, read about them in the scores of novels and stories set in fictional public schools.

Even though patriotism is lauded in *The Wouldbegoods,* it is never talked about openly, as if national pride were somehow too private and too sacred to be spoken of overtly. This is another way Nesbit parallels Kipling, who devoted an entire Stalky story to this issue. In "The Flag of Their Country" Mr. Raymond Martin, a Conservative Member of Parliment, comes to address the boys on the subject of patriotism. The boys are appalled at the M.P., who by speaking aloud of patriotism devalues it for the boys: "In a raucous voice he cried aloud little matters, like the hope of Honour and the dream of Glory, that boys do not discuss even with their most intimate equals" (218). This same philosophy underlies Nesbit's treatment of the soldiers in *The Wouldbegoods,* although she romanticizes soldiery far more than does Kipling.

The romanticizing of war continues after the soldiers have left the Bastable children behind. The next story Oswald tells us is of the poor woman who believes her soldier son Bill has been lost "in the Southern hemisphere" (60). Oswald "only hopes if he falls on the wild battlefield, which is his highest ambition, that somebody will be as sorry about him as he was about Bill, that's all!" (61).[32] The children make a tombstone for Bill, who then miraculously appears on the road, not dead after all, so the children give him tobacco left over from their gifts to the other soldiers, and we are told that "Father is going to have [Bill] for under-gardener when his wounds get well" (63).

It is both the nature of Bill's story and its placement in the narrative that illuminate the presence of Bill's story in Nesbit's narrative. The story of Bill appears directly after the regiment of soldiers has headed off to the Transvaal, and of them Oswald merely says, "We have never seen those brave soldiers again" (54), which certainly hints at the serious and fatal nature of warfare and might be seen as undercutting the naïve patriotism of the children. But in the very next paragraph Oswald tells us that "I have told you all this [about the soldiers] to show you how we got so keen about soldiers, and why we sought to aid and abet the poor widow at the white cottage," the widow who is also the mother of the missing, presumed-dead, Bill (54). The entire story of the children's desire to help the widow, how they first annoy and anger her, then please her with their tombstone, and then how both children and widow are astonished and delighted at the resurrection of Bill, has the effect of muting the fact that not all soldiers return, and indeed of muting the brutal nature of military, imperial conflicts in the Transvaal and elsewhere. Instead, the probability of soldiers' return to hearth and home is held out, and Bill's homecoming is sweetened by the promise of a job as underling on the estate of those people who stand to profit from soldiers' sacrifices of both health and life on the battlefield.

Here we have a combination of imperialism and class at work. The Bastables take for granted a class system in which the working classes should be grateful for a chance to be servants to the upper classes, and where the upper classes benefit from the labor not only of gardeners, but also of the working-class soldiers who cleared the way for imperialism and foreign commerce, which enrich the middle classes far more than the working classes. The attitudes of all the Bastable children, especially evident in Oswald, are decidedly bourgeois. Julia Briggs has noted that Oswald is "very much a small boy," but he also "speaks for the adult males of his society" and is set up "as a target for comic irony, the complacent Victorian patriarch in embryo."[33]

When the children in *The Wouldbegoods* are not playing at soldiers and empire, they are playing at being explorers. The imagery of exploration, and particularly of Arctic and Antarctic exploration, gained increasing importance in English literature for both adults and children as the twentieth century progressed. By the turn of the century, after the Boer War and before the World War I, there was not much more empire to amass: nearly every inch of the earth's land surface was either claimed by a Western nation or was imagined useless and inaccessible. But the inaccessible places—even if one did not want to annex them, even if they did not have natural resources nor native workers to exploit—could be put to patriotic use. One has only to look at the British response to Robert Falcon Scott's Antarctic expeditions, particularly the last and fatal push for the South Pole, to see how fighting against geography and climate could be used to emphasize British grit and superiority. Indeed, the British never forgave the Norwegian Roald Amundsen for reaching the South Pole first, partly because he was ungentlemanly enough to eat his sled dogs for food—and for having planned to do so before he ever reached Antarctica—but also because Amundsen was Norwegian and a symbol of a fledgling nation, not of a long-standing empire like Britain's. But Antarctic exploration had not really begun at the time Nesbit was writing: it is Arctic exploration that has a pull on the Bastable children.

Chapter Seven of *The Wouldbegoods* is entitled, "Being Beavers; Or, the Young Explorers (Arctic or Otherwise)," and in it the children make "two expeditions to discover the source of the Nile (or the North Pole)" (128). Whether they play at Northern or Southern expeditions does not matter: what matters is the romance of exploration, the glory of being "first" even in make-believe, and the expansion of the British not only around the globe, but from pole to pole. The children know that explorers often become national heroes. David Livingstone, for example, died while exploring Africa. His native companions salted and preserved his body and shipped it home to England to a spectacular funeral in Westminster Abbey. Oswald might be just as happy to die a "glorious" death as an explorer as to die gloriously as a soldier, and he and his siblings would certainly know the tales of explorers like Livingstone, not only through reading newspapers and listening to adult conversation, but also from publications like *Magnet Stories,* which Oswald specifically mentions, or in nonfiction accounts like that of "that big book . . . Mr. Nansen wrote" (131), a reference to Nansen's *Farthest North* (a text the Swallows and Amazons are also familiar with). Their imaginative play includes an adventure with real leeches, leaving Denny with bandaged legs and all the children looking like "wounded warriors returning" (145). Exploration and imperial war are intertwined here.

*The New Treasure Seekers* expands upon the themes of the first two books in the series. The children's dog is stolen, or so they think, and as they search for him "Over the Water to China," they again imagine themselves as having "the true explorer's instincts" (76) and they do discover China, or at least a kind of Chinatown, complete with an aged Chinese man who speaks in dialect: "Nicee lilly girlee, some piecee flowlee" (79), and whom the children rescue from some Caucasian street children. Their charitable impulse comes not out of sympathy for the Chinaman's Otherness, but out of respect for his age. Like all good middle-class persons, they abhor unfairness and disrespect, and help the Chinaman even though he lives in a "dirty" room with a "dirty" cloth on the sideboard, which also contains "an idol" (80-81). The entire room is filled with an odd smell that "seemed to have all sorts of things in it— glue and gunpowder and white garden lilies and burnt fat, and it was not so easy to breathe as plain air" (81).

This brief excursion to what is essentially a foreign land to the children emphasizes the dangers of exploring new lands and encountering the Other. The children ask a sailor if he has seen their missing dog, and the sailor tells them that if they are captured by the Chinaman "'e'll 'ave a pie as'll need a big crust to cover it" (70), and although the children know that the "Chinese are not cannibals," they also know that "the Chinese really do eat dogs, as well as rats and birds' nests and other disgraceful forms of eating" (70), and they know their father "wouldn't like us being in these wild, savage places" (73). Exploring lands that are already inhabited by natives poses different threats than are posed by the nearly empty Arctic or the completely empty Antarctic. The "savages" one meets—even Chinese "savages," whose civilization is vastly older than Britain's—are dirty, disgusting, unintelligible, and pose a threat to life and limb.

The exploration theme continues later in the book, when the children explore the Red House of some of their adult friends. The chapter is entitled "The Intrepid Explorer and His Lieutenant," and in it the children discover a hidden basement. In the process, referring to Kipling once again, they fear there might be "serpents guarding the treasure like in the Cold Lairs" (113), and even when they discover the basement and show the owner of the house the antique furniture stored there, Mr. Red House (as the children call him) says, "Nansen is nothing to you! You ought to have a medal for daring explorations" (114). One of the items the children discover and Mr. Red House takes away to restore turns out to be an antique cradle, which Mr. and Mrs. Red House use for their new baby. Exploration, then, may turn out to have benefits for coming generations, Nesbit suggests.

Nesbit also links this exploratory expedition to British nationalism, Nansen notwithstanding. The children have first made friends with the owners of the Red House when they have been playing at being antiquarians, writing out "historical papers" on the subjects of Agincourt; the Norman conquest of the Saxons and the eventual merging of the two into "Britons"; King John's concessions to the nobles, the beginning of the English parliamentary system; and the struggle between Mary and Elizabeth for control of the crown. They plan to read their finished papers to the occupants of the Red House, a house they know is quite old and was inhabited "in more ancient years" by "Sir Thomas What's his name" (88). The entire episode links themes that run through all the Bastable books: the importance of the past; the significance of exploration; and the importance of fighting for one's nation. Nesbit further implies that these will remain important, embodied in the antique cradle of the newborn Red House baby.

Although the Bastable books are largely conservative and even nostalgic in their treatment of Britain and its past, Nesbit does not entirely gloss over some of the difficulties of Edwardian life. The early part of the twentieth century was a time of labor disputes and an uncertain economy in Britain, facts which filter into the *Treasure Seeker* books in the form of tramps on the road, tramps who often threaten the children. Two such threats appear in *The Would-begoods,* in "The Benevolent Bar" and "Tower of Mystery" chapters. In the former, the children set up a refreshment stand for roadside travelers, offering free drinks. Unfortunately, some of the rougher passersby assume this means free alcoholic drinks, and they turn nasty when they discover lemonade in their glasses. Likewise, in "The Tower of Mystery" chapter, a tramp who feels he has been insulted by the children locks them in an abandoned tower. In both cases, the children are saved by a properly loyal and obedient member of the lower classes, or by a combination of British pluck and help from the better sort of yeoman farmer, as they are in "The Tower of Mystery" chapter, when Alice thinks of "the lion of the English nation which does not know when it is beaten" (80) in the children's struggle with the tramp, before they are rescued by the pig farmer. Nesbit, despite being a socialist, relies for the story's resolution not on social change, but on the restoration of an older, more feudal order.

Although Burnett and Nesbit are contemporaries of one another, they hardly seem so, at least in terms of their narrative techniques. Burnett's heroines are much more Victorian than Nesbit's, and the entire tone of Nesbit's work is more modern. Yet both writers demonstrate the way tropes of empire and nationalism are part of even the most domestic fiction of the era. Burnett and

Nesbit also are in general agreement that empire and nationalism are good things. Empire is the source of wealth and comfort to those home in Britain. Foreigners from the colonies may be useful servants, but are dangerous if left to live on their own terms in places like Chinatown. Military intervention in colonial lands is dangerous and demanding for the British, but is necessary and is worth some sacrifice. Empire provides fabulous stories, either to tell friends or to incorporate into one's imaginative play. Empire is something that will last until the children in these books are adults and can take a more active role in maintaining the empire. This last wish, of course, does not come true, although it takes the British a long while to accept that their dominion is shrinking, and that acceptance is even slower to take hold in children's books, as we shall see.

## NOTES

[1]Shirley Foster and Judy Simons, *What Katy Read: Feminist Re-Readings of "Classic" Stories for Girls* (Iowa City: University of Iowa Press, 1995), 5.

[2]Gillian Avery and Margaret Kinnell, "Morality and Levity," in Peter Hunt, ed., *Children's Literature: An Illustrated History* (Oxford: Oxford University Press, 1995), 48.

[3]Jacqueline Rose, *The Case of Peter Pan: The Impossibility of Children's Fiction* (London: Macmillan, 1984), 48.

[4]Jenny Sharpe, *Allegories of Empire* (Minneapolis: University of Minnesota Press, 1993); Susan Meyer, *Imperialism at Home: Race and Victorian Women's Fiction* (Ithaca: Cornell University Press, 1996); Julia Bush, *Edwardian Ladies and Imperial Power* (Manchester: University of Manchester Press, 1998).

[5]Julia Bush, "Edwardian Ladies and the 'Race' Dimensions of British Imperialism," *Women's Studies International Forum* 21:3 (1998), 277-78.

[6]Roderick McGillis, *A Little Princess: Gender and Empire* (New York: Twayne, 1996).

[7]Frances Hodgson Burnett, *A Little Princess* (1905; London: Puffin, 1994).

[8]See especially Elizabeth Lennox Keyser, "'Quite Contrary': Frances Hodgson Burnett's *The Secret Garden,*" *Children's Literature* 11 (1983): 1-13, which argues that the novel reflects Burnett's ambivalence towards accepted sex roles; Phyllis Bixler's response in "Gardens, Houses, and Nurturant Power in *The Secret Garden,*" in James Holt McGavran, Jr., ed., *Romanticism and Children's Literature in Nineteenth-Century England* (Athens: University of Georgia Press, 1991, 208–33; and the discussion in Shirley Foster and Judy Simons, *What Katy Read: Feminist Re-Readings of "Classic" Stories for Girls* (Iowa City: University of Iowa, 1995).

[9]Mike Cadden, "Home is a Matter of Blood, Time, and Genre: Essentialism in Burnett and McKinley," *Ariel* 28:1 (1997), 55.

[1·]Jerry Phillips, "The Mem Sahib, the Worthy, the Rajah and his Minions: Some Reflections on the Class Politics of *The Secret Garden,*" *Lion and Unicorn* 17 (1993), 182.

[11]Frances Hodgson Burnett, *The Secret Garden* (1911; New York: HarperCollins, 1990), 1.

[12]Penelope Tuson, "Mutiny Narratives and the Imperial Feminine: European Women's Accounts of the Rebellion in India in 1857," *Women's Studies International Forum* 21:3 (1998), 294.

[13]Quoted in ibid., 294.

[14]The yellow face as a consequence of and marker of the colonial English is common in fiction. Most of the colonial officers in *Vanity Fair,* for example, return to England with yellow faces, the mark of both physical infection and, perhaps, moral infection in the colonies. Yellow faces are also connected with the darker elements of orientalism: opium addicts are often described as having yellowed faces, for example.

[15]Cadden, 62.

[16]Phillips, 173.

[17]Ibid., 187.

[18]Marcus Crouch, *Treasure Seekers and Borrowers: Children's Books in Britain 1900–1960* (London: Library Association, 1962), 12.

[19]Marcus Crouch, *The Nesbit Tradition: The Children's Novel in England 1945–1970* (Totowa, NJ: Rowman and Littlefield, 1972), 16.

[20]Suzanne Rahn, "News from E. Nesbit: *The Story of the Amulet* and the Socialist Utopia," *English Literature in Transition* 28:2 (1985), 124.

[21]Anita Moss, *"The Story of the Treasure Seekers:* The Idiom of Childhood," in Perry Nodelman, ed., *Touchstones: Reflections of the Best in Children's Literature* (W. Lafayette, IN: Children's Literature Association, 1985),191.

[22]Ibid., 192-3.

[23]Maria Nicolajeva, *Aspects and Issues in the History of Children's Literature* (Westport, CT: Greenwood, 1995), 54.

[24]E. Nesbit, *The Story of the Treasure Seekers* (1899; London: Puffin 1982).

[25]Martin Green, *Dreams of Adventure, Deeds of Empires* (New York: Basic Books, 1979), 3.

[26]E. Nesbit, *The Wouldbegoods* (1901; London: Puffin, 1987).

[27]W. W. Robson, "E. Nesbit and *The Book of Dragons,"* in Gillian Avery and Julia Briggs, eds., *Children and Their Books: A Celebration of the Work of Iona and Peter Opie* (Oxford: Clarendon, 1989), 259.

[28]Crouch, *Treasure Seekers and Borrowers,* 20.

[29]Anita Moss, "E. Nesbit's Romantic Child in Modern Dress," in John Holt McGavran, ed., *Romanticism and Children's Literature in Nineteenth-Century England* (Atlanta: University of Georgia Press, 1991), 225.

[30]Quoted in Allen Warren, "Citizens of the Empire: Baden-Powell, Scouts and Guides, and an Imperial Ideal, 1900–40," in John M. MacKenzie, ed., *Imperialism and Popular Culture* (Manchester: Manchester University Press, 1986), 233.

[31]J. A. Magnan, *The Games Ethic and Imperialism* (New York: Viking, 1986), 64.

[32]One of the unconsciouss ironies of this is that Oswald, were he a real young man, probably would grow up to die on the battlefield, during World War I. Nesbit, of course, did not intend this irony.

[33]Julia Briggs, "Women Writers and Writing for Children: From Sarah Fielding to E. Nesbit," in Julia Briggs and Gillian Avery, eds., *Children and Their Books: A Celebration of the Work of Iona and Peter Opie.* (Oxford: Clarendon, 1989, 247, 245.)

# CHAPTER 4

# Imperial Fantasies: Lofting and Milne

Imperialism exists as subtext not only in domestic fiction of the Edwardian era, but in fantasy fiction as well, where again its appearance seems unlikely. Children's fantasy had steadily grown in popularity throughout the Victorian era, particularly the fairy tale, which influenced fantasists like Ruskin (*The King of the Golden River*, 1851), Thackery (*The Rose and the Ring*, 1855), McDonald (*At The Back of the North Wind*, 1871), and Wilde (*The Happy Prince and Other Tales*, 1888). This was also the era of Andrew Lang's colored Fairy Books. Fantasy not so heavily influenced by the fairy tale also grew in popularity, spurred on particularly by Carroll's *Alice's Adventures in Wonderland* (1865). By the late nineteenth century, animal fantasies were becoming a genre in themselves. Anna Sewell's *Black Beauty* (1877) combines the moral tale with that of an anthropomorphized horse, the reader being urged not to be cruel to animals. Kipling's *Just So Stories* (1902) and *The Jungle Books* are examples of animal fantasies of the period, and of course there are the works of Beatrix Potter, Kenneth Grahame, and many others. Even R. M. Ballantyne contributes to the genre with *The Dog Crusoe* (1861).

Fantasy does not always have a serious message beneath the surface. Sewell's *Black Beauty* and Orwell's *Animal Farm* certainly have important social messages to convey to the reader, but one does not expect Potter or Milne, for example, to be cloaking social or political messages beneath the whimsy of talking animals. Fantasy, more than realistic fiction, is often considered to be escapist in the most negative sense of the word, and hence to be devoid of any serious purpose whatsoever. It is this attitude towards fantasy— and especially children's fantasy—that made possible Frederick Crews's witty *The Pooh Perplex* (1963), whose humor rests on the assumption that serious commentary of the Pooh books is comical by definition.

But fantasy is written in the real world, by real writers who are influenced by the world they live in, as well as by the world of faerie (in Tolkien's sense of the word). *The Wind in the Willows* is not only a charming fantasy of talking woodland animals, but also a reflection of the upper-class masculine values held by the author and many of his peers. Animal fantasies were becoming a popular genre of children's fiction at the same time the British empire was reaching the height of its powers, and it would be surprising if references to empire did *not* find their way into animal fantasies of the period. The references are not always immediately apparent, however. The two fantasists I want to examine here are Hugh Lofting (1886–1947) and A. A. Milne (1882–1956). Both were veterans of the World War I; both began their children's books for their own children and not for a popular audience; both published their best-known books within a few years of one another. One of these writers, A. A. Milne, is as beloved today as he was in the twenties, and in fact, Pooh has become an emperor of sorts in the commercial kingdom: there is a plethora of Pooh-related merchandise available to consumers, everything from bubble bath to videos. The other, Hugh Lofting, is nearly forgotten, except for the two films based, however loosely, on the Doctor Dolittle books.

Hugh Lofting was enormously popular and respected earlier in the century, but today the Doctor Dolittle books are little read, at least not in their original form. Only the first two of the twelve volumes of stories remain in print, and as Lofting's son Christopher notes in the Afterword to the Dell editions, the editors faced the problem of "whether or not to delete or rewrite portions of the *Doctor Dolittle* stories."[1] The editors did choose to rewrite and delete. The books may not have survived in print at all if not for the fact that Lofting won the Newbery Award in 1923 for *The Voyages of Doctor Dolittle*. Despite his status as only the second winner of the Newbery (he qualified because, although British by birth and education, he had become a naturalized American citizen), there has been only one critical essay devoted to his work[2] and several brief parenthetical remarks in general histories of fantasy or of children's literature. On the other hand, quite a bit has been written about the filmed adaptations of the stories, one starring Rex Harrison and the other Eddie Murphy. The two stars of these very different adaptations hint at one of the reasons the books themselves have fallen out of favor: the original texts, illustrated by Lofting himself, reflect their times, and both text and images are considered "politically incorrect," in the current unfortunate terminology. Casting a black man as Dolittle is one way Hollywood tries to convince itself and us that it has moved beyond racism—something I believe is a dubious claim at best.

The editing done by Dell in the 1980s removes much that is relevant to a discussion of Lofting's attitudes towards imperialism. For example, the original volume of *The Story of Doctor Dolittle* has a frontispiece with a profile of a rather forbidding Doctor surrounded by four miniature portraits, one of which is a caricature of an African prince, complete with over-large lips, bulging eyes, and a tiny crown upon his nappy head. The current Dell edition has substituted the more familiar W. C. Fields like portrait of the doctor in the middle of the frontispiece, and the African prince has been replaced by an inoffensive, if somewhat stern, white official of some sort, in uniform. When Doctor Dolittle and his animals land in Africa, the 1988 Dell reprint does not reproduce an illustration that is clearly based on the figure of the Hottentot Venus, and further expurgates the language. In the original, Polynesia the parrot says, "But do not forget that although I am only a bird, *I can talk like a man* [Lofting's emphasis]—and I know these darkies."[3] The Dell reprint changes this to "and I know these people" (45). Likewise, the original edition of *The Voyages of Doctor Dolittle* describes the African Prince Bumpo as dressed "in a fashionable frock coat with an enormous bright red cravat . . . He was very smart in every respect except his feet. He wore no shoes or socks."[4] The Dell revision describes Bumpo as "a black man . . . very fashionably dressed" (128). Here the attempt seems to be not only to change language based on its offensiveness, but also based on its supposed inaccessibility to contemporary child readers.

Lofting began to write his stories while he was on the Western Front, serving in the Irish Guards during the World War I. The stories began as illustrated letters to his children, and Lofting later explained that "There seemed very little of interest to write to youngsters from the Front; the news was either too horrible or too dull."[5] But he was struck by the plight of the horses and other animals who sacrificed their lives in the war, and imagined what a "Casualty Clearing Station" for horses would entail; hence, the stories of Doctor Dolittle and his knowledge of animal language and physiology.

Lofting's Doctor Dolittle books not only reflect his experiences in World War I, but also the experiences he had had in Cuba and in Lagos, where he worked as a civil engineer, building railroads on the frontiers of empire. Like Kipling, he had direct experience of British colonialism, and also like Kipling, his books reflect personal knowledge of and affection for a colonial outpost, in Lofting's case Africa rather than India. Both his wartime and his colonial experiences inform the ethos that Lofting presents to his readers in the twelve volumes of Doctor Dolittle tales that were published between 1920 and 1948, especially in the volumes with African or South American settings and characters.

Africa was an uncommon setting for children's fiction in the late nineteenth and early twentieth centuries, although it certainly had a prominent place in the British imagination.[6] Africa was more mysterious, more dangerous, and altogether more frightening than India. Africa was the "dark continent," a metaphor that reaches all the way from early missionary accounts (William S. Naylor's *Daybreak in the Dark* or James Stewart's *Dawn in the Dark Continent,* for example; and Stanley's book of his travels in Africa was titled *Through the Dark Continent*) all the way to Conrad's *Heart of Darkness* (1904). Africa was "the white man's grave," doing in missionaries and explorers by malaria, geography, tribal warfare, or a combination of these factors. Patrick Brantlinger summarizes British attitudes towards Africa quite neatly when he writes, "By the time of the Berlin Conference of 1884–85, which is often identified as the start of the Scramble for Africa, the British tended to see Africa as a center of evil, a part of the world possessed by a demonic darkness or barbarism, represented above all by slavery, human sacrifice, and cannibalism, which it was their duty to exorcise."[7] No wonder Africa and Africans make only rare appearances in children's books.

Children—especially adolescents—were attracted to sensational tales of Africa, as evidenced by the large juvenile audiences for the novels of Rider Haggard and John Buchan, but sensationalism was frowned upon in serious writing for children; hence, Africa is not nearly as common as India as either setting or metaphor in serious children's fiction. Africa also came into the British empire much later than India, which also helps account for its relatively rare appearances. When Africa does appear in serious children's books, as it does in Nesbit's stories of the Bastables, it is almost always the relatively white and civilized South Africa, rather than the more troubled interior, that is featured. Lofting does tackle Africa in some of the Dolittle books: *The Story of Doctor Dolittle* (1920), *Doctor Dolittle's Post Office* (1923), and *Doctor Dolittle and the Secret Lake* (begun in 1923, but only published posthumously in 1948). A fourth Doctor Dolittle book (the second published volume), *The Voyages of Doctor Dolittle* (1922), takes place among a tribe of South American Indians, but also includes an African prince as a character.

*The Story of Doctor Dolittle* begins in Puddleby-on-Marsh, an English coastal village, but quickly moves to Africa when the doctor receives a message that the monkeys are desperately ill and need his help. The doctor—ever compassionate and ever-willing, despite his chronic lack of funds—borrows a ship and heads to Africa with some of his animal friends. Although Doctor Dolittle is traveling to help cure the monkeys, and not to save the health or souls of African natives, his impulses mirror those of missionaries who went out to Africa. Like the missionaries, he travels as a minimally-funded private citizen who puts the welfare of foreign strangers above his own comfort and safety. Lofting has Dolittle treat monkeys, albeit civilized monkeys, rather than African natives primarily because he is writing a fantasy and not a missionary tract, but the blurred line between civilized monkeys/not very civilized natives reflects late nineteenth-century views that Africans were more closely related to monkeys than were Europeans. In some ways Doctor Dolittle reflects not only European missionaries, but also early European ethnologists and anthropologists. He brings help and medicine to Africa and the animals, but he is just as curious about animal culture and animal language as he is about animal health. Doctor Dolittle treats the animals the way an ethnographer of the period might treat native peoples: as curious subjects worthy of study, if not exactly human just like you and me.

Dolittle's first view of Africa is described this way: "And about half an hour later, sure enough, they thought they could see something in front that might be land. But it began to get darker and darker and they couldn't be sure" (39). The darkness is caused by an approaching storm, but grammatically "it" apparently refers to "land," and Lofting seems to be echoing the common motif of "darkest Africa." The darkness referred not to the physical darkness of Africans, but rather to the spiritual and moral darkness that Europeans perceived in Africans. Lofting's novels are comedies and thus, steer clear of most of the nightmare images of dark and impenetrable Africa, but in this brief description and in some of the doctor's other adventures with Africans, we see that even comic texts cannot fully escape the nightmare qualities of Africa.

In the first volume of the stories, Doctor Dolittle is brought before the African King of the Jolliginki, who explains that Doctor Dolittle may not travel through his lands, because "Many years ago a white man came to these shores; and I was very kind to him. But after he had dug holes in the ground to get the gold, and killed all the elephants to get their ivory tusks, he went away secretly in his ship—without so much as saying 'Thank you.' Never again shall a white man travel through the lands of Jolliginki" (47–48)—and he promptly throws the doctor into prison. The king may have gotten off lightly at the hands of Europeans, if one considers a report of the Cape Colony governor in 1837, in which he states that in a skirmish the natives lost 4,000 men to the British losses of a mere one hundred, and "There have been taken from them also, besides the conquest and alienation of their country, about 60,000 head of cattle, and almost all their goats; their habitations have everywhere been destroyed and their gardens and cornfields laid waste. They have, therefore, been chastised, not extremely, but sufficiently."[8]

The king (who, interestingly, is not demoted to "chief," as most African kings were by European invaders and writers) gives a native perspective on European activities in Africa—highly unusual in fiction from the end of the nineteenth century and into the twentieth. John Buchan's *Prester John* (1910) presents an African rebellion led by the Zulu John Laputa, a plot suggesting that Westernization is not necessarily desired or appreciated by Africans, but Laputa's rebellion is equated with savagery and must be put down at all costs. Rider Haggard's fiction clearly presents Europeans as being the destroyers of African civilization, yet in the end whites are still culturally superior to black Africans. All of these characters may be native, but they are all created by white Europeans and cannot speak for themselves: their ideas must be filtered through a Western consciousness.

Lofting is no champion of black Africans or of African self-rule, however. For all that the King of the Jolliginki is presented as having a valid grievance against the white man, he is also presented as comic and childlike. There were three common stereotypes of African natives prevalent in writing by the British: the noble savage; the bestial savage, prone to cannibalism and other unnamed "savage rites"; and the childlike savage. The noble savage is the best-known of these stereotypes, and the bestial savage was briefly summarized by W. Winwood Reade when he wrote that one might infer that the barbarity of a "negro" is "mere ignorance and thoughtlessness . . . But negro barbarity is not ignorance alone . . . It cannot be denied that the Africans are connoisseurs in cruelty, that murder is one of their fine arts."[9] The native-as-child was a common stereotype for Indians as well, but Indians tended to be treated more kindly than were Africans: Kipling's lama is childlike, yet still admirable, for example. The British treatment of Africans-as-children is touched with disgust and loathing. As a brief example, consider the words of the explorer Richard Burton: "The cruelty of the negro is, like that of a schoolboy, the blind impulse of rage combined with the want of sympathy. Thus he thoughtlessly tortures and slays his prisoners, as the youth of England torment and kill cats . . . he mentally remains a child, and is never capable of a generalization."[10] Lofting is more inclined to focus on the comic child-like native rather than the savage, although he includes elements of both.

The King of the Jolliginki does have legitimate complaints against Europeans, but the narrative undercuts these complaints with the child-like behavior of the king, which diminishes his moral authority. He is able first to be fooled by a parrot and second to be fooled by the doctor when the latter says, "If you don't let me and my animals travel through your kingdom, I will make you and all your people sick like the monkeys. For I can make people well: and I can make people ill—just by raising my little finger" (53). Natives— superstitious by nature, as Victorian missionaries and explorers would tell you—easily believe the lies of magic presented by the West, as susceptible as children at a magic show. When the king recaptures Dolittle, the doctor is saved by the king's son, Prince Bumpo, who reads fairy tales and sighs, "If only I were a *white* prince!" (97; Lofting's emphasis). He will settle for having only his face made white, because he "shall wear shining armor and gauntlets of steel, like the other white princes, and ride on a horse" (102). Bumpo is presented as comic first because he literally believes in fairy tales, and second because he aspires to be what the reader knows he never can be: a white man. This is a larger fairy tale than the one Bumpo is reading.

Bumpo is one in a long string of native figures who aspire—comically— to be white. We have already seen Hurree Babu, and we will see Missee Lee in Ransome's novel. Adult novels also include such figures, both as minor characters (the black servant in Thackery's *Vanity Fair,* for example) or as major characters (Dr. Aziz in *A Passage to India*). The prince's desire for a white face is presented comically in the first volume of Doctor Dolittle tales, and his desire to be culturally white is presented comically in its sequel. In *The Voyages of Doctor Dolittle* Bumpo has come to study at Oxford, and he has all the trappings of the comic native would-be European: his clothes mimic European clothing, but are not quite right (he wears a frock coat, over-sized cravat, a straw hat, and carries a green umbrella—but wears no socks or shoes), and his language also attempts European civility to comic results. He says to Doctor Dolittle when they meet in England, "I am sublimely ecstasied that I did not miss you" (149). In *Doctor Dolittle's Post Office*[11] we meet another African king, King Koko of Fantippo. Koko constantly sucks on a lollipop, being excessively fond of sweets, and occasionally peers through the lollipop in imitation of Europeans peering through monocles. He is incurably vain, having many different portraits of himself printed on a never-ending succession of postage stamps. In other words, he is presented as an oversized and egotistical child, a not-uncommon portrayal of African natives.

The cruel side of the African-native-as-child shows up not in these two African kings, but in the figure of the Emir of Ellebubu, who imprisons Doctor Dolittle after the doctor has resolved an intertribal conflict by showing the natives how to harvest pearls. The emir, wanting the wealth of the pearls for himself, captures Doctor Dolittle and throws him into a windowless prison, threatening to "give orders that you shall get no food . . . You shall be starved to death" (298). When the doctor holds out (being secretly fed, of course, by his animal friends), the emir says, "then let him starve. In ten days more the fool will be dead. Then I will come and laugh over him. So perish all wretches who oppose the wishes of the Emir of Ellebubu!" (302). Once again Doctor Dolittle gets out of prison by claiming that he has magic he can use against the emir—and makes the emir promise to put windows in the prison and to return stolen lands and properties to his rival tribe.

The incident elucidates several elements of imperialism in Africa. First, the troubles for the tribes and for Doctor Dolittle begin over a conflict that is intertribal and that is based on territory and wealth. Such conflicts were common in Africa, and often considered by Europeans to be indicative of the African's less-civilized status, since the tribal issues as stake were often incomprehensible to Europeans, or considered to be trivial. The doctor is the figure who brings to his chosen tribe the secret of the pearls and how to harvest them, and thus, acts the part of European capitalist adventurer. A true capitalist adventurer would harvest the pearls, pay little or nothing for them, and ship them to Europe at a great profit. But Doctor Dolittle is more interested in teaching the tribe something of trade, so that they may make a profit for themselves, not for a European middleman. Second, part of the urge to turn Africans into traders with the West was connected to attempts to destroy the slave trade in Africa: Africans had to be both Christianized and had to be given a means of making a profit that did not involve selling human beings. Here again we can see some of the missionary influence that underlies Doctor

Dolittle's doings in Africa, although he is preaching capitalism rather than Christianity.

Doctor Dolittle, in short, carries the "white man's burden," neatly summarized by Buchan in *Prester John:* "I knew then the meaning of the white man's duty. He has to take all the risks, recking nothing of his life or his fortunes and well content to find his reward in the fulfillment of his task. That is the difference between white and black . . . the gift of responsibility, the power of being in a little way a king; and so long as we know this and practice it, we will rule not in Africa alone but wherever there are dark men who live only for the day and their own bellies."[12]

Doctor Dolittle's success in carrying out the "white man's burden" is made especially clear in *Doctor Dolittle's Post Office.* The doctor's adventures begin when he comes to the aid of Zuzana, a woman whose husband is being sold into slavery. Lofting gives a simplified, but accurate, explanation of the slave trade: "These were the days, you must understand, when slavery was being done away with. To capture, to buy or to sell slaves had, in fact, been strictly forbidden by most governments. But certain bad men still came down the west coast of Africa and captured or bought slaves secretly . . . Some African kings sold prisoners they had taken in war to these men and made a great deal of money that way" (6). Here Lofting echoes the Western sentiment that if the Africans are to be civilized, they must be taught to trade in something other than human flesh. Zuzanna's husband, in fact, has been captured and sold by King Koko, but is rescued by the doctor and his animals, with the aid of a man o' war from the British navy. Doctor Dolittle then ends up in King Koko's kingdom, where he brings civilization through the invention of a post office for the kingdom, and Koko gives up the slave trade.[13]

Making a post office the emblem of civilization is a wonderful invention on Lofting's part. Another name for post office is the "government mails," and of course the government regulates the post office. It is the means by which not only personal, but also political, communication is made. A post office suggests a literate nation, and a nation willing to communicate rather than to war within its own borders or with its neighbors. Above all it suggests order and the bureaucracy needed to maintain that order. But King Koko has a difficult time grasping the realities of a postal system. He is much taken with the idea of post boxes and has them erected around his city, but then must face irate citizens who put letters into boxes yet never receive replies: the king has failed to hire and train postal workers to collect, sort, and deliver the mail. Like a child, he is playing at post office, and not inventing a true postal system. For that he needs the wise Doctor Dolittle, who explains how a post office works while the two of them sit over a cup of "China tea"—a useful emblem of both British civility and British imperialism.

Once Doctor Dolittle takes control of the postal system, the domestic mails in Fantippo begin to work quite well, and before long the post office needs to expand into foreign mails, to provide for the Fantippans, but also for the wild animals themselves. What Doctor Dolittle says of the benefits of a postal system for the animals is also true for the Fantippans. The doctor's idea, he says, is "firstly an educational one. With a good post-office system of their own, I feel that the condition of the birds and animals will be greatly bettered" (76), just as Fantippan society has been bettered.

Interestingly, Dolittle has not had to teach the Fantippans to be literate and to write letters, although if his were a realistic missionary account of life in Africa, literacy would have had to have been the first step, since most African languages were oral and not written. But Lofting displaces the need to civilize the natives onto the animals, just as he did in the first volume of tales, where Doctor Dolittle goes to Africa to save monkeys, not natives. Displacing the literacy problem onto animals suggests either that Lofting wanted to portray the African natives as innately more civilized than commonly portrayed in fiction, or that the animals are innately more human: it is difficult to tell which is the case, or if both are true at the same time. Certainly the animals in the Dolittle books are wise beyond the ways of animals in the real world: Cheapside the sparrow speaks in cockney and knows the streets of London better than a cabbie; Polynesia the parrot has lived long, traveled widely, and speaks more than one language; even the fairly slow-witted pig can tell a story around the fireplace of an evening. Lofting elevates the animals very nearly to human status in the Dolittle books.

The Africans, on the other hand, do not seem to be equal to Dolittle or to other Europeans by way of social, cultural, or economic organization. They are often treated kindly, but condescendingly, as innocent naïves. There is certainly no recognition of African society being different, although equal, to European society. The Fantippans, for example, know how to read, but like Prince Bumpo they read European texts: they are literate, but apparently have not created a body of their own literature. Yet the Fantippans, and even the more "savage" natives that turn up in the books, are never treated as if they are animals, beasts of the jungle, as they are in much other literature about Africa. Lofting's portrayal of Africans is certainly, by today's standards, racist—but by the standards of the time, his portrayal can be seen as progressive. After all, in the twenties, when women were just getting the vote, not all men and women, not even the white ones, were considered equal to one another: a class system was seen as natural, even Darwinian.

Lofting's most sustained treatment of imperialism in Africa, and the book that most clearly articulates its author's ambivalent attitudes towards imperialism, is *Doctor Dolittle and the Secret Lake*.[14] Lofting took thirteen years to write the book, and it was only published posthumously, in 1948. In this novel, Lofting is increasingly critical of empire and armed conflict, due not only to his experiences in World War I, but also to the rise of yet another global war begun by a would-be imperial leader: World War I was not, after

all, the war to end all wars. In *The Secret Lake,* Dolittle returns to Africa to
rescue an old friend, Mudface the turtle, who is so ancient he predates Noah,
which is why Dolittle wants to find him again. While still back in England,
Doctor Dolittle has been working on ways to prolong the human lifespan, and
remembering biblical patriarchs who were described as being hundreds of
years old, hopes Mudface will be able to tell him something of the diet and
behavior of these biblical characters that might both explain their longevity
and be of help to modern humans. The doctor, as always, is interested in making life better, for animals and now for humans. His interest in increasing the
lifespan of humans is ironic in this novel, which has war and empire as its
central theme, and was written largely in the years between the two world
wars. It is not difficult to imagine Lofting—whose earlier Dolittle books are
far more optimistic than the later ones—becoming increasingly distraught
and pessimistic as the world headed towards another global conflict. He, like
Dolittle, was essentially a pacifist, which was not an easy stance to maintain
in the first half of the twentieth century.

The internal struggles Lofting may have been dealing with are reflected
in the narrative weakness of *The Secret Lake,* which introduces characters
and then drops them, tends to be long on exposition and light on action, and
raises questions it does not answer. It is also a very curious example of the
influence of the Bible upon Lofting's life and work. There is no biography of
Lofting, and no easy way to determine his religious beliefs, but as the twentieth century progressed, seemingly without the world having learned any
lessons from World War I, Lofting seems to have despaired of finding any
solace or inspiration in the Bible. Noah is an important figure in *The Secret
Lake,* but he is described as being "cross-eyed with stupid conceit" (212) for
believing he and his family are the only righteous people on earth. He is also
seen as a poor planner, despite God's supposed help in designing the ark:
Noah fails to provide sufficient fodder for his ark of animals, thus paving the
way for strife and warfare among them. The novel is too unfocused to draw
any sort of conclusion about whether or not Lofting meant Noah and the ark
to be seen as a metaphor of Europe in pre–World War II years, but he certainly comes off badly in Mudface's account of the Flood. He is not quite as
evil a figure as King Mashtu, however, the despotic emperor of nearly the
entire world of Noah's time, whose excesses bring down the wrath of the
"Someone" Mudface thinks created the Flood. Mashtu is the evil, savage
human of this tale, and Noah is the bumbling, foolish human. They both are
overthrown in Lofting's peculiar retelling of the Flood by other humans
entirely.

In Mudface's version of the story of Noah, Noah was enslaved by King
Mashtu to run the King's zoo, since Noah could understand the animals. As
Mudface says, "He was the first and only man, besides yourself, John Dolit-
tle, who could understand animal talk" (182), but unlike Dolittle, Noah can

only understand and cannot talk back to the animals. Mudface says, "He was not so wise and clever as he was cracked up to be. In fact often he was downright stupid" (182). Mashtu has many other slaves, but the two who matter in the story of the Flood are Eber and Gaza. They are lovers, but from different ethnic groups, so that they have difficulty communicating in a common language. They are saved by Mudface and his wife—a pair of animals who survive the Flood without the help of Noah. In fact Noah, once his boat is beached on dry land, finds himself facing an animal rebellion among the starving animals on the Ark. These rebellious animals learn of Gaza and Eber and wish to eat them for dinner, rather than allow them to live to replant and replenish the earth so that there will eventually be food for everyone. Mudface refers to these animals as being an "animal empire" that refuses to listen to the "emperor" elephant any longer (280). Eventually Eber and Gaza are saved, thanks to Mudface, and end up on the shores of America, described in these words: "From the level of the sea, upward and upward, to where the mountains sloped into the white clouds, it was all colours. Land, fertile land in blossom—land as it had been before the coming of the Flood!" (328). America is the new Eden, to be populated by the offspring of Eber and Gaza, who themselves are escaped slaves from Africa.

If this brief account seems a bizarre recasting of the Bible, it is, and is even more so in the novel itself, where the telling of this tale occupies more than one hundred and fifty pages of text. In a simplified plot summary, one could almost believe Lofting was suggesting that the world would be better off if white people (symbolized by Noah and his family) were wiped off the face of the earth and we began again with freed blacks in America, but I do not think this is what Lofting had in mind. Race is not the uppermost issue for Lofting in this novel: the urge for imperialism and domination is, and it gets replayed in various guises throughout the novel.

First we have Mashtu's empire. When Doctor Dolittle tours the ruins of his city, he is impressed by the "vast planning" and "beauty and magnificence" of the ancient city (348). But both Doctor Dolittle and the reader learn that the beautiful city—like Rome, perhaps—was built at great human cost. Much of Mashtu's wealth came from taxation upon his citizens, "But most of it he took from the kings and princes he captured or killed on the battlefield. He was crazy about money—not for itself so much—but he needed it to make war—more and more wars. And he didn't care how he got it" (353). Mashtu desires to be "King of the World," but he must conquer one last, small, faraway nation, that of the Zonabites. After winning the war, Mashtu plans to be "ruler of the Universe" and "Master of Mankind" (357). His plans are thwarted, however, when the Flood begins five days before his planned war.

Mashtu's is not the only empire, however. He has been very proud of his zoo, which both Noah and Eber had a part in maintaining. Both Noah and Eber are Mashtu's slaves, but from the animals' point of view they are masters, enslaving the animals. When the rebellious animals of the ark catch up with Eber and Gaza, the elephant leader says angrily, "Didn't they make a beast of burden out of me? . . . Did they not make slaves of the horses and oxen?" (265). Mudface argues that it was all King Mashtu's fault: "It was King Mashtu who did it—he who almost enslaved the whole world, Man and Beast" (266). The other animals are unconvinced, wishing to have a world free of humans altogether. They are finally convinced not to eat Eber and Gaza, but to keep them as human slaves to till the land and plant fodder for the grass-eating animals to eat: they allow the humans to live, but only as slaves.

So Eber and Gaza, until ultimately freed by Mudface, begin as slaves to the human Mashtu, help him enslave the animals, then end up enslaved by the animals. And over all of them is Noah, and over Noah is God, who orders the Flood and the clean sweeping of the earth of sinners, even if Mudface (and Lofting) seem to think he hasn't done a very good job of it. God may have planned the Flood in part to thwart Mashtu's desire to rise to a godlike status in the world, but neither God nor his servant Noah come off particularly well in this account of the Flood. The only survivors survive by happenstance, not by divine will, and go off to the Americas to start over again in a new Eden that seems curiously devoid of any god whatsoever. The new Adam and Eve are a multicultural pair who have many babies and do very well for themselves. Noah and his sons remain stranded in the beached ark, as far as the novel tells us, and disappear from the story altogether.

Doctor Dolittle hears this story, and toward the end of the novel has a chance to explore the ruined palace of Mashtu himself, in which he finds the treasure-horde of the long-dead emperor. Dab-Dab the duck urges the doctor to take the jewels with him, to alleviate the chronic insolvency of the Dolittle household. But Doctor Dolittle asks, "What would I do with pearls and rubies? . . . All this treasure has been stolen, taken from conquered kings and murdered princes. Their gold coins cry out with the voice of suffering—of innocent men, and women, and even children slaughtered in war. Money! Bah! it is the curse of the world!" (356). The doctor will take with him only the worthless bronze crown of the emperor.

Mudface tells Doctor Dolittle, "If you do write what I have told you into a book for all the peoples of today to read—who knows?—maybe war may stop altogether and no leaders like King Mashtu will ever rise again." But the doctor is doubtful: "For men are deaf, mind you, Mudface—deaf when they do not wish to hear and to remember—and deafest of all when their close danger is ended with a short peace, and they *want* to believe that war will not come back" (360). One could hardly ask for a clearer statement about the author's state of mind about his own world, where the horrors of World War I did bring a short peace and hopefulness, shattered by the time Lofting finished writing this novel.

In trying to puzzle out Lofting's philosophy in this novel, it is clear enough that empire and the urge for power and domination bring evil almost beyond imagining to the world. Mashtu lusts for total domination and nearly achieves it; when his animal slaves are released, they react by forming a despotic empire of their own, turning the tables on their former human keepers; and both Mashtu and the animals end up dead, defeated, or starving. The novel links desire for power and empire with selfish individualism, something the doctor stands squarely against, and has throughout the series of Doctor Dolittle tales. Doctor Dolittle always, in every book in the series, has the welfare of others uppermost in his mind. He sacrifices his own comfort and sometimes safety for the comfort and safety of others, even if those others are often animals; he learns the languages of other creatures not so he may give them orders, but so he may understand their lives and their cultures. Dolittle and Mudface both urge diplomacy and compromise upon others, rather than warfare and battle. When the emperor elephant is astonished that the meat-eaters turn on him in rebellion, Mudface comments that the elephant did not have the skills of a leader: "What he should have done of course was to talk pleasantly to these rebels till the rhinos, the hippos, and the other big grass-eaters should come to help" (291).

These diplomatic and pacifist views are not limited to this last and narratively jumbled novel. A more simplified presentation of some of the same issues can be found in the second volume of the Dolittle stories, *The Voyages of Doctor Dolittle*. The earlier novel is published in the twenties, when there is still the hope that World War I had ended all wars, and this optimism shows in *The Voyages,* unlike *The Secret Lake,* which seems to be a despairing cry against the state and future of the world.

*The Voyages of Doctor Dolittle* takes the doctor off to Spidermonkey Island, his choice of destination because he has already been to the North Pole, which Tommy Stubbins has recommended as a port of call.[15] Spidermonkey Island floats unanchored off the South American coast, and on it Doctor Dolittle must rescue the "Red Indian" Long Arrow, whom Doctor Dolittle considers to be the greatest naturalist in the world, surpassing even Darwin and Cuvier, although the doctor says, "I fancy Mr. Darwin doesn't even know he exists" (71). Long Arrow is described as "an enormous red Indian, seven feet tall, handsome, muscular, slim and naked," whose eyes have "a curious piercing gleam in them—like the eyes of an eagle, but kinder and more gentle" (256). Long Arrow is the noble savage, a figure we do not find in Lofting's African stories, but who shows up to be admired when the setting shifts to the Americas.

But not all Indians are noble. Long Arrow's tribe, the Popsipetals, occupy the northern half of the island, and their enemies to the south are the Bug-jagderags, whom Long Arrow describes as an "idle shiftless race" (275). The two tribes come to war, and the Popsipetals win with the aid of Dolittle and Prince Bumpo, who has come all the way from Africa to help the doctor. The battle is fierce, "but the strength and weight of those three men [Dolittle, Bumpo, and Long Arrow] of different lands and colors, standing close together, swinging their enormous war-clubs, was really a sight for the wonder and admiration of any one" (280). The Popsipetals win with the help of an army of parrots, the Peace of the Parrots is declared, Doctor Dolittle becomes "King Jong Thinkalot" of the now-united tribes, and the business of rebuilding civilization gets underway.

When Dolittle lands on the island, he discovers it is hollow and filled with air, drifting towards Antarctica, and largely underwater. It is a failing island, and its precarious geography accounts for some of the struggle between the two tribes who inhabit it. The floating island is a reference to the flying island of Laputa in Book III of Swift's *Gulliver's Travels,* whose inhabitants were addicted to impracticable visionary and utopian projects.[16] Dolittle is certainly a visionary, and he manages to get the island anchored safely and to end the conflict between the tribes. The nature of the island also perhaps suggests to the reader that the kind of peaceful society Dolittle brings to Spidermonkey Island is nothing more than a utopian pipedream. Certainly by the time readers finish *Doctor Dolittle and the Secret Lake,* they will find that the good animal doctor is no longer optimistic about the future of humankind.

The differences between the conflicts of *The Voyages* and *The Secret Lake* underline the cultural shift between 1914 and 1948. For one thing, the conflict in the earlier novel arises not from the despotic urges of an emperor, but from one tribe's famine and need for food: neither side seems to have a significant leader, and both tribes learn to compromise and to get along with the help of Doctor Dolittle, who urges the tribes to help one another rather than to raid and war when either tribe is suffering from drought, famine, or any other sort of difficulty. Second, the kindness of Doctor Dolittle, who does not order anyone from the losing tribe beheaded after the war, so impresses the natives that they first offer him gold from the mines, which Dolittle refuses, telling them to "Be true to the terms of the Peace and from yourselves shall come good government and prosperity" (242).

The optimism here is remarkable: the natives are left to their own devices, the assumption being that their underlying nature is good. Dolittle will end up staying to help the Indians along the road to civilization, but the fact that the Indians are seen as inherently good is testimony not only to Lofting's optimistic view of human nature in the twenties, but his progressive thinking about Others, who certainly have the means to live peacefully and democratically, if only shown the way. Third, Lofting has the winning tribe win by virtue of having warriors from three different races work together, helped in the end by an army of parrots, suggesting that togetherness across cultural (and even species) lines makes one stronger, not weaker. The novel is not exactly a parable of multicultural equality—the white man gets to be king, after all, and Prince Bumpo has cannibalistic tendencies and needs to be put in his place by the parrot—but it is difficult to believe that a story of such multinational togetherness—a fantasy story, let us not forget—could have been imagined before World War I. Certainly by the time Lofting writes the later passages of *The Secret Lake,* he is far less optimistic: in that novel, animals and people war, people and people war, and devastation is brought to the planet.

Even though Doctor Dolittle stays on with the Popsipetals as king for a time, and shows them "what town-sewers were, and how garbage should be collected each day" (315) and also teaches them the uses of fire and cookery, he is uneasy being a king, uneasy with anything that smacks of one person having too much power over others. As king, Dolittle "tried his hardest to do away with most of the old-fashioned pomp and grandeur of a royal court . . . if he must be a king he meant to be a thoroughly democratic one" (315). He outlines the reason behind his uneasiness towards the end of the novel, when he says to his friends as they finally leave Popsipetal for England, "I told you it was not easy to shake off responsibilities, once you had taken them up. These people have come to rely on me for a great number of things . . . we . . . have changed the current of their lives considerably . . . And whether the changes we have made will be, in the end, for good or for bad, is our lookout" (325).

Lofting, in a few sentences at the end of a children's fantasy, articulates late-imperial anxieties and uncertainties about the effects of imperialism and colonialism. He has taken up the white man's burden with the Popsipetals, and finds it a heavy burden indeed. From the first novels in the twenties, through to the posthumous *Doctor Dolittle and the Secret Lake,* there is a progression from optimism to pessimism, from certainty about the role of whites in bringing civilization to Others to uncertainty, from confidence to doubt. Lofting's novels mirror the shifting cultural attitudes of the period. There is, after World War I, a brief moment of peace and optimism, where the League of Nations is founded and war seemed to be gone forever, but the moment was only brief. In the wake of World War I Britain's status as the single greatest imperial power on earth was shaken. Native Others were not always thankful for government from London, and were agitating for self-rule and independence. War seemed all too likely to erupt again, as it did in the thirties. Lofting's Doctor Dolittle books are influenced both by the imperial desire of whites to impose western civilization upon native peoples, but also by the anxieties of World War I and its aftermath. The war and empire were two parts of the same knot of Western ethnocentricity and perceived European superiority, and both have a role in the development of Lofting's fantasy world. For him, hope seems to lie not in Europe, destroying itself in warfare and imperial competition, but in America, where he made his home for most of his life, a place the novels—and especially *Doctor Dolittle and the Secret Lake*—see as somewhere a more democratic and peaceful society might have room to grow.

The first Doctor Dolittle book appeared in 1920, and the first of the Pooh books in 1926, but two more dissimilar texts could hardly be imagined. The Dolittle books pay little attention to the kingdom of childhood: Tommy Stubbins is the only child character, and he does not appear in all the volumes, nor is he always a child when he does appear, but at times is a grown-up reminiscing on his past travels with Doctor Dolittle. Lofting's interest in presenting the reader with animal fantasy is to present a series of parables about human nature. Milne's books are something else again. Whereas Lofting's novels present real adventures (even if they are fantasies), the Pooh stories can be seen as parodies of adventure stories, containing as they do comic versions of expeditions, kidnappings, and so forth.[17] The child Christopher Robin may not appear often in the books, but the books are centered on the imaginative life of a child, on inner life and not on outer life, as the Dolittle books are. In fact, one could say that Lofting and Milne together give us two possible reactions to World War I and to the decline of imperialism. Lofting looks outward, struggling to find explanations and parallels for what had happened, strongly influenced by nineteenth-century British imperialism, but also marked by the horrors of the war. Milne looks inward, blandly seeming to ignore the tidal shift in the larger adult world, retreating to the safety of childhood and the inward life.

The world of Pooh provides an escape into an arcadian utopia for both child and adult readers of the book. The Hundred Acre Wood has no motor cars or telegraphs or other signs of modernity; no serious conflict, but instead a variety of creatures, all of whom respect and get along with each other; there is little bad weather, and when it arrives, it brings the possibility of adventure, not of crisis; the outside world barely impinges at all, and when it does, it does so benevolently in the figure of Christopher Robin. We should not be surprised to find that the Pooh books had at the time, and continue to have today, as much or more appeal for adult readers as for children. The books are meant for very small children, after all, children who perhaps can read on their own, but who are certainly not capable of going to the local bookshop to ask and pay for their own books. The Pooh books present an idealized world, an idealized *children's* world, that continues to have enormous appeal for adults. Roger Sale notes that when he teaches these books to undergraduates, "they like these books better at twenty-odd than they did as children,"[18] and the several dozen web pages devoted to Pooh are adult-generated and maintained and show little, if any, inclination to share the world of Christopher Robin with children.

Milne is nostalgic about lost childhood, both his own and his country's, and this nostalgia pervades the world of the Hundred Acre Wood. Britain is losing her importance on the world stage; Milne felt his own career as playwright stalling after the war; and the birth of his own son no doubt caused him to think about his own childhood and adulthood, and what his son's adulthood might be. Neither the real Christopher Robin nor his literary namesake was growing up in the same England Milne had grown up in.

Milne's two books about Pooh, *Winnie-the-Pooh* (1926) and *The House at Pooh Corner* (1928)[19] are cozy, domestic retreats into an apparently safer and more innocent world than that of post-war England. The portrayal of Christopher Robin as a sweet, androgynous young boy who plays with stuffed animals and infuses them with lives and minds of their own is a nostalgic portrait not only of childhood-as-we-wish-it-might-be, but also a kind of narrative attempt to protect young children (particularly boys) from the twin horrors of war and of domesticity. Christopher Robin, safe in the Hundred Acre Wood, can rule over the animals and avoid the recognition that he, in turn, is ruled by the adults in his life, particularly the father who articulates the imaginative play of the son. Christopher can play at being grown up, without in fact having to grow up at all. He can be a kind of parent to the animals, but can also escape the attentions of a real mother, who might want to control his actions much as Kanga tries to control the actions of both Roo and Tigger.

Christopher Robin, as a number of critics have pointed out, is both character and observer in the Pooh books, a person who often shows up as *deus ex machina* to solve troublesome situations the animals have gotten themselves into. When Piglet finds himself surrounded by water, he wonders "what Christopher Robin would do" (*Winnie* 133); it is Christopher Robin who knows what an "Ambush" is, as opposed to a gorse bush (*Winnie* 119); Christopher Robin who finds the solution when Tigger is stuck up a tree. For all his importance, however, Christopher Robin's appearances in the stories are rare: the focus is kept on the animals, who, after all, are the literal possessions of Christopher Robin, his nursery toys brought to life. Christopher Robin's interactions with the animals mimic the imaginative play of children, where they often position themselves as rulers of imaginative worlds, a comfort when they are not rulers in their own, realistic worlds at all: they are children, small and relatively powerless in a land of giant adults.

Yet Milne undercuts Christopher Robin's power in these books. Yes, they are Christopher's toys, and the stories are presented as products of Christopher's playful nursery imagination, but in important ways, they are not Christopher's inventions at all, but Milne's. Milne is literally the creator of these stories, of course, but beyond that he inserts his adult voice and adult control over both the fantasy lives of the animals and the imaginative life of his son. Milne looks back to narratives of the nineteenth century, where authors often "self-consciously admit[ted] their own role as mediators between the states of childhood and maturity."[20] What Nesbit tried to go beyond when creating a believable child narrator in the Bastable books, Milne goes back to.

When we first meet both Christopher Robin and Pooh, we meet them not in the forest, but in the domestic confines of the house, as boy and bear bump down the stairs. The adult narrator invites the child listener/reader of the stories into the book: "When I first heard his name, I said, just as you are going to say, 'But I thought he was a boy?' " (*Winnie* 3). Milne asserts his narrative power here not only over Christopher Robin, but also over the reader, telling the reader what the reader is thinking and is going to say, denying the child reader a question of his/her own. The reader's responses are controlled by the narrator, who then invites the reader to identify with the child Christopher Robin, because Christopher says, directly after this, "So did I." Christopher Robin and the child audience are both put on equal ground on the first page of the stories. But the adult voice, not the child voice, has control of the fantasy stories, the reader, and Christopher Robin himself. It is the child who requests stories of Pooh from the adult speaker, and the adult speaker who obliges. As he begins the first tale, he is interrupted by Christopher Robin, who wants to know what "under the name of" means, and who then asserts that it is Winnie-the-Pooh who doesn't understand the phrase, not himself. As the story of Pooh's attempt to get honey from the bees continues, Christopher Robin appears as a character in the story, and an italicized parenthetical dialogue follows: " '*Was that me?*' said Christopher Robin in an awed voice, hardly daring to believe it. '*That was you*' " (*Winnie* 10).

Whose imaginative life is being conveyed here, that of the child, or that of the adult narrator? The issue of control here is crucial. Within the stories, within the Hundred Acre Wood, Christopher Robin is the most powerful of the characters, the human leader of the animals, when he chooses to be. But the only reason Christopher Robin is in the stories at all is because he has been inserted into them by Milne. Christopher Robin himself does not remember the stories: they are not his stories, but an adult's stories, based upon the supposed imaginative play between child and stuffed animals.

In a sense, Christopher Robin has been colonized by the adult narrator. He is not free to tell his own stories, or to have the starring role in them, but must depend upon the colonizing adult narrator to tell him what his stories are. In fact, it is not entirely clear that the stories are his in any sense. Christopher Robin does not remember the stories, even the ones in which he has a role, and instead accepts the stories the adult narrator tells, stories the narrator imagines the child might have told himself. If, as Perry Nodleman has suggested, all children's literature is an imperialist endeavor,[21] then Milne in the Pooh books is one of the most successful of adult imperialists. Christopher Robin is as colonized and voiceless as any native in India or Africa—with the crucial distinction that as a white British boy he will eventually grow into adulthood and out of colonial status.

Nodelman's essay lifts several key concepts of Edward Said's *Orientalism* (1978) and explores their application to child psychology and children's literature. If we look at the Pooh books in the context of Nodelman's essay, we can see that Milne is colonizing both Christopher Robin and the reader. The first category Nodelman borrows from Said is "inherent inferiority," and the narrator points out Christopher Robin's inferiority in his lack of understanding of certain words and phrases. The animals suffer in the same way, being inferior to Christopher Robin and thus, doubly inferior to the adult narrator. The second category is "inherent femaleness." The figure of the oriental was often feminized, and Shepherd's illustrations for the Pooh books feminize the little boy as well, portraying an androgynous figure with a bowl haircut, shorts, and a blousey sort of tunic top. The third category is "inherent distortion." Nodelman suggests that "adult interpretations of children's behavior . . . are always contaminated by previously established adult assumptions about childhood" (30). Christopher Robin's behavior is based not so much on accurate adult observation of child play (although some of this is at work) as it is on adult assumptions that children are innocent and sweet, and thus, play innocently and sweetly.

The fourth category is "inherently adult-centered": "As Orientalism is primarily for the benefit of Europeans . . . children's literature [is] primarily for the benefit of adults" (30). Pooh, far more than Doctor Dolittle, is of interest and benefit to adults. There are made-for-adult books like *The Tao of Pooh,* for example, and endless web sites for adults to wax nostalgic about what Pooh means to them. The fifth category is "silencing and inherent silence." When we speak for someone else, we silence that someone else. Adults frequently do this to children, in everything from ordering food for a child in a restaurant to saying, "Oh, she didn't mean she doesn't like Barbie, she means she doesn't like Sally's Barbie." Christopher Robin, as noted above, is effectively silenced by the adult narrator in the Pooh books.

The sixth category is "inherent danger." In Said's examination of orientalism, rationality is undermined by Eastern excesses, excesses that are nonetheless tempting, seductive. Nodelman applies this to adults' behavior towards children: "If adults have a secret desire to act childishly, and if that dangerous desire is engendered by the childish actions of children, then we must protect ourselves and our world by making children *less* childish" (31). Not only do the animals and Christopher Robin practice and play at adult behaviors, but Christopher Robin himself is inexorably moved from the world of play to the world of responsible school, which he enters by the end of the books. There are sixteen categories in all, and over half of them have direct parallels to the world of Christopher Robin and his animals, suggesting that—if Said and Nodelman are accurate in their reading of the Orient and of childhood—Milne and his narrator are as guilty of colonizing and silencing children as the West was of colonizing and silencing the East. This is, to put it mildly, ironic in a book intended for children.

There is another layer of imperialism in the stories. Within the stories— if one looks at the stories amputated from adult narrative control, if we ignore that adult narrative voice and focus solely on the actions of Christopher and the animals—Christopher Robin morphs from colonized to colonizer. He may be colonized by the adult narrator, but he is the literal owner of Pooh and his friends and has the power to exert control over their behavior, although he rarely chooses to exercise that control, and tends to do so at the request of the animals themselves and for their own good. This is one of the primary myths of empire, that imperial powers act infrequently and only for the good of the natives. The play that Christopher Robin indulges in with his animals is play that prepares him for the adult role of imperial ruler of children or of child-like colonial subjects. The irony is that the world was altered forever by World War I, and Christopher Robin's training as would-be imperial leader is ill-suited for a world moving further and further from empire. He may be able to rule in the static, ideal, enclosed world of the Hundred Acre Wood, and may grow up to be a colonizer of his own children, but the values he learns in the wood are likely to cause him grief in the modern world of suffrage, motor cars, and Indian national rule—not to mention the increasing numbers of "natives" who come to England as immigrants.

And there is yet a third level of imperialism present in the Pooh stories, present in the nature of the animals themselves. They are an odd mix of domestic and wild animals: we have Pooh himself, a bear who is more teddy bear than grizzly, who keeps company with wild animals (Kanga and Roo, Tigger, Rabbit, and Owl) and with domestic animals (Piglet and Eeyore). The animals live together, with occasional visits from their human friend, in the peaceable kingdom of the Hundred Acre Wood. All of the animals are an imaginative combination of child-like and adult-like characteristics, with the emphasis on the child-like in most cases. Pooh, like many children, is egotistical, in the sense that all stories revolve around him, and (for Pooh), Pooh's point of view is the only true one. If he loves honey, the Heffalump must love honey; when Christopher Robin says, "Oh, Bear! How I do love you!" Pooh responds, "So do I"—love himself, that is (*Winnie* 71). Owl appears more adult, as do Rabbit and Eeyore, but even these adult-like characters have child-like insecurities: Owl never wants to appear to be less than wise, and develops strategies by which he can appear to know more than he does (a technique repeated by Christopher Robin himself, who often says, "I knew that," "carelessly"). Eeyore has a cynical adult glumness, but is delighted in a child-like way when he receives a present.

The only truly adult animal is Kanga, mother to Roo and eventually adoptive mother to Tigger. Kanga and Tigger both exist in Christopher

Robin's nursery as visitors from the colonies: Kanga is a kangaroo, indigenous to Australia, and Tigger is a tiger, the emblem of India. There is a third invisible imperial animal in the nursery, the Heffalump (elephant), indigenous to both Africa and India. As stuffed animals, kangaroo, tiger, and elephant suggest that the wild natives of the colonies have been fully domesticated and de-clawed, safe for even children to handle. Although it may seem a stretch to consider Kanga and Tigger as figures of empire, I would argue that it is not a stretch. It certainly is not conscious on Milne's part—the stories were concocted based upon real toys the real Christopher Robin possessed, after all—but that is precisely the point. By the twenties empire is so interwoven into British life, social and private as well as political and public, that it makes an almost unavoidable appearance in children's nurseries and in children's stories. Empire, by the twenties, no longer presents the possibility for high adventure and heroic deeds: empire has been literally domesticated into nursery toys, stuffed tigers and kangaroos and elephants. The real world might be increasingly anxious about the state of empire, but in children's books we get the comforting image of an empire totally tamed, so tamed it can be handled even by a British boy. We are a long way from Ballantyne's *The Coral Island.*

Or is empire quite so domesticated? The two most upsetting creatures in the Hundred Acre Wood are Tigger and the invisible Heffalump. Tigger makes his first appearance in *The House at Pooh Corner,* awakening Pooh, in whose house Tigger has insinuated himself. Tigger's first major action in the story is to attack an invisible invader in Pooh's house, and in the process to bring down the tablecloth and upset Pooh's domestic comfort. In fact, the main complaint the other animals have about Tigger is that he is too "bouncy" and unpredictable, alarming to some extent and not at first accepted by the other animals. The timid piglet is alarmed by Tigger, "who had been hiding behind trees and jumping out on Pooh's shadow when it wasn't looking" (*House* 26), and when Pooh says that Tigger isn't really very big, Piglet replies, "Well, he *seems* so" (*House* 32). When Tigger gets himself caught in a tree, Pooh mistakes him for a "jagular" and solemnly announces to Piglet that "They hide in the branches of trees, and drop on you as you go underneath. Christopher Robin told me" (*House* 66). It is Tigger who bounces Eeyore into the river during the game of Pooh-sticks, and Tigger whom the other animals want to teach a lesson by losing him at the North Pole.

Tigger, although presented playfully in the stories, is clearly an uncontrollable and somewhat upsetting animal, one whom the other animals recognize as needing further domestication and who they leave in the capable paws of Kanga. He is dangerous, and might jump out of trees: his confusion with "jagular" animals suggests both his wildness and his potential life-threatening qualities, since predators (jaguars, for instance) often "go for the jugular" when they kill. He is also childlike, and unaware of his potential for disruption. These characteristics, along with his literal tiger-ness, link him with India. India was part of the British empire and, as we have already seen, often represented as being childlike and dependent—but always with the capability of turning vicious and disruptive. The childlike natives might, in a moment, turn mutinous and attack Cawnpore or Amritsar. Further, in the Pooh books Tigger is both part of and not-part-of the domestic nursery kingdom: he is a late-comer, and must be kept to one side with a stable adult figure in order to be safely contained. India may have been one of the first of Britain's imperial possessions, but in the history of Britain itself India is a latecomer. Furthermore, Britain wanted not only to exploit the riches of India, but wanted also to domesticate India in Western ways, through Christianizing the natives and banning such native cultural traditions as suttee.

Tigger, then, is emblematic of both India and of childhood, and must be domesticated through the ministrations of Kanga, the only one of the animals who behaves, always, like an adult, and specifically like a mother. She is an interesting choice of domesticating influence for Tigger, because if Tigger suggests India, Kanga certainly suggest Australia, another of England's colonial possessions, one of the settler colonies. But Australia, despite its origins as penal colony, always had closer ties to England than India could hope for. The British had largely decimated the aboriginal population and had populated Australia with white colonists. Australia, unlike India, could hope to achieve—and did achieve, by 1901—full dominion status. Colonies where the native population significantly outnumbered the white population (India, Africa, and elsewhere) could not hope to achieve such dominion status. When the nonsettler colonies like India gain independence (as India does in 1947), it signals a complete separation from British political control and influence, not a rise to equal status with Britain, which is what happens eventually in Canada, Australia, and New Zealand. Tigger/India needs to come under the training and control of a more successful and mature Kanga/Australia and needs to emulate the behavior of Kanga/Australia more than the behavior of "jagulars." Just as convicts were sent from England to Australia in the hopes they might repent, Tigger is also exiled to "Australia," in the form of Kanga.

Kanga is not entirely a positive figure, however. Yes, she is an emblem of civilizing power and domesticity, but domesticity can be seen as a threat by children. Like Tigger, she is an outsider because none of the other animals knows where she and baby Roo come from. In *Winnie-the-Pooh* the original animals plot to kidnap Roo and to return him only if Kanga promises to leave the forest and never return. They do kidnap Roo, replacing him with Piglet in Kanga's pouch, but Kanga gets the best of the other animals in the end. When Kanga discovers Piglet in her pouch, she takes revenge by refusing to acknowledge that Piglet is not Roo and subjecting him to a cold bath.

This incident is instructive on a number of levels. Its appeal to children cannot be denied: the plot to switch babies is comical; the punishment of a cold bath—of a bath of any kind—is ideally suited to the child audience who loathes baths; and the refusal of both Kanga and Christopher Robin to recognize Piglet as Piglet speaks to children's fear of being abandoned or forgotten by parents. But if we put the story into the imperial context I have been suggesting here, we can see that Kanga must prove her right to exist in the forest both by showing them that Christopher Robin is the real ruler of the wood and approves of her, and by showing that she is capable of playing along with the animals and being part of their community. Just as British women were held up as a symbol of British moral superiority within the empire, Kanga has a kind of moral, maternal superiority within the Pooh stories. Like real British (or white colonial) women, however, Kanga is marginalized. Throughout the stories she remains at home and does not participate in the animals' adventures, and she provides a faintly threatening presence within the otherwise all-male preserve of the woods. One of her primary goals is to get Roo to take his medicine, and she also likes giving baths and telling children what to eat and otherwise trying to effect maternal control over children. In other words, she is the antithesis of adventure, an echo of the outside control of the world that Christopher and the animals would prefer to avoid.

The third imperial animal making an appearance in the Pooh stories is the Heffalump, who appears only in the imaginations of the characters and is not fully developed. The Heffalump suggests both India and Africa, but more specifically Africa. The Heffalump is emblematic of the fear and mystery and mythology of the Dark Continent. It is Christopher Robin who introduces the idea of the Heffalump to both Pooh and Piglet, and Pooh who decides that he and Piglet must catch the Heffalump in a "Cunning Trap." The two dig a pit for the Heffalump and try to lure him into it with honey, on the assumption that since Pooh likes honey, so must the Heffalump.

The Heffalump is a mysterious creature to both animals, and especially fearsome to Piglet, who wonders if the Heffalump is "fierce" and whether or not it likes pigs—the implication being, does it like pigs to eat? Pooh and Piglet's plan to catch the Heffalump is both comic and imperial: what better way to catch a native or a native animal than to offer it something it wants? And of course it must want exactly the same things we want. This is, in fact, one of the classic assumptions of imperialism, that what is good for the imperialists is good for the colonized. This particular imperial fable has a comic twist at the end, however. The honey disappears, but only because Pooh himself has gone back to eat it, obsessed as he is with honey. Pooh gets his head stuck in the honey jar and is mistaken by Piglet for a Heffalump until Christopher Robin solves the mystery and frees Pooh. Pooh's greediness here suggests the greed of imperial powers, but the greed gets a comic turn and ends up costing Pooh his dignity and his honey jar. There is, in this story, a hint both that the mysterious and perhaps mythical Heffalump, an emblem for Africa, may never be caught or controlled, and that there are limits to empire:

that imperial greed may in fact turn on imperial power and undo it. This was certainly the case in post-war Britain, no longer powerful enough to control her extensive empire, and gradually no longer able to control both white colonies and native colonies, in both of which there was increasing agitation for self-rule.

The Pooh books also contain a hint of what was to replace acquisition of foreign lands as a marker of national superiority: exploration of foreign lands and geographical exploits. By the end of World War I nearly all available lands had been claimed by a foreign power or were themselves strong imperial powers. The British national imagination needed to gain proof of British superiority in some way other than by acquiring colonies. If one could no longer acquire colonies, one could prove national prestige by being the first to discover the source of the Nile, the first to reach the South Pole, the first to climb Everest. References to geographic exploration are common in children's books published after 1900, and almost nonexistent before. Of the writers discussed here, only Kipling and Burnett fail to mention polar exploration (although Kipling does set "The White Seal" story of the *Jungle Books* in the arctic). Nesbit's children play at being arctic explorers; Tommy Stubbins is surprised to learn Doctor Dolittle has been to the North Pole; Ransome's children play at climbing the Himalayas and discovering the North Pole. Pooh and his friends also go on an "expotition" to the North Pole.

In *Winnie-the-Pooh,* it is Christopher Robin who suggests the expedition to the North Pole—the only adventure that he, rather than the animals, initiates. Going on an expedition is both adult and imperial behavior, and the adult-in-training is a more logical leader than one of the animals would be. Christopher himself seems uncertain of what the North Pole is: when asked by Pooh he says, "carelessly," "It's just a thing you discover" (*Winnie* 113). Christopher explains that an expedition means "a long line of everybody," and sends Pooh off for "provisions" (*Winnie* 113). The long line of everybody, in real expeditions, usually included native bearers (as in African and Himalayan exploration), or working-class underlings, as in Scott's and Shackleton's explorations of Antarctica. In the Pooh books, Christopher gets to play at expeditionary leader, and the animals fulfill the roles of bearers or underlings, thus emphasizing Christopher Robin's higher status in the hierarchy of the Hundred Acre Wood.

As the animals progress in their adventure, Milne provides us with a shorthand account of expeditionary dangers: the party worries about an "ambush" (which Pooh confuses with a gorse bush), they climb "cautiously" from "rock to rock" (*Winnie* 120), and the leaders keep some information to themselves, not wanting inferiors to hear and misinterpret, or hear and panic. Christopher and Rabbit walk away from the group because, as Christopher says, "I didn't want the others to hear." Rabbit asks, "What does the North Pole *look* like?" (*Winnie* 122), a question to which Christopher Robin has no ready answer. The conversation is amusing on two levels. First, as the characters decide that the North Pole must be a pole stuck in the ground, they imitate the literal quality of young children's understanding of language. The idea of a magnetic or geographic pole is too complex for small children to understand, but a pole in the ground is understandable. Hence, a reference to the North Pole must be to a particular pole in the ground.

Second, adults would find it amusing that the characters are searching for the North Pole, and that they don't know "where it is sticking" (*Winnie* 122). Whereas the South Pole does have a geographic center on land, the North Pole is notoriously difficult to pin down. "[T]he North Pole in some ways is virtually designed for hoaxery. There is no fixed land at the spot . . . thus no claimant's marker left at the North Pole would remain there long . . . The scenery is no different from that for hundreds of miles around, so no surface description of it can provide a decisive basis of judgment of claims."[22] Indeed, there is still some confusion about who made it to the North Pole first, Richard E. Peary or Frederick A. Cook. British adults would have been well aware of the various struggles to reach both North and South poles, and would have been amused by the shifty quality of the pole Milne's characters are searching for. When they find the pole—a literal, stick pole—they erect a sign declaring Pooh as its discoverer. Even if one could not claim literal possession of poles or mountain tops, one could claim first conquest, or furthest north, or furthest south.

The end of the Pooh books, the conclusion of *The House at Pooh Corner,* brings together the imperialism of adults over children as well as of children over toys. Christopher Robin is about to leave the Hundred Acre Wood and the kingdom of childhood for the adult-supervised kingdom of school, and is walking with Pooh. Christopher Robin begins to tell Pooh about "People called Kings and Queens and something called Factors, and a place called Europe, and an island in the middle of the sea where no ships came . . . and when Knights were Knighted, and what comes from Brazil" (173–175). Christopher Robin's lessons are laden with elements of empire: with kings and queens and knighthoods, with travels abroad, and with exports from foreign lands to England. Christopher Robin ends by knighting Pooh—thus, positioning himself as emperor and Pooh as loyal dependent, and signifying his movement from the world of the child to the world of the adult. Christopher Robin is beginning to move from playing king or emperor in the Hundred Acre Wood to being trained to act as agent of king or emperor in the larger adult world, as a British citizen in what was still an empire. The irony, of course, is that literal children trained in school to be leaders of empire were growing into an adulthood in a Britain whose empire was shrinking, not expanding or even remaining stable. Christopher Robin, though neither he nor Milne could have known it, hasn't got a prayer of growing up to be an imperial leader. But in the fictive world of the Pooh books and of other books of the period, empire, its values and its endurance, are rarely if ever questioned. Lofting's troubled view of empire is unusual in this period, and although his books have been bowlderized for their supposed insensitivity to racial issues, they are far more liberal in spirit than the beloved Pooh books and far more cognizant of the implications of empire. But for Milne, remaining in a mythical land of childhood and learning the values of a declining empire still seems more appealing than sailing off to Africa to confront troublesome issues of empire and imperialism. The Pooh books allow us to remain in a mythologized world of childhood, to retreat from adult responsibilities; Lofting's novels push us to confront those responsibilities.

## NOTES

[1]Christopher Lofting, Afterword to Hugh Lofting, *The Story of Doctor Dolittle* (New York: Dell, 1988), 152.

[2]Gary D. Schmidt, "The Craft of the Cobbler's Son: Tommy Stubbins and the Narrative Form of the *Doctor Dolittle Series,*" *Children's Literature Association Quarterly* 12:1 (1987): 19–23.

[3]Hugh Lofting, *The Story of Doctor Dolittle* (Philadelphia: Lippincott, 1920).

[4]Hugh Lofting, *The Voyages of Doctor Dolittle* (Philadelphia: Lippincott, 1922), 148.

[5]Quoted in Helen Dean Fish, "Doctor Dolittle: His Life and Works," in *Horn Book Reflections: On Children's Books and Reading,* ed. Elinor Field (Boston: Horn Book, 1969), 219.

[6]The most obvious exception to this are the Babar books by Jean de Brunhoff, but these date from the 1930s, not from earlier in the century. Since they are not British books, I have not discussed them here, although there are several excellent discussions of the books available, including Herbert Kohl's *Should We Burn Babar?* (New York: New Press, 1995).

[7]Patrick Brantlinger, *Rule of Darkness: British Literature and Imperialism, 1830-1914* (Ithaca, NY: Cornell University Press, 1988), 179.

[8]Quoted in John Hatch, *The History of Britain in Africa* (New York: Praeger, 1969), 101.

[9]Quoted in Dorothy Hammond and Alta Jablow, *The Myth of Africa* (New York: Library of Social Science, 1977),69.

[10]Richard Burton, *Lake Regions II,* quoted in ibid., 65.

[11]Hugh Lofting, *Doctor Dolittle's Post Office* (Philadelphia: Lippincott, 1923).

[12]John Buchan, *Prester John* (New York: Houghton Mifflin, 1928), 264. First published in 1910.

[13]There is still some controversy over the role of Africans in the selling of other Africans into slavery, although there is no doubt that such sales were common. Henry Louis Gates has been quoted as saying, "The image of slavery we had when I was a kid . . . was that the Europeans showed up with these fish nets and swept all the Africans away. Rubbish. It's like they went to a shopping mall. Without the Africans there wouldn't have been a slave trade" (quoted by Ariel Swarley, "Television Focuses on Africa's Human History"), *New York Times,* October 24, 1999, Section 2:1, p. 46.

[14]Hugh Lofting, *Doctor Dolittle and the Secret Lake* (Philadelphia: Lippincott, 1948).

[15]Lofting is the second writer in this study who mentions polar exploration (Nesbit is the first), but Milne and Ransome pursue polar imagery much more vigorously than Lofting does. Here, the reference serves simply as a reminder that Dolittle is indeed quite the world traveler.

[16]John Buchan also makes reference to Swift in his African novel *Prester John*. The rebellious African leader is John Laputa, who is a visionary and a prophet, and whose plans to raise all of Africa against the white man are certainly utopian.

[17]Anita Wilson makes this point in "Milne's Pooh Books: The Benevolent Forest," in Perry Nodelman, ed., *Touchstones: Reflections of the Best in Children's Literature* (W. Lafayette, IN: Children's Literature Association, 1985): 163–72.

[18]Roger Sale, *Fairy Tales and After: From Snow White to E. B. White* (Cambridge, MA: Harvard University Press, 1979), 16.

[19]A. A. Milne, *Winnie-the-Pooh* (1926; New York: Puffin, 1992); *The House at Pooh Corner* (1928; New York: Puffin, 1992).

[20]U. C. Knoepflemacher, "The Balancing of Child and Adult: An Approach to Victorian Fantasies for Children," *Nineteenth Century Fiction* 37:4 (1983), 498.

[21]Perry Nodelman, "The Other: Orientalism, Colonialism, and Children's Literature," *Children's Literature Association Quarterly* 12:1 (1992): 29–35.

[22]Dennis Rawlins, *Peary at the North Pole: Fact or Fiction?* (Washington & New York: Robert Luce, 1973), 10–11.

# CHAPTER 5

# Swallows and Amazons Forever?

From Kipling's novels at the turn of the century, through Lofting and Milne, British children's fiction is full of references to empire, even as authors become more troubled about imperial matters and empire becomes more encoded after World War I. Even if imperialism, in the strict sense of the exertion of commercial and political power over foreign nations, begins to disappear in British children's fiction, its close cousin, nationalism, does not. In some ways, the rise of nationalism, of the sense that Britain is stronger than and superior to other nations, might be seen as a defensive reaction to Britain's dwindling influence as imperial power. Saying it is so makes it so—a tactic any child would recognize. Britain begins to assert its national superiority not through acquiring colonial possessions, but through exploration and exploit.

Arthur Ransome (1884–1967) was a writer perfectly situated to mirror British attitudes and anxieties about empire and its loss. He was born in 1884, only eight years after Victoria was proclaimed Empress of India and three years before her Golden Jubilee. His childhood and young adulthood coincided with the mad scramble for African territory, as well as with the Boer War and, in China, the Boxer Rebellion. When Ransome was thirty World War I broke out, but because of poor health he was unable to serve. Instead, he went to Russia as a journalist to cover the Bolshevik Revolution, and after about a dozen years as a foreign correspondent, he came home to an England much changed from that of his youth—no longer the domineering imperial power of the globe, but a diminished and somewhat disheartened Britain after the brutalities of World War I.

But England, and especially the Lake District, was Ransome's spiritual home, the place that had spoken to him since his own childhood, and his series of books set mostly upon its lakes and fells are both nostalgic for arcadia and hopeful of the future. They are highly realistic in the details of sailing, signaling, birding, and other activities of the children, but also somewhat fantastic in the way adults leave the children largely to their own devices. And although Ransome's books are original and innovative, they owe clear debts to earlier writers, especially to Nesbit and Kipling and earlier adventure writers like Ballantyne and Stevenson. All of the novels are concerned with questions of the nature of childhood and growing up, many of them incorporate issues of empire and imperialism, and all of them suggest a hopeful future for Britain, despite the shrinking empire and the threat of another world war. The novels under discussion here—*Swallowdale, Winter Holiday,* and *Missee Lee*—are those where empire, or at least nationalism, lie closest to the surface, although nearly all of the books in the series touch upon these issues, however lightly.

The four Walker children are the central characters of the series, the offspring of an obliging mother and a conveniently off-stage father. Walker Senior is a naval officer, posted to unnamed foreign parts, but still the family's authority figure: the children must wait for him to telegraph his permission before they can begin to learn to sail. His eldest son, John, is already considering a naval career, following in his admired father's wake. Mr. Walker's status as naval officer links both him and his family with traditions of British might and empire. The nature of the play his children (and their friends, the Blacketts and the D's) indulge in further suggests that the children are comfortable with both the values and the language of empire—and that contemporary readers of their adventures must be comfortable with the same values and language, in order to vicariously enjoy the adventures of the Swallows and Amazons.

The very first volume of the series, *Swallows and Amazons* (1931) opens with an uncredited quotation from Keats's famous sonnet, "On First Looking Into Chapman's Homer," and one of the landmarks on the island the children claim as theirs is known to them as "Darien." Keats hardly seems an obvious source of epigraph for a children's novel, but in the world Ransome is creating (both consciously and unconsciously), the epigraph allows him to combine adventure, empire, and heroism as the background for his stories. Keats's poem celebrates Homer's epic accounting of Odysseus's voyages and of the battle for Troy, both of which are, in part, stories of empire building. Keats's poem ends with a reference to Cortez, another great explorer and empire-builder. Further, the fact that Keats is a Romantic poet allows Ransome to suggest that there is something "Romantic" about the children, primarily their connection with the natural world. They are rarely portrayed indoors, preferring to be out of doors and in natural settings. And finally, Keats is among the greatest of English poets, in fact among the greatest poets in the world, indicating Britain's literary strength, if not her military or political strength.

So the entire series begins with a poem fraught with implications of empire and tradition, then quickly introduces the Walker children and makes clear their father's importance as a naval officer, and sends the children off to colonize and rename the lake they are summering on, in the manner of all proper English colonizers. Indeed, the children consciously position themselves as colonizers in their references to all adults as *natives,* a term Ransome may have lifted from Kipling's *Stalky & Co.,* in which the schoolboys refer to bothersome adult locals as "natives" who stand in opposition to the boy "Collegers." In *Swallowdale,* for instance, the Blackett girls have their adventures thwarted by the grim and offstage Great Aunt. They explain to the Swallows :"[D]on't you understand? We put it in the message we left with the wood. We told you there was native trouble."[1] In the same volume, the Blacketts' Uncle Jim is referred to as a "native porter", which "all explorers" have (168). Titty, the romantic storyteller of the children, thinks that she can use a native ritual to disable the Great Aunt: create a voodoo doll.

The references to natives and their doings is omnipresent in the series. On the one hand, this device has the happy effect of making children—usually the subordinates in a family—the dominant ones. The children are subjects and actors, not objects to be acted upon. On the other hand, all of the references to natives seem to have been drawn (by the children) from literature that presents real natives, indigenous people, as less intelligent, less resourceful, and less capable of noticing and dealing with the important aspects of the world. The children appear to have read books like *Robinson Crusoe, The Coral Island,* and other classics that consistently position the indigenous as not only object, but as animalistic, barbarian, non-Christian, and exotic. To the children, who imagine adults as natives, this makes exploration and colonization exciting and dangerous. But their play is based upon a troubling British history with indigenous peoples.

The series has other minor allusions to things imperial. Captain Flint (the children's Stevensonian nickname for the Blacketts's Uncle Jim) is the childlike adult figure who, from time to time, is allowed to participate in the children's adventures. Although his profession is not made clear, he is a world traveler whose trunk bears labels from around the globe, and whose book *Mixed Moss* has, according to a note in *Swallowdale,* gone through eight printings. Like Albert-next-door's uncle in Nesbit's Bastable books, Captain Flint appears to make his living by publishing tales of his adventures around the empire and around the globe. Whether he has been soldier, trader, colonial official, or—like Ransome himself—a newspaperman, he has clearly benefited from, if not directly participated in, Britain's imperial conquests. The Walker children's youngest sibling, too young to join them on their adventures, is known as "Vicky" because she looks like Queen Victoria—as if the glory of Victorian empire-building were being reborn through the Walker family.[2]

The first novel in the series that makes explicit and extended use of empire and exploration is *Swallowdale* (1931), the second book in the series. Although critics have noted that this is perhaps the most discursive and loosely plotted of the series books, it is, in fact, held together by the children's desire to conquer unknown territory, in the manner of all great British explorers. The premise of the novel is that the Amazons cannot break free of the native trouble caused by the visit of their Great Aunt, thus leaving the Swallows to their own devices for much of the novel. But the Swallows are also stymied, because John has made a serious sailing error and smashed the children's boat, which spends the majority of the book in dry dock. Unable to sail, the children make plans to camp on the fells and to do some climbing and exploring instead.

While I hesitate to put too heavy a metaphoric burden on a children's novel, and while I am certain that Ransome had only the adventuresome possibilities of the wrecked boat in mind when he plotted his novel, I also think it is possible to read the smashing of the boat—under the command of John, after all, who is a proto-naval officer—as an emblem of the waning of British imperial strength. If, for a moment, we imagine the children as being a miniature British Empire unto themselves, it has been their fleet of boats that has allowed them both to explore and conquer the wider world, and to subvert the authority of the native adults. At the same time their naval power wanes, native uprisings in the form of the Great Aunt and other troublesome adults are on the increase.

The children, or empire in miniature, react just as the larger British public did as empire waned: they turn their attention to the conquering of geographical obstacles rather than of cultures and territories as evidence of their superiority over the natives or over foreigners. The children make a camp on the fells and set plans to reach the summit of "Kanchenjunga" (in actuality Coniston Old Man in the Lakes). The real Kanchenjunga is one of the eight-thousand-meter peaks in the Himalayas, the third highest in the world after Everest and K2. It was not summited until 1955, two years after Everest, and again the conquerors were British. Indeed, the British had been mountaineering in the Himalayas, and writing books about their exploits, since the mid nineteenth century.

Ransome's children, in the early 1930s, seem well aware of British mountaineering feats, suggesting how important such feats were in the public imagination. The children not only know of expeditions in the Himalayas, but also seem conversant with some of the details of those expeditions, details they no doubt gleaned through press coverage, overheard in adult conversations, and perhaps read in explorers' accounts. (That they read such accounts is made clear in *Winter Holiday,* when they have been perusing Nansen's descriptions of his North Polar expeditions.)

And if the children themselves haven't read explorers' accounts, Ransome certainly had. The hike the children make to the top of Kanchenjunga is a child-sized, summertime, low-altitude version of the stages of an assault on an eight-thosand-meter peak. When the children look up at the mountain, they look "at the peak of Kanchenjunga towering into the morning sunlight. It was hard to believe that they were going to the top of it" (276). The first day, they hike halfway up the mountain and make a camp, what a mountaineer would refer to as a base camp. "Halfway up . . . It's a fine place for a camp, just above the tree level" (306). As the children climb higher, Titty says, "Isn't he a beauty? . . . He's the finest mountain in the world" (314), and indeed Ransome's descriptions of the view and the countryside are very nearly rhapsodic:

> The sun set in a golden cap on the head of Kanchenjunga, and the morning glow, creeping down, found out the creases and wrinkles of his old face almost as well as it does in winter when the sunshine makes every crevice and gully a blue shadow in the gleaming snow. The light crept lower and lower down the mountain sides and lit the tops of the pine trees in the woods below the camp. (320)

This description captures Ransome's strong emotional attachment to the Lake District, but is also reminiscent of early mountaineers' descriptions of views from the tops of mountains. For example, Mallory writes of the 1921 expedition to Everest:

> Presently the miracle happened. We caught the gleam of snow behind the grey mist. A whole group of mountains began to appear in gigantic fragments . . . like the wildest creation of a dream . . . To the left a black serrated crest was hanging in the sky incredibly. Gradually . . . we saw the great mountain sides and glaciers . . . now one fragment now another through the floating rifts, until far higher than imagination had dared to suggest the white summit of Everest appeared . . . [W]e were able to piece together the fragments, to interpret the dream.[3]

When the day for the final assault comes, all six children are able to participate, since the native trouble has been quashed and the Great Aunt is on her way back home. The children have a rope, which they carefully tie around each other, leaving about five yards between each individual, in imitation of real mountaineering technique. Titty, however, says, "We ought really to have ice-axes" (326), remembering, no doubt, something she has read in reports of real mountaineering. The children scramble up the mountain, grateful for the rope, when Roger slips and nearly goes over a precipice (or into a crevasse, although Ransome does not use this word), until he is hauled back to safety by the others. They make a point of climbing over, rather than around, boulders, in order to make the climb truly challenging and new, just as mountaineers today search for new routes in order to claim some sort of "first" on a mountain.

The final accomplishment of reaching the top of Kanchenjunga/Old Man Coniston is given to the reader in these terms:

> All this time the explorers had been climbing up the northern side of Kanchenjunga. The huge shoulder of the mountain had shut out from them everything that there was to the west. As they climbed, other hills in the distance seemed to be climbing, too . . . But it was not until the last rush to the top, not until they were actually standing by the cairn that marked the highest point of Kanchenjunga, that they could see what lay beyond the mountain. Then, indeed, they knew that they were on the roof of the world. (331–332)

"The roof of the world" is a phrase has been used to describe the Himalayas and Nepal since the mid-nineteenth century. Dozens of books, dating from the nineteenth century and continuing up to the present, use the phrase in titles of books about the Himalayas, or Nepal, or Tibet.[4] Ransome is underlining that, for the children, conquering Old Man Coniston is the equivalent of conquering the Himalayas, none of which were conquered until the mid nineteen-fifties. Thus, the children are made truly heroic, miniature versions of British national heroes. In fact, although perhaps Ransome did not realize it as he wrote, he has quite literally written the future of British nationalistic exploration in the story of these children. The children are, in 1931, close to the age Hillary himself must have been at the time. John, if he doesn't grow up to be a naval officer like his father, might well opt to be a member of a British expedition to the high Himalayas.

But it is the moments just after the successful summiting that are the most telling, and that shed the most light on Ransome's uses of the imagery and language of empire and exploration. The children discover, beneath the cairn, "a small round brass box with the head of an old lady stamped on the lid of it. Framing the head of the old lady were big printed letters: 'QUEEN OF ENGLAND EMPRESS OF INDIA DIAMOND JUBILEE 1897' " (334). Inside the box is a note, stating that in 1901 the parents of the Blacketts and Uncle Jim (all children at the time) had climbed "the Matterhorn" (335).

This is a significant moment for several reasons. First of all, the relic at the summit makes specific reference to Queen Victoria, to her status as Empress of India, and to the Diamond Jubilee of 1897. The Jubilee year (of which the brass box is a souvenir) provoked a significant outpouring of Victorian patriotism and pride in the empire and the British role in claiming and ruling it. By 1897 Britain held sway over a quarter of the landmass of the globe and a quarter of the global population. During Victoria's reign eighteen territories and countless minor possessions were acquired by the British. However, this "new imperialism" during the last half of the nineteenth century had significant differences from the purer colonial expansionist policies of early empire-building. Classical colonialism uses colonial territories as sources of raw materials and as new markets for domestically produced goods. The "new imperialism" of the mid- and late- Victorian era often did not involve actually colonizing countries in this way, but instead set up protectorates, or treaty ports, or other, looser kinds of associations with the Crown.

The empire at the end of the nineteenth century and the end of Victoria's reign had no central governing authority. There were white-settled colonies like Canada and New Zealand, both of which achieved Dominion status by the late nineteenth century. (Dominion status meant these countries still swore allegiance to the Crown, had dominion over their own boundaries, but no dominion over British policy at "home.") Possessions of the British Crown were ruled either by bureaucracy, by military, by some sort of self-governance, or, at times, by the presence of some lonely colonial governor thousands of miles from home. While this sort of ad hoc, haphazard way of ruling its empire generally worked for the British, it certainly posed difficulties, and in fact, by the end of Victoria's reign, the edges of the empire were beginning to fray. Possessions, which had never been forced to supply troops for the British, became increasingly reluctant to volunteer to do so, and there were agitations of various sorts for home rule, independence, or some other sort of loosening of the reins from England. While the Jubilee Year certainly gave Britain a chance to wave the flag and proudly celebrate its vast empire, there was also a certain uneasiness beneath the celebration. These last years of the century, after all, were also the years of the great land grab in Africa, with Britain and other nations racing to annex African territory for fear some other nation would beat them to it. There were no good economic or strategic reasons for expanding into Africa, but lands that could be annexed were running out, and European nations felt the urge to accumulate what was left as quickly as they could.

So the souvenir the children find at the top of the mountain is more than an old brass box: it is an emblem of both the height of British empire and the beginning of its decline. It is linked to the children's explorations of new territories, as well as to the British explorations of new territories that might be annexed or colonized. Further, it is linked to some initial disappointment for the children, whose fantasy play has involved being the *first* to discover the top of Kanchenjunga—and now they learn some other people, natives from the past, have beaten them to it.

But Titty points out that for those other explorers the mountain was the Matterhorn and now it is Kanchenjunga, so they did it first anyway—a typical bit of childlike logic. But the disappointment at not being first would, for the British reader in the thirties at any rate, resonate with Scott's profound disappointment at having Amundsen beat him to the South Pole, disappointment that ended in "heroic" death for the expedition as they tried to make their exhausted way back eight hundred miles to camp. *Swallowdale* focuses on

Himalayan exploration and not arctic or Antarctic exploration (polar exploration has a specific role to play in *Winter Holiday*) not only because doing so makes a happy ending possible, but because by the 1930s, Himalayan exploration had begun, to a large extent, to replace polar exploration as a national obsession.

The return journey from the peak also mirrors that of many expeditions: the descent is more arduous than the ascent, and for a reason familiar to many mountaineers: weather. Unexpectedly, fog rolls in, the children become separated, and Roger sprains an ankle. The disorientation Roger and Titty feel is similar to that of many lost explorers. Their senses seem to tell them one thing, and their compass another, and they unwisely choose to believe their senses. Titty finds help from local men, charcoal burners who are working on the fells and who are referred to as friendly natives. In fact, the hut the men have built for shelter, a conical structure made of logs, is called a "wigwam" by the children, and in it the woodsmen make a poultice, a bed, and a cup of tea for the rescued Roger and Titty. Titty thinks that "It was very pleasant after being lost in the fog to be sitting there in the quiet wood having tea with a medicine man and other friendly natives" (366).

The charcoal-burning natives are interesting minor characters when looked at in the light of empire. In this particular context, the natives are friendly and helpful, more aware of the ways of the mountain than the exploring children are, and capable of carrying the injured Roger down the mountainside. In fact, they are sherpas to the mountaineering children, even if they haven't helped them find the way up the mountain. Second, these natives are portrayed by Ransome as being ancient, long-lived, and exotic. Young Billy, one of the men, entertains Roger by telling him (in local dialect or, metaphorically, a foreign tongue or "pidgin" English) wrestling stories of long ago, stories Roger does not understand, but that "left him with the feeling that the old man was very much stirred up by something or other that had happened a long time ago" (372). The old man also boils his eggs in a kettle, something Roger has been taught is not wise, "and he was just going to ask a question about that, but stopped himself, remembering that different tribes have different customs and that he really knew very little about this one" (373). Roger shows a certain amount of respect and consideration here for the natives—but he does so at least partly because he is, for the moment, dependent upon them for his health and well-being. As in real empires and colonies, the colonizers tend to treat the indigenous people better when the indigenous are central to the survival of the colonizers.

These natives, of course, are also representatives of a vanishing culture. Their nontechnological, labor-intensive ways of harvesting wood and burning it into charcoal were fading even in the 1930s, and have now vanished altogether. And, in fact, these natives work for the neighboring farms, one of which is working in turn for the Walker family by providing a holiday house and servants for them. There is a very neat hierarchy here of both class and culture, one that mirrors much of the British colonial hierarchy, where the white colonists (represented here by the Walkers and Blacketts, who either own property or can afford to rent holiday property) are at the top of the ladder, the "sepoy" class of trusted servants is next, and the indigenous and unassimilated are at the bottom of the ladder. When the children are at imaginative play, they put themselves at the top of the ladder and include the white adults as natives, even if they are "the best of natives"—but when we step out of imaginative play and into the real world, it becomes clear that the children (or Roger, at any rate, in this particular volume) actually have the least power of all.

A stretcher party is formed to bring Roger down the mountain after his night in the wigwam, and his ankle heals in time for him to take part in a final sailboat race. *Swallow* has been repaired and is better than new, and she races the *Amazon* at the closing of the novel. I think it is significant that the novel ends back on the water, back in a "naval" setting—and that John and the crew of *Swallow* beat out the more experienced Amazons in their sailboat. Metaphorically, the conquest of Kanchenjunga and the successful resolution of the rescue party have reasserted British pride and accomplishment, and the mini-Empire of children can once again rule the seas of Lake Windermere.

Ransome makes even more explicit use of exploration as metaphor for national pride and precedence in *Winter Holiday* (1931).[5] This novel introduces a new pair of children to the Swallows and Amazons: the D's, alias Dick and Dorothea. All of the children are spending their winter school holiday on the lakes, and Dick and Dorothea rather wistfully wish they could get to know the Amazons, who appear to them to have exciting adventures, as indeed they do. The D's are city children, very inexperienced in the sort of outdoor adventures the other children take for granted: they can't see any important difference between sail and rowboats, use paper to start fires, and commit any number of other mortal sins that make the Swallows and Amazons look askance. If we think of the original six children as the original colonizers of this lake landscape and its natives, Dick and Dorothea are tenderfeet, newcomers to this strange world of child (colonial) imaginative domination over the landscape. They must both prove themselves and be initiated into this new world in the course of the novel.

Part of the reason they are successful, and the entire reason the children have adventures at all, is that Captain Nancy comes down with mumps and is quarantined, as are all the children. They can't return to school for term opening until they are certified disease-free. Nancy is the only child who actually develops mumps, and she is effectively closed off from the other children for the bulk of the novel. This allows her younger and weaker sister Peggy the chance to develop some leadership, and it also allows the D's a chink in which to assert themselves into the group. Nancy is the *de facto* leader of the group, along with John ( once he proves that he is a good sailor). She rules by virtue of greater experience and age—gender does not appear to have much effect upon the possibilities of her leadership—and also because she is a year-round resident of the district, rather than a holiday visitor. Again, if we think of the children within the metaphor of colonialism, Nancy would be the permanent colonial governor, her sister would be her loyal assistant, and the other children would be the more temporary colonial employees. Without Nancy's leadership, the entire group seems lost and adrift, constantly wondering, "What Nancy would do" or expect, and trying to communicate with her by means of semaphore. Nancy's absence allows a space for the D's to insert and assert themselves.

The children in this volume, as in *Swallowdale,* are kept from sailing by the weather. A hard frost sets in, the hardest in decades, and the lake begins to freeze from end to end. Sailing is not possible, so the children concoct a scheme to travel to "the North Pole," or the furthest northern reach of the lake. They plan to skate to it, once the lake freezes entirely.

Polar expeditions at the end of the nineteenth and early twentieth centuries, the so-called "heroic age" of exploration, provided much drama and national excitement for the British, even if they failed to be first at either pole. The British had been involved in arctic exploration since at least 1587, when John Davis pushed north as far as 72° 12 min N. But the British were outdone by both the Americans and the Norwegians, the Americans at the North Pole and the Norwegians at the South. The American Richard E. Peary claimed to have reached the North Pole in April of 1908, but he had a noisy and public dispute with Frederick A. Cook, who claimed to have achieved the pole some months earlier. The dispute reached all the way to Congress, where an Act of Congress was needed before Peary could be promoted to Rear Admiral. To this day there is still some contention about which man reached the North Pole first, although generally Peary is thought to have miscalculated and missed the pole itself by about a hundred miles. There was no such confusion over the South Pole. The British Shackleton had tried for the pole and failed in 1908–09, and Roald Amundsen of Norway and Robert Falcon Scott of Britain were in a race for the pole in 1911–12, with Amundsen beating Scott by a month on December 14, 1911. Scott and his party died of starvation and exposure during their eight hundred mile journey back from the pole.

Ransome chooses neither the Americans nor the British as a model for his child explorers, but rather the Norwegians, in the person of Fridtjof Nansen. Although the choice of a Norwegian model may seem odd, given the bitterness Britain felt towards Amundsen's success at the South Pole, it really is not. Ransome cannot have his children emulate Scott, because Scott died and failed; he cannot have them emulate the Americans, whose honor is questionable. The British had not been major players in the quest for the North Pole, but the Norwegians had been, and Nansen's remarkable arctic adventures were both dramatic and well-documented, by Nansen himself and by others. Nansen never quite made it to the North Pole, but some of Ransome's children do, suggesting metaphorically that the British have what it takes to beat the Norwegians to *a* pole, if not the South Pole. But the major reason for choosing Nansen as model is the sheer drama of his story.[6]

In the novel itself, the children (not the narrator) choose Nansen as their model. It is not the controlling voice of the narrator that foregrounds Nansen's exploration, but the children themselves who are aware of his exploits and use them as a base camp of sorts for their own. When Captain Nancy, isolated at her home, learns that Captain Flint's houseboat has been frozen into the lake, she sends a one-word message: "FRAM," and the other children need no other direction in order to turn the houseboat into the *Fram* and to begin to organize their expeditionary forces. Nansen is a logical model for the children. Not only do they have access to the absent Captain Flint's frozen-in houseboat, but the houseboat itself contains Nansen's two-volume account of his time in the arctic, *Farthest North . . . The Voyage and Exploration of the Fram, and the Fifteen-Months Sledge Expedition.*[7] Dick, when he discovers this text says, "This'll tell us everything we want to know" (171). The children already have sledges and skates, and soon accumulate "bearskins" in the form of sheepskins and rabbit skins that they attempt to fashion into arctic wear. They, like Nansen before them, must wait for proper conditions before they can set out for the pole—in their case, the "farthest north" point of the lake.

The written word, the text, obviously plays a role in the kind of play these children are involved with, just as the written word provided a spring-board for the imaginative play of Nesbit's Bastables, whose sibling together-ness is a strong influence on Ransome's sibling groups. In *Swallowdale,* there is not a specific textual reference, as there is in *Winter Holiday* (and, later, in *Missee Lee*). None of the important texts that Ransome depends upon as foundations for his fantasy are specifically English texts. The texts underly-ing the adventures in *Swallowdale* may—or may not—have been written by English explorers; *Farthest North* is a Norwegian text; and the text behind *Missee Lee* is *The Aeneid.* Yet each of these texts involves exploration, if not exploitation, of lands or people or of both, and all are appropriated by these English children for their own uses. In a sense, Ransome is appropriating or annexing these texts and using them in order to give British children the chance to imaginatively practice exploration and exploitation through their play. In *Winter Holiday,* he effectively ignores the fact that Nansen (and Amundsen, the other great Norwegian explorer) were used by Norway for the same sorts of nationalistic purposes that Britain had used Scott, and would later use Hillary. British children—and effectively, Britain's future—will win what Nansen could not, and will once again be able to fly the Union Jack above foreign territory. This is the subtext underlying *Winter Holiday,* and similar subtexts underlie other volumes in the *Swallows and Amazons* series.

The description of the inside of the houseboat-cum-*Fram* indicates quite specifically the connections between empire and exploration. In the first place, the children are appropriating and exploiting property and territory that belongs to a native adult, Captain Flint. Although they do feel some twinges of apprehension about occupying the houseboat with no knowledge or permission from any of the adults, as soon as they make themselves comfortable, their apprehension vanishes, and they think of the boat as their own. When Captain Flint unexpectedly returns to claim his territory, he discovers that his cupboards have been stripped bare by the children: being children of empire, they have exploited the natural resources of the foreign territory they have occupied as their own.

Of course, they are not the only exploiters. The adults in these novels tend to veer between being "the best of natives" from the children's point of view, and bona fide adults who exist within an adult world, with adult experiences and adult acculturation. Thus, Captain Flint may be seen as a native whose goods the children exploit, but at the same time elements of his boat reveal that he himself has connections with the British empire and its exploitative past. Within the cabin of the boat, the children see Captain Flint's souvenirs of his travels: "a knobkerry, a boomerang, a model catamaran from Ceylon, a bamboo flute from Shanghai" (170). Knobkerries are short round clubs that were used in battle by tribesmen in South Africa; boomerangs are native weapons from Australia; and catamarans and flutes are cultural artifacts from Asia. While for the children these are simply exotic and fascinating objects that hint at Captain Flint's adventuresome past, they also carry symbolic weight. From about the 1880s onward, Britain had been involved in a series of wars with native Africans, including those in South Africa, and had struggled with colonial competition during the Boer War of 1899–1902. The fact that Captain Flint has brought back a trophy of these encounters, a captured weapon, underlines not only his identity as a traveler, but also his close connection with conquest and Empire itself. The same can be said of the boomerang, which could be used as a hunting weapon or a weapon in battle by the indigenous Aborigine. The Asian artifacts are more cultural than military, and suggest a kind of diminution of indigenous culture and autonomy. The catamaran, a crucial tool for fishing and transportation in Ceylon, is turned into a toy in Captain Flint's cabin; the flute is "primitive" bamboo rather than metal, clearly not suitable for playing Mozart, and it has been struck into silence, lacking a player to bring it to life. The children, in a sense, are colonizing the colonizers, appropriating—and being appropriated by— emblems of empire and imperialism.

In *Winter Holiday,* however, the children are less intent on conquering natives and their lands than they are in pretending to be the first to reach the

North Pole: the imperial and colonial implications of their play are the sub-text to the primary text of playacting Nansen's exploratory feats. Like all serious explorers, they plan their expedition carefully, and one of the chief tasks is to choose the team of explorers permitted on the expedition. The D's are new to the lakes and to the other children, and more used to solitary literary and scientific pursuits than they are to vigorous play in the out-of-doors. Dorothea is a would-be writer, who often looks at events and transforms them into the beginnings of romantic novels, to which she gives titles like *The Riddle of the Sands* (170). Dick is slightly more outward looking—he is a would-be scientist, who carefully writes things down in his notebook and who owns a telescope and is trying to learn the stars. He is, in miniature, the absent-minded professor or scientist, who vanishes into another world when thinking about anything scientific. Between them, Dick and Dorothea exemplify two aspects of Ransome's literary world: the realistic and the romantic. Ransome provides plenty of accurate detail about sails and sailing, primus stoves and tents, which has the effect of making the romantic adventures of the children seem realistic, as if they could—and did—happen. The other six children also exemplify the dual aspects of Ransome's fictional world: the youngest, Titty and Roger, mirror Dorothea and Dick. Like Dorothea, Titty likes to make up and tell stories, and like Dick, Roger is drawn to technology and things mechanical, and so on.

The Swallows and Amazons do not at first see the worth of the inexperienced D's. Dorothea overhears the other children, whom she thinks of as "elders" even though she is nearly the same age as they, discussing whether or not she and her brother will be allowed to join the expedition:

> "An astronomer might be quite useful."
> "But what's *she* going to do?"
> "We'll soon know if they're any good." (47)

Here the "elders" sound as stuffy and elitist as any member of the Explorers' Club. Like real explorers, they must be convinced that their team members will be able to contribute to the expedition, rather than become a burden to it. As it turns out, the D's are far more resourceful and adventuresome than they first appear, and end up the true heroes of the expedition, in the best underdog tradition.

In order to play out their fantasy, the children must rename the landscape they know so well from summers on the lake. No longer are "Rio" and "the Amazon" suitable place names. Natives become "Eskimos"; the children set out from Spitzbergen (like real polar explorers before and after them); and skaters on the ice are variously polar bears or seals. While on one level this transformation is merely an indication of the flexibility of the children's imagination, on a deeper level it reflects the colonial imperative to name places according to European names, or after European leaders or explorers. One need only think of "Rhodesia" in Africa (named for Sir Cecil Rhodes), or "New Amsterdam" under the Dutch, later "New York" under the English. Naming a place gives the namer power over it, or at least the illusion of power and control. Colonial powers literally transform a landscape once they rename it and begin reshaping it. The colonizing children in *Winter Holiday* have a less deleterious effect on the landscape and the cultures inhabiting it, but they almost instinctively function according to colonial imperative by renaming the landscape, thus, re-visioning it and appropriating it for their own needs.

The children, having read Nansen's work, follow his lead closely. While they wait for Captain Nancy to get better and join them for the final push to the pole, they make exploratory marches up the frozen lake, to a point they call their "farthest north," just as real explorers did. Furthermore, they make a cache. Although real explorers would have left food and supplies in a cache, the children merely leave a message in a discarded ginger-beer bottle that reads, "Cache Island. Reached this point of northern latitude, 28 January. S., A., and D. North Polar Expedition" (180). Their message is as terse and scientific as anything Nansen himself might have left behind.

The Swallows and Amazons, sailors at heart, inspired by the ice yachts on the lake, rig a sail to a sledge and career down the ice, ending in a tumble that does the children no real harm. The scientific and mechanical Dick, however, is inspired not so much by a desire to sail even if the lake is frozen (he knows nothing of boats) as he is by drawings and photographs in Nansen's own book about his winter on the *Fram,* during which he rigged sails to sledges, in hopes of moving more quickly across the ice. Nansen and his crew had had to kill all of their dogs; their kayaks needed constant repair and were not very seaworthy; their sledges were cumbersome and difficult to maneuver over pressure ridges in the ice. Sledges with sails seemed like a reasonable mode of transportation to try to move over frozen ground. Nansen's *Farthest North* not only contains an account of the making of sails for the sledges, but also an illustration showing exactly what these sailing sledges looked like. Dick makes a "careful drawing of one of the sledges in the Nansen books," and then sits up with his host "Eskimo," Mr. Dixon, planning how to recreate a similar sledge. He and his sister say nothing to the others of what they are up to, in case their plan is unsuccessful. But it is not.

Dick and his Eskimo friend (who here functions not unlike one of the Eskimo helpers Peary had on his Polar expeditions, or like a sherpa on a Himalayan expedition) secretly and successfully fashion a sledge, and like his real-life native counterparts, Mr. Dixon will receive little or no credit for his part in the expedition. None of the other children (except for Dorothea) know about the sledge—a critical point in the climax of the novel, where the heretofore more dominant Swallows and Amazons, and Nancy in particular, make a crucial error in their signaling instructions. Dick and Dorothea take off for the pole in their sledge, thinking the other children have left before them, when in fact they are still safe at home.

The climax of the book is the hair-raising sledge yacht race up the lake, accomplished by Dick and Dorothea on their own. Having taken the signal flag to mean the others have already started for the pole, the brother and sister hurry off in an attempt to catch them, not realizing that the others have not set off at all. Their journey begins safely enough, on skates, with the sledge being towed behind. Having learned some lessons from the other children, Dick and Dorothea stop at the cache and leave a note saying they have been there. They wonder why the others have not left a message, but assume they are racing to be first, and dismiss the fact that there is no evidence that their fellow expedition members are, indeed, preceding them. Dick is anxious to set the sail on the sledge, once they are on new ice "that they had seen only from High Greenland." He looks behind and says "There's more wind coming. I'm sure John would say wind was coming. Just look at that cloud" (272). More than wind is coming—snow is coming with it, a real blizzard, and the children are on a frozen lake, and neither their fellow children nor the adults have any idea where they are. Furthermore, although they have the sledge and a rudimentary idea of how to handle it under sail, they are otherwise inexperienced explorers, unaware that the cloud behind them means serious weather is moving in. Ransome has set up a situation that is genuinely dangerous and difficult for the children, one that mirrors real experiences arctic explorers have had, and one that, if the children are successful, will give them full membership into the circle of the Swallows and Amazons.

Dick fastens the ropes "as he had seen them shown in the Nansen pictures" (273) just before the wind hits, and the children are blown up the lake, not really knowing where they are going, and going too fast to have any control over their sledge. As they career up the ice, Dick lifts his head and tries to look into the blizzard: "In a moment his glasses were crusted over with driven snow" (291) and he is blinded, just as arctic explorers were often struck snow-blind on the ice fields. Dorothea, frightened, thinks that Dick might be looking at her, "but instead of his eyes there were only those round white splashes of snow. His hand, the one that had lost its rabbit-skin mitten, was looking wet and blue about the knuckles. . . . She, too, began to feel cold . . . [L]ying upon [the sledge], being blown along, she felt that the cold was finding its way through everything that was meant to keep it out" (292). Ransome is clearly familiar with descriptions of Scott's final desperate days in Antarctica, of Greely's horrific time in Starvation Camp on Ellesmere Island in 1884, as well as with Nansen's descriptions of desperate days on the *Fram*.

The children finally tilt and crash as the sledge slams into land—but what land? The children have no way of knowing where they are. Dick wisely secures himself to a rope, to the sledge, and to Dorothea before he begins to explore in the dark and the storm, and before long he discovers a little hut, which, of course, turns out to be the North Pole. Nearly the first thing Dick does when he realizes that they have successfully beaten the other, more experienced children is to raise a flag—not the Union Jack, but the quarantine flag the children have been using all winter:

> There, close by one of the windows, white halyards, new and stiff, came down from the top of the flagstaff and were fastened loosely round a cleat. Captain Flint had known that the discovery of the North Pole would be nothing without the hoisting of a flag. (304)

The children claim the pole for themselves—for children—with a children's flag, and are grateful to the helpful native Captain Flint for making the hoisting of the flag possible, but give him no further credit for help in getting to the Pole, despite having used his boat and his supplies for most of the winter and depending upon the cache of food he has left for them at the North Pole. They have also successfully beaten their competitors, something the British never managed to accomplish in polar expeditions.

Both the children and the adults gradually figure out what has happened to the D's. John assumes the children would have gotten off the ice when they saw the storm coming, but Susan says, "If only they had any sense. But they haven't got any, not that sort" (308). Even this late in the holiday adventure, the more experienced children have gained no respect for the newcomers to their group, and always assume the worst of their actions. But Dick and Dorothea have, quietly, been learning from their elders, and even if they still can't tie a respectable seaman's knot, they know enough Morse to signal with a lantern from the North Pole, and to stay put until the others arrive. Captain Nancy is the first, and her reaction to their achievement clinches their acceptance into the larger group of children. She says of their sledge trip, "Well, it's the best thing I ever heard. You couldn't have made it more real" (324). The other children show up shortly after Nancy, and at first give the D's the cold shoulder, assuming that the D's own stupidity took them onto the lake and into danger. But Nancy, showing good sportsmanship, notices this and says, "It's not their fault at all. It's mine, really," (326), and she explains how the signaling became confused due to her own forgetfulness. Scott of the Antarctic would have been proud of her.

The children celebrate the achievement of the "pole," the new expertise and status of the D's, and Nancy's return to the world of the well, with a grand feast that Captain Flint has left to greet the children, even though they arrive in an unexpected fashion and at an unexpected time. Their food may not be as exotic as the "lobscouse made of potatoes . . . pemmican, dried bear's and seal's flesh, and bear tongues" that Nansen's team ate upon a celebratory occasion ( 320), but it is no less festive, and more of it arrives with the adults, whose rescue team is slower off the mark than that of the children.

At the end of the novel, Dick and Dorothea have proved themselves to be worthy explorers and worthy members of the ruling class of children. Peggy, too, has gained some status, as the surprised Nancy learns when Peggy reveals that she has been using Nancy's pet phrases, such as "Jib booms and bobstays!" and "Barbecued billygoats!" Considering the colonial and imperial subtext of Ransome's series of novels, it is logical that full acceptance into the empire of children is reached through exploits of exploration, and that at least in fantasy the less-prepared, less-knowledgeable British team of explorers should reach the pole first. It is not only wish fulfillment for the child characters in this novel, but for adult readers as well, who can vicariously see the British win at empire and exploration.

It is *Missee Lee* (1941)[8] that provides the clearest example in the Ransome canon of his complex attitudes towards imperialism, empire, and children themselves. It appears late in the series, and is apparently not a "real" adventure the children have but one that they make up as a story during winters away from their holiday haunts. In brief, the novel is about the Swallows, Amazons, and Captain Flint and their sailing adventure in the South China Sea. They are shipwrecked, temporarily separated from one another, and end up on the shores of an island run by a fierce female Chinese "taicoon," Missee Lee. Although threatened not only with being held for ransom, but also with potential violence and perhaps even death, the children find a way to escape their Chinese captors and to sail back to England.

The novel's place in time is not entirely clear. The fact that Missee Lee and the other Chinese taicoons are running independent island kingdoms and that they fear the possibility of invasion from the British suggests the uneasy Chinese Republic after the overthrow of the Manchu Dynasty in 1911, although it is also reminiscent of the China of the Opium Wars of 1839–42. The novel is purposefully unclear on its temporal placement not only because this is a children's book about a fantasy adventure, but because historical placement does not matter to the story. What matters is the fact that the British have greater power than the Chinese, are feared by the Chinese, and have a foothold in China in Hong Kong, Shanghai, Kowloon, and elsewhere. The exact point in imperial history does not matter; the underpinnings of empire and colonization do. Ransome had firsthand experience with the British in China, having met and admired Madame Sun-Yat Sen in both 1927 and 1929, and having written a book about his Chinese experiences, *The Chinese Puzzle* (1927). His Chinese experiences certainly lend verisimilitude to the descriptions of Chinese life presented in the novel, although how realistic a character Missee Lee might be is questionable.

Our very first clues about Missee Lee set the reader up for the ironic interplay of colonizer and colonized. Whereas Ransome does not seem entirely aware of the imperial subtext to *Swallowdale* and *Winter Holiday,* he does seem aware of it in *Missee Lee,* since the interplay of colonizer and colonized underlies much of the intended humor of the novel. The children have heard of a fierce "Missee Lee," a kind of Chinese pirate, but their first real introduction to her is by way of a copy of *The Aeneid* in which she has written her name, Miss Lee, and her academic titles (B.A., M.A., and so forth) both in Chinese and English. The children at first do not make the connection between the legendary "Missee Lee" and Miss Lee, but they turn out to be one and the same.

This first glimpse of the major Chinese character, mediated through another narrative text, is an important one. *The Aeneid* is a text explicitly about conquest and colonization, written for the ruling class of one of the world's most successful imperial empires (whose language gave us the very words *imperial* and *empire*), and used in Roman schoolrooms of Virgil's time. These children of the British Empire find the text in what appears to be an abandoned summer house, and at first assume the tenant is English, since *The Aeneid* is the Cambridge tutorial version. The text, furthermore, is inscribed with a famous Latin schoolboy verse that begins *"Hic liber est meus,"* or "This book is mine." The owner of the book is laying claim to the text and by implication, to all that the text stands for: empire both Roman and British; British university education for the children of the upper-class; British superiority and imperialism. The British, after all, once conquered by the Romans, had themselves conquered more than the Romans could dream of. But the owner of the text is a female Chinese warlord, not some British colonial official brushing up on his Latin. Her claims to the text and what it stands for are false.

Roger reappropriates what is, imperially speaking, his, by adding the last line and a drawing to the inscription in the textbook. His sister reprimands him: "Roger! In someone else's book!" and Roger's response is, "I haven't made a mess of it. She'd have put it in herself if she'd known it" (83). Roger is breathtakingly imperialistic here. Were he an adult British colonial administrator, he might just as dismissively have said, "I haven't ruined the country. The natives would have done the same if they knew how." Roger's knowledge of Latin and his defacement of *The Aeneid* will, ironically, turn out not to condemn them but to save them from immediate death. Missee Lee, we discover, aspires to be a scholar and recruits the children (and Captain Flint) to be Latin students, much against their will.

Ransome is not the only children's author to refer to *The Aeneid*. Kipling's schoolboys in *Stalky & Co.* know they must pass a Latin test as part of the Army Examination for entrance to Sandhurst and a military career, and as Judith Plotz has argued, *The Aeneid,* Horace's *Odes* (which also have a place in *Missee Lee*), and nineteenth-century British imperialism "all assume the need for imperial domination of a barbarian other."[9] *The Aeneid's* first eight books confirm the prophecy of a Roman Empire as depicted in the Shield of Aeneas and were the parts of *The Aeneid* most often taught to British schoolboys. Books nine through twelve, which tell of the often savage means by which Aeneas subjugates Italy and the barbarian Other, were generally omitted from schoolboy study: the emphasis was to be on imperial might and right and not on the often unsavory and dishonorable means by which such might was gained.

When we finally meet Missee Lee in person, the situation becomes more complicated still. She not only has no rights to the Latin text and its symbolic powers, but she has questionable rights to her place as chief warlord and Taicoon of the islands over which she rules. She is, for one thing, female. For another, she has inherited her position from a father who was himself a refugee from battle: he was *adopted* by a taicoon, inherited the taicoon's property and power, brought peace and cooperation to the three islands over which he now ruled, and when he died passed his power and authority to Missee Lee, who had been educated in Britain at both boarding school and at Cambridge. She is an outsider in the hierarchy of Chinese power because of lineage, gender, and education at the hands of the "enemy."

The relative peace that Missee Lee has inherited has come through both conciliation with the other taicoons and with a promise never to take British prisoners, since that will lead only to gunboats and British intervention, if not colonial expansion. Hence, the arrival of seven British shipwreck survivors complicates her political life. She should behead them and be done with it, but she is no savage native at ease with barbaric behavior, but a British-educated woman nostalgic for her lost British scholarly past. Instead of beheading them, she wants to stuff their heads with Latin: she makes them attend Latin classes, with herself as mistress, in a room that was "like walking into Europe out of Asia" (174).

The tables are turned. The children, who style themselves pirates and explorers and who have been playing at being adults, are rudely pushed back into the territory of childhood, along with the adult Captain Flint, who is also forced to join the class. They are, in a sense, "colonized" by Missee Lee, a female member of a race that the British have colonized elsewhere in Asia. Perhaps because they are children, and hence relatively impotent, they are able to be colonized by someone who is herself potentially colonized by both gender and race. Yet throughout the novel, the reader remains confident that the children will escape their colonized status, that Missee Lee will find her proper colonial place, and that the imperial reversal of the central part of the narrative will be put right by the end. Partly this is accomplished through the discourse of the novel and its genre: we depend upon a book that is part of a series to end happily, if not conclusively; and we especially depend upon children's books of the period to allow children to have deliciously supervision-free adventures, yet to remain safe and sound. But another, deeper part of the discourse is the imperial discourse. We can enjoy the discomfort of the recolonized children and laugh at the humor of a Chinese woman teaching British children Latin because, indeed, Missee Lee poses no threat. The understood rules of empire rule the understructure of the novel: British superiority will, we know, win in the end.

Our earliest clue that Missee Lee is not suited for emperor status, over her own people or over the children, is that she is not readily accepted by the other taicoons because she is female and because she has been educated in England. In her mind, her "superior" education makes her eminently suitable to rule her three islands, but from the point of view of the native Chinese islanders, she is suspect. She is the colonized subject who has put the values of the colonizers above the values of her own people. It is not only her Anglophilia that will get her in trouble, but her insistence upon nurturing the culture of the colonizer, rather than the native culture. In fact, nurturing this foreign culture in her European-style study directly threatens the stability and future of the native culture.

Missee Lee, then, appears to have imperial status, yet she harbors a potential colonizer within her boundaries. She assumes—wrongly—that the children's status as impotent *children* supersedes their status as British subjects. She is capable of this self-delusion because she also—mistakenly—believes she has gained a legitimate imperial status both as an alumna of Cambridge and as a Chinese taicoon. Race and gender will ultimately be the undoing of Missee Lee.

This confusion over who is colonizer and who is colonized forms the center of the humor of the novel. Missee Lee is part of this tradition of comic native that we have seen in Kipling and Nesbit. Here she is, in remotest China, in a sitting room filled with photographs of girls' hockey teams and the green lawns of Cambridge, serving tea and toast and lecturing her "students" in the required "comic" accent. She says "bimbey" for "blimey," and explains the local geography: "There are thlee islands here, Dlagon, Turtle and Tiger. This is Dlagon Island. Now the men of these thlee islands have lived by what you call pilacy since the world began" (176). She is clearly, even to the child reader, an inappropriate Latin teacher and has no obvious authority over the children except her authority as native leader—authority that, as we have seen, is shaky and becomes shakier as she insists upon keeping the children, against the advice of the other taicoons.

Missee Lee is playacting at being an emperor, and does not have to put her colonized subjects into a dependent, childlike state because they are already children. In fact, the children are spared having to act like colonizers because their work has already been done for them by the great institution of British education. Missee Lee did not have to wait for the empire-building British to invade her island kingdom. She went, instead, to their island and allowed herself to be individually colonized or infected by British culture, so that when she returns to China she becomes the enemy within. This is, of course, an economical way of building empires. If you can convince prominent people within the society you wish to take over that your way is best, you can save yourself the cost of armies and of building a colonial infrastructure. The natives you have won over will do your work for you.

The resolution of this comedy of empire begins when Missee Lee's unhappy rival taicoons discover that the English not only have a sextant, but have taken measurements and have a good idea of where they are, which makes them dangerous: they could escape, reveal the location of the islands, and send British gunboats. It is the threat of discovery and colonization by adult imperial forces that ultimately forces the Chinese to force Missee Lee to dispose of the children. She apparently, if reluctantly, agrees, but the Swallows and Amazons concoct an ingenious plan to escape. They plan to take part in the dragon dance ceremony, disguising themselves as one of the dancing dragons. They then will sneak to the junk Missee Lee has agreed to give them and navigate a narrow, rocky river gorge in pitch blackness, heading to the open sea, where they will be free of Chinese pirates and would-be Latin teachers. They will appropriate Chinese culture in order to escape it, leaving behind a potential empire for which they do not yet have the skills to rule. They will return to a proper English formal—and informal—education in what we might term "imperial studies," the implication being that as adults they will be better colonizers than they are as children.

The children could not complete their escape, however, were it not for Missee Lee's complicity. She has shared with them her knowledge of the dangerous gorge they must sail; she makes a junk available to them; and during the climactic scene we learn she has stowed away on board with the children, hoping to go back to Cambridge and her British life. That she stows away is good for the children and Captain Flint, who can safely negotiate the gorge with her help, and who at first are delighted that Missee Lee wants to sail with them: they have grown fond of her. But as they reach the end of the gorge and wait, becalmed, for sunrise and the wind, Missee Lee's old Chinese amah and her counselor find them and plead for Missee Lee to return. There is the sound of fighting from the islands, and the peace that her father worked so hard for seems to be unraveling. At the realization that there is fighting in Dragon Town, Missee Lee "gripped her Horace as if the book were a pistol holster and she were about to pull a pistol from it" (343).

This single image captures the conflict within Missee Lee. She is gripping yet another of her precious texts, this one by a contemporary of Virgil, as if it contains the weapon she needs. Horace's *Odes* were written for Horace's imperial patron, the Emperor Augustus, and were "intended to indorse [sic] and support the emperor in the social and religious reforms he had inaugurated for promoting the stability and perpetuity of the Roman State."[10] Horace's *Odes* may have helped the Roman Empire maintain stability, but an ancient Latin text is an inappropriate ideological weapon for a female Chinese taicoon. She needs her pistols and her hard-earned knowledge of her Chinese enemies to reclaim her place as a Chinese leader, not as a would-be

British leader. She opts, at the end, for her Chinese heritage and duty and heads back to reunite the three islands. Captain Flint says it's probably a good thing, and she'll be happy "if only she stops hankering after Cambridge" (346). The taicoon and the British sailors part company, and the children sail Missee Lee's junk back to England, to amaze and delight family and friends. They have brought home an even better souvenir than Captain Flint's model of a Ceylon catamaran.

What is the imperial lesson the reader is to draw from this children's narrative? One lesson is that imperial subjects always win, even if they are only children. Yet they win only with the help of their Chinese captor and potential colonial subject. What, precisely, do they win? They win the sort of adventure that not only children, but explorers of "exotic" lands have always dreamed of. They win a complex narrative of empire with which to entertain and perhaps inform their fellow imperial subjects, who might then be tempted to pursue their own imperial dreams. They gain an ally in a land that is a potential British colony. They gain favorable trade relations: they leave China with a junk, with provisions, with maps and navigational equipment that they were given by Missee Lee. There is no mention of paying her back for these expensive gifts. They gain childhood experience in the discourse of empire, which will make them strong adult imperial leaders—or would, if Britain still had an empire.

## NOTES

[1]Arthur Ransome, *Swallowdale*. (Boston: Godine, 1985), 51. First published 1931.

[2]Interestingly, later in the series, she reverts to her given name of Bridget, since she no longer resembles Queen Victoria. This, of course, makes sense since she has left the pudgy domain of babyhood, but it also is an indication that the Victorian era is truly gone forever.

[3]Quoted in Walt Unsworth, *Everest: A Mountaineering History* (Boston: Houghton Mifflin, 1981), 49.

[4]One of the earliest, if not the earliest, books to use the phrase is T. E. Gordon's *The Roof of the World,* an account of travels through Tibet to "the Russian Frontier and the Oxus Sources on Pamir" (1876). The subtitle has interesting connections to Ransome, who had spent several years in Russia and who had helped two young schoolgirls publish their own Ransomesque book about pony-trekking youth, entitled *The Far-Distant Oxus.*

[5]Arthur Ransome, *Winter Holiday* (London: Puffin, 1971). First published 1931.

[6]Arthur Ransome had actually met Nansen in the Baltic in 1921, where Nansen was working with war refugees.

[7]Fridtjof Nansen, *Farthest North* (New York: Harper, 1898).

[8]Arthur Ransome, *Missee Lee* (London: Puffin, 1971). First published 1941.

[9]Judith Plotz, "Latin For Empire: Kipling's 'Regululus' as a Classics Class for the Ruling Classes," *Lion and Unicorn* 17 (1993), 154.

[10]Allyn and Bacon's College Latin Series, quoted in Plotz, 155.

# CHAPTER 6

# Empire Then and Now: Conclusions

Arthur Ransome is the last writer I will discuss in detail. He wrote just before and during World War II, and is the last children's writer to reflect issues of empire in easily recognizable and definable ways. But the desire for empire does not go away after World War II—or perhaps it does, to be replaced by its close cousin, nostalgia for a lost and more powerful Britain and a more perfect British past. Empire becomes generalized into a longing for past glories. Fred Inglis, writing of Kipling's Puck books, asserted that "The idea of England transcends the real history of empire, devastation, invasion, and colonization,"[1] a statement that applies as readily to later twentieth-century British children's books as to Kipling's.

Nostalgia for a vanished and powerful Britain takes many forms in children's books both during and after World War II, but is most likely to show up in either historical fiction or in fantasy works. This alone is a shift from the earlier, pre-World War I Period. Before World War I, images of empire are more likely to appear in realistic fiction than in fantasy; whereas directly after the war, in Milne and Lofting for example, empire has receded into the world of fantasy. Partly this has to do with the rise and fall of the popularity of fantasy as a genre in children's writing, but I think it also has to do with increasing disquietude about empire and its effects, disquietude that is perhaps too disturbing to look at realistically and is more safely approached in the realm of fantasy or in the safety of the distant past.

Perhaps the most famous of World War II-era fantasies is Tolkien's tale of Middle Earth, beginning with *The Hobbit* (1937) and continuing in the three volumes of *The Lord of the Rings* (written 1936-1949). The four volumes, taken together, provide an epic tale of the struggle of democratic and largely disenfranchised people—the hobbits in particular, but also in different ways the elves and the dwarves and other magical beings—against the Dark Lord Saruman, a despotic and totalitarian ruler. Tolkien wrote the bulk of the trilogy during World War II, posting parts of it off as serial reading for his son Christopher, stationed in South Africa with the R.A.F.: an airman in a colonial outpost defending Britain against the rise of a would-be German empire. Tolkien emphatically denied that his books were in any way an allegory of World War II, but war and the loss of empire certainly had an effect on Tolkien's thinking. In the foreword to the American edition of *The Lord of the Rings* Tolkien writes that "as the years go by it seems often forgotten that to be caught in youth by 1914 was no less hideous than to be involved in 1939 . . . By 1918 all but one of my close friends were dead."[2] The next sentence denies that the devastated Shire at the end of the trilogy had any reference to England's post-blitz, post-war, battered condition.

Tolkien is being honest here, I think, but also disingenuous. He may not have had an allegory of wartime Britain in mind in *The Lord of the Rings,* but he was certainly thinking of the diminution of a once-great empire, as well as of the effects of industrialization and warfare upon green and pleasant England. The world of the Shire, before outside events intervene, is (as many critics have noted) an idealized rural England.

The hobbits and Middle Earth itself are close relatives to simple English folk who love their villages, their pubs, and their gardens, and don't really pay much mind to outside worlds unless they encroach upon their own comfortable lives. The hobbit world is a fantasy, an arcadian image of the perfect rural English life, life as it was before industrialization (something the Dark Lord makes use of, thus demonizing technology and the modern world) and before war, both World War I and II.

The fact that it is outside interference, battles and warfare beyond the Shire's borders, that brings enormous change, has an analogy in Britain's experiences with events outside the borders of England. Events in Africa, particularly during the Boer Wars, had a direct impact on British policies and politics at home; struggles for control of the Suez Canal led to international conflict and tenuous political agreements with France and Germany; the vulnerability of Indian trade routes led to complex (and often secret) interventions—all of which provided the build-up to World War I and an England changed forever. Britain overreached itself in the Empire, and ultimately paid the price. In Tolkien's trilogy, the hobbits do not over-reach themselves— they are properly insular—but outside events overtake them nonetheless, as they did Britons who never went to the colonies, but stayed home with pipe and pub.

The hobbits themselves, like ordinary Englishmen, seem harmless and even foolish at times, but rise to heroic stature when needed. Frodo is a wounded mythic hero, nearly Arthurian by the end of the tale, and Merry comes home with a sword, a soldier's reputation, and even some additional inches of physical height. The hobbits rise up against empire and totalitarianism, rather than fighting for it, suggesting that Tolkien's view of empire had been colored by the experiences of World War I: empire becomes a bad thing in these books, even if order and hierarchy are good things. And empire is thwarted by "stalky" behavior, by the Fellowship's decision to destroy the Ring rather than use it against Saruman. Just as *The Lord of the Rings* is a reverse quest story, in many ways it is a reverse tale of imperialism, raising questions not unlike those raised by Hugh Lofting in the Doctor Dolittle books.

The medieval and Arthurian tone of Tolkien's work reflects back to the late nineteenth-century interest in chivalry and muscular Christianity, both of which were important influences upon children's books of the period. The appeal shifts in the post-World War II period, however. In the late nineteenth century, Arthurian chivalry and courage were seen as values that young boys, in particular, should emulate in order to become strong leaders of a Britain once again as strong and noble as Arthur's Britain. After World War II, chivalric and Arthurian imagery is used not so much to encourage children to incorporate these values for the good of a present and future Britain, but rather to impress upon children the glories of the British past and to suggest that it is gone now, though still longed for, and perhaps possible again in the future. There is a melancholy to the uses of chivalry and Arthur after World War II.

This can certainly be seen in some of the best-known of the post-war historical novels, Rosemary Sutcliff's books about both early Anglo-Saxon England and the Arthurian legend. Her works were enormously popular and influential in the fifties and sixties when they were first published. Sutcliff's telling of the Arthurian legend, for example, takes the story all the way to its sad ending: she does not stop with Galahad's achievement of the Grail, but goes on to Arthur's betrayal and death, and in fact the entire last volume of her retelling focuses upon betrayal after betrayal of Arthur and his court. Her tale of the battles between Britons and Saxons, *Dawn Wind* (1961)[3] is a more hopeful novel, in that by the end Saxons are being integrated into British life and are being Christianized through the twin forces of King Aethelbert and Augustine of Rome, who comes from Rome to spread the word of God to the heathen.

The novel begins with the aftermath of a horrific battle between Saxons and Britons: "They had died at sunset, under a flaming sky, with all that was left of free Britain behind them, and their faces to the Saxon hordes. It was all over; nothing left now but the dark" (2). It ends with our Briton hero, Owain, reunited with the suggestively named Regina, heading back to Saxons who had once sheltered him, to start a homestead and family of his own as the "dawn wind" of a new, Saxon-inclusive Britain rises. The invaders who had hoped to take Britain for their own are lost through a combination of internecine warfare and assimilation to the stronger values of the Britons and—significantly—of Rome. It may be Christian, post-imperial Rome that influences Britain, but Owain largely succeeds because he considers himself still attached to the Roman Empire and can still speak Latin. Imperialism is presented as not inherently evil, but possibly good if led by the right sort of (British) people, an attitude towards imperialism familiar to nineteenth-century readers.

Sutcliff's novels are certainly more realistic than the pseudo-chivalric tales of the Edwardian era: she does not stint on the details of thralldom, of battle, or of the harshness of life in those times. And her novels have the feel of the period through both the rhythm of her prose and her use of Anglo-Saxon words. Yet one wonders at their popularity—and the popularity of other historical works about the same period—in the fifties and the sixties in Britain. Britain had suffered enormously during World War II, for the first time in centuries invaded by foreigners (in the form of V2 rockets from Germany). Great damage was inflicted upon English cities, children were evacuated to the countryside and overseas (including the United States), and in some ways Britain took as long to recover from the war as did the rest of Europe: food and gas rationing, for example, lasted in Britain well into the 1950s. Children's books—books in general—had been in short supply during the war due to paper and labor shortages, and when they reappear, many of them present the British past as something to be admired. Britain is on the winning side of World War II not because she is the major world power, but largely because of aid from the other allies, primarily the United States. A former colonial possession must be depended upon to save a formerly imperial Britain from being overrun by invaders. No wonder books that look back to an historical past or a fantastic realm in which those invaders are repelled by Britons alone appealed to post-war writers. They are reassurance that Britain has a glorious past, and may still consider itself to be a glorious and powerful nation.

But even when children's books are not looking nostalgically at Britain's Arthurian or Roman past, they are still nostalgic for an arcadian, pre-industrial, peaceful past. The "idea of England," in Inglis's phrase, is conveyed not only through historical fiction, but also in fantasies set in modern times. We can see this in works like Lucy Boston's *The Children of Green Knowe* (1954) and in Phillipa Pearce's *Tom's Midnight Garden* (1958). Both are time-travel fantasies set in old houses in the English countryside: Tom's garden no longer exists in his present, but he can travel to it in the past, and Tolly's garden exists in the present much as it did in the past. Both novels take place in the Fen district of England (as does a later Ransome novel, *The Coot Club*), and both concern lonely children who discover ghost-children for playmates. But both Tolly and Tom discover more than playmates: they discover a door into a largely utopian past.

*Tom's Midnight Garden* shows the unappealing nature of postwar England more so than does *The Children of Green Knowe*. Tom must spend the summer holidays with his childless aunt and uncle in a garden-less flat rather than at home with his brother, who has come down with measles. Not that home is all that desirable: Tom's city home does have a garden, but it is "small" with a "vegetable plot and a grass plot and one flower-bed and a rough patch by the back fence,"[4] and his parents are not as well-off as his aunt and uncle, since they have two boys to raise. But his home is certainly prefer-able to the block of flats where Uncle Alan and Aunt Gwen live. The flats have been converted from an old, large house that is now "crowded round with newer, smaller houses that beat up to its very confines in a broken sea of bay-windows and gable-ends and pinnacles . . . [It was] oblong, plain, grave" (4), has only a short drive, and no garden at all, only an alley with ashcans. Tom, understandably, is depressed by the thought of being quarantined here for weeks, with only his adult relatives to keep him company.

Tom's rescue comes in the form of a magic garden that he learns to access, the garden that was once attached to the house and that he still can, through the fantasy of time travel, visit. And it is no ordinary garden, but in the arcadian tradition is a garden closer to paradise than to earth: the weather is nearly always perfect, there are broad lawns, flower beds, vegetable gar-dens, a summer house and a greenhouse, shaped hedges, large yew trees to climb, and—as he eventually discovers—the young girl Hatty to play with. Tom's escape from the dreariness of post-war life is an escape to—where else?—the late Victorian period, when England was more stable, more pow-erful, and could afford many more grand houses than it can in Tom's time.

The connection between the nineteenth century and Tom's twentieth cen-tury is a crucial one, and shows up in more than one children's book. Pearce gradually makes clear that Hatty and the garden exist in the golden age of the Edwardian period, before World War I and the beginnings of the end of En-gland as empire, England as utopia, England as arcadia. Tom, in his search to discover Hatty's time period, asks his aunt when women wore long skirts, and Aunt Gwen says, "long skirts were always the fashion, until not so long ago. Up to World War I, certainly" (113). When Tom finally discovers that the old lady who owns the house is the adult Hatty, Hatty (now Mrs. Bartholomew) says, "I was born towards the end of the Queen's reign. She was an old lady when I was a girl. I am a Late Victorian" (218). Mrs. Bartholomew fills in the history for Tom, explaining that she married happily and lived on a farm in the fens with her husband, while the family fortunes of her cousins (with whom she had been raised) declined. Her life has had sorrows though—her sons "were both killed in the Great War—World War I they call it now . . . Then, many years later, [my husband] died, and I was left quite alone. That was when I came here; and I've lived here ever since" (224). But as an old woman, Hatty lives largely in the past, and it is her dreaming memories of a Victorian girlhood spent largely in an idyllic garden that draws Tom into the past and allows him to experience the idyll as well. Both the Late Victorian and the post–World War II boy prefer to live in the time period before the

Great War, when life is presented as having been if not perfect, more perfect than it is in the twentieth century. The late Victorian period functions metaphorically as Britain's cultural and historical apex, a period when the country and the people in it were more stable, more powerful, and certainly happier than they are in the twentieth century. The Edwardian period begins to take on a patina of perfection for twentieth-century writers, battered by war and the loss of empire.

The nostalgia of *Tom's Midnight Garden* is an example of the way images of empire begin to soften and blur into a generalized nostalgia for Britain's glorious past. The same sort of nostalgia can be seen in *The Children of Green Knowe,* where Tolly can explore a garden and a home largely unchanged over the centuries—a home that is an old manor house with much history to it, and where he can become friends with the ghosts of children who died during the Great Plague. Although Boston's novel and Pearce's have some striking similarities, Boston is, perhaps, more nostalgic even than Pearce. Whereas there are frequent references to the daily ordinariness of twentieth-century life in *Tom's Midnight Garden,* once Tolly is delivered to his great-grandmother's house, he might as well be living in the past as in the present. Tolly's Christian name—Toseland—is an ancient local name reflected in many place-names of the area; the house is filled with furniture and paintings and toys and stories of the past; the very servant man in charge of the grounds has the same name as the family men who have preceded him for generations, and so on. There is very little modern about Green Knowe: there are lamps and candles rather than electric lights, and fires in fireplaces rather than central heat, and no real concern with the modern world that lies beyond the estate. And although one can infer that Tom's old Victorian house gained some of its wealth from imperial business (the nineteenth-century version of the house has a tiger skin rug), the imperial connections are clearer for Tolly's house, whose former owners, we are told, included Captain Oldknow "who sailed all over the world. He used to bring home presents for the family. From one journey he brought the [Japanese stone] mouse for Toby . . . and that great silk Chinese lantern that hangs in the Music Room."[5]

The wealth that Captain Oldknow accumulated also supported the lovely house and its even more lovely gardens, as expansive as those of Pearce's novel, but even more arcadian. The emphasis on old folkways and the symbolic importance of animals links Boston's Green Knowe to a much older Britain than we see in Hatty Bartholomew's Victorian house. Indeed, in the flute-playing Alexander, the tame deer and fox surrounding the ghost-children in a secret arbor in the garden, in the frightening greenwitch figure of Old Noah, one feels old Pan again and some of the magic of Kipling's Dan and Una in their own arcadian paradise, hearing of the British past. Tolly discovers the children's books, which include *Merlin the Sorcerer* and Malory's *Morte d'Arthur,* as well as *The History of Troy*—works specifically con-

cerned with the mythic British past (specifically the unification and strength-
ening of Britain under Arthur) as well as the mythic Greek past, in a story that
has much to do with unification, betrayal, and empire building as well.

Like Kipling's Puck books, Boston's novel includes stories-within-
stories, but hers have to do with family history, rather than with the history of
Britain, although of course the family she is concerned with is one that seems
to have been of some importance in the past. Indeed, Tolly witnesses the per-
formance of one of the ghost-children, Alexander, who is chosen to sing for
the entertainment of the king. The emphasis is on the importance of this occasion to a single child and a single family: there is little, if any, metaphoric
reaching for images of empire, whether positive or negative, in *The Children
of Green Knowe*. But Boston does make clear that history is one cause of the
estate's decline in fortune over the years. Boggis, the estate's factotum,
whose identically named forbears have also been estate employees for generations upon generations, answers some of Tolly's questions. Tolly asks if
Boggis has a grandson, and Boggis says, "I had, but he was killed in the last
war." Tolly then asks if he has a son, and Boggis says, "I had, two. But they
were killed in the first war" (117). Tolly is upset by this, because "How would
things go on if there wasn't a Boggis?" (117). It is war—specifically modern
war—that threatens the continuity of life at Green Knowe, more so than the
Great Plague that killed the ghost-children ever could. Boggis explains that
"My son was batman to your grandfather in the first war. They were killed
together. In the second war it was my grandson as was the sergeant and your
father was his corporal. He carried my grandson across an open bridge when
his legs were shot off" (119). It is not only the continuity of Boggis at Green
Knowe, but the continuity of the master/servant relationship that has made
the estate possible, and that is threatened in the modern world.

One would think nostalgia for an arcadian, sometimes feudal, English
past would become dimmer and dimmer as the twentieth century progresses,
but it does not. One of the more popular series of the seventies is Susan
Cooper's *The Dark Is Rising* series, which as Michael Drout has demon-
strated has British nationalism at its heart.[6] Cooper's fantasy series—another
time-travel tale—gives the reader a sense of British history as a history of
invasions by the Other and ultimately showing that England holds a "central
and privileged position" in the world (Drout 243). It comes as no surprise that
Cooper depends not only upon the folkloric past of Britain, but especially
upon the Arthur legend to frame her tale, whose entire point is that King
Arthur will come again to restore Britain to its former glory. Like Sutcliff,
Cooper sees the only hope for Britain's modern future in the feudal past.
While there is no mention of empire per se in the series—no more so than in
*The Lord of the Rings,* which likewise has a Dark Lord who wishes to con-
quer the world—giving England a "central and privileged position" in the
contemporary world can be considered a desire to return to an imperial past.

What is an imperial power, after all, if not a power with a "central and privileged" position?

Cooper's series, like that of many British children's books before hers, has a house as a central metaphor. We have seen the importance of old manor houses before, in Dan and Una's ancestral home, tended by generations of Hobdens; in the Bastables's Moat House; in Misselthwaite Manor; in the houses of Tom and Tolly in *Tom's Midnight Garden* and *The Children of Green Knowe.* Cooper's books, particularly the second in the series, *The Dark Is Rising* (1973) are also centered on houses, the ancient manor house of Miss Greythorne, specifically linked to Britain's historical and mythic past, and the Stantons's ancient farmhouse, symbol of English domesticity and comfort. Houses very often become metaphors of "the house of England" in children's books where nationalism or imperialism is part of the narrative.

A more recent fantasy series where a house serves as metaphor for country is Lynn Reid Banks' *Indian in the Cupboard* series, (1981-93). These books are also nostalgic for the glories of the British past, and like *Tom's Midnight Garden,* look to World War I as the turning point when British strength and might in the world begin to fail. Omri, the hero of the books, has a series of adventures with his animated toys, but it isn't until *The Mystery of the Cupboard* (1993) that Banks provides us with an explanation of the magic that enlivens the toys. Omri will come to learn the secret not in London, where he has spent most of his childhood, but in Dorset, where his family has inherited "a real Dorset longhouse," with thatched roof, in the Hidden Valley, behind hedges, in what Omri's mother calls a "magical" setting.[7] The family has escaped a London where there is not only insufficient room for an arcadian garden, but there are also threats by burglars and street thugs who are described in terms familiar from earlier adventure fiction: they are "animal like," with "cropped heads" and "five gold rings" in each ear, and although Banks makes clear that they are white, they are described in language that links them to descriptions of "savage" others in former British colonial holdings.[8]

It is the Dorset longhouse that holds the secret of the magic of the cupboard. Omri finds a diary that links his family's history with the larger history of Britain. The diary explains that an ancestor was enraged when his toy business of making "beautiful and realistic little lead model [soldiers] . . . heavy to the hand, well-balanced, infinitely rewarding to set up—and to knock down in the excitement of mock battle" (84) is destroyed by industrialization and particularly by the invention of plastic toys, "cheap, mass-produced, ugly, lightweight rubbish" (84) that begins to appear in the late nineteenth and early twentieth centuries. The ancestral toy-maker puts his rage into the cupboard, and thus the cupboard has the ability to bring toys to life.

Here, in the late 1980s and 1990s, is yet another children's novel that looks to the arcadian British past for inspiration. Like the novels of Pearce,

Boston, and Cooper, Banks has at the center of her books a historic house that in many ways is emblematic of the house of Britain itself. Like her predecessors, Banks presents the late Edwardian period as the apex of British power and prestige, and longs for her nation to return to this past glory. The ideal past for British children's writers, well into the twentieth century, is the past where England still ruled the waves and ran an empire. This nostalgia for the past is not really so surprising, when one considers British history from the post-World War II period through the 1980s and into the nineties. In the 1950s England provided one-fifth of the world's manufactured goods, but by the end of the 1960's it provided only one-tenth, and the trend of importing more and exporting less continued through the 1970s and into the 1980s.[9] Throughout the 1970s inflation in Britain rose, labor strikes and even riots occurred (most spectacularly the coal miners' strike of 1972), and Britain found herself struggling uneasily with an immigrant population. People of color from former colonial possessions were immigrating in large numbers to England, prompting the proposal of the Nationalities Bill of 1981, which, if passed, would have created different classes of citizenship, with immigrants at the bottom of the ladder. There were riots by people of color in Bristol and in Brixton in the 1980s. Far from being an imperial power with long-reaching powers over Other and darker people in other lands, Britain found herself possessing only a few tiny territories of little commercial or military importance, invaded by former colonial subjects who were now demanding a place in Britain. No wonder the British elected the very conservative Margaret Thatcher as prime minister, and no wonder it was Thatcher's leadership that led to British naval intervention in the Falklands War of 1982. Thatcher was the longest-serving prime minister since 1827, and her leadership during the Falkland War was a factor in her landslide re-election in 1983. The empire—what is left of it—must be defended.

Cultural and political ideologies are expressed everywhere in our daily lives, often in unlikely places, and often unrecognized by us. Whether people as a whole passively incorporate the ideology of an elite upper class, or actively participate in creating ideology and sometimes dismissing such ideology, the evidence of ideology is everywhere. The ideology of capitalism, for example, is inescapable in the United States and in most Western nations: commercials constantly interrupt television; the characters on television own and consume enormous amounts of goods; films (even in the United States) are preceded not only by commercials for soft drinks and future films, but are infiltrated by "product placement" of Coke cans or Apple computers or Ford cars. In such a world, one does not have to teach children to be consumers and to value capitalism: it is a lesson they can learn by the age of two, if not through books through other media. Perhaps the purveyors of film and television are conscious of the capitalist ideology they present viewers, and perhaps not. Many viewers claim not to be influenced by commercials, yet any number of studies link certain marketing campaigns with dramatic rises in sales of various products. Certainly the writers I have discussed here, whose ideologies are formed more by imperialism than by capitalism, are largely unconscious of the ideology of imperialism that pervades their works and makes its way into the minds of children. But the ideology exists nonetheless, woven into some of the most important and influential British children's books of the late nineteenth and early twentieth centuries.

If children's fiction is one way of acculturating children into an acceptable ideology, then classic children's texts from the Boer Wars to World War II suggest to children that Britain's imperial rule over other countries is a good thing, for both Britain and for imperial outposts. That issues of empire are so closely woven into fiction by Kipling, Nesbit, and others is an indication of how closely empire was woven into the everyday lives of the middle classes who produced this literature for middle-class children. Empire is a given in these book and only rarely is it questioned or does it raise questions about empire for readers. Just as a separation of gender roles was an unspoken "truth" in most children's fiction until fairly recently—a given of the world as presented to children—so too is empire a given truth.

Children's fiction also presents the reader with the lives of children who will grow up to be adults, and the adult lives, either imagined for these children or that the children are likely to grow into, reflect the wishes of their adult creators more than the wishes of the children themselves. Children's fiction provides, as I wrote in the introduction, a mirror of adult desires. The desires of the adult creators of classic children's books include a desire that children grow up not only to be honorable and respectable, but that they grow up into the kind of adult who can maintain Britain's strength—and that strength was an imperial strength. There is a desire, from Kipling through Ransome, for Britain to maintain imperial strength and the hopes for that strength lie in children, the future adult leaders of Britain.

Children's books of the period I have discussed here were as important and perhaps as influential for middle-class children of the time as television and film are today. Books for children carried much more cultural weight in the pre-World War I period than afterwards, when their importance has been diluted by other media influences. The essentially conservative and imperial ideology these children's books convey reflects not only the ideologies of individual writers, but also, I would argue, the ideology of the majority of the British middle class. It is an ideology adult writers pass on to child readers, in ways not inconsistent with the ways in which Western ideologies were imposed upon colonial subjects in India, Africa, China, and elsewhere. Children are treated as colonial subjects of adult intentions, just as colonial subjects were treated as children by adult imperialists. There is, on the whole, a refusal to confront the changing world in the twentieth century, a desire to keep children in what is perceived as the idyllic past—or to give them both the belief and the skills necessary to recreate that idyllic British imperial past.

Books written earlier in Britain's imperial history, and especially those by Kipling, are perfectly frank about the nature of empire and the need for future imperial leaders. I began this study with Kipling because, among other things, Kipling provides a microcosm of both the themes and techniques of other writers of classic children's books. He is both a realist and a fantasist; he provides readers both with Britain's historical past in the Puck books and its imperial present in *Kim* and *Stalky & Co*. He values the nature of childhood and its promise for the future, made clearest at the end of *Stalky & Co.*, when the "old boys" reunite and tell tales of brave imperial deeds of their fellow schoolmates out on the imperial frontier. Other writers are less frank and open, though no less approving of empire and its values. This is apparent in the way empire provides fairytale endings for Burnett's novels; in the imperial play of the Bastable children in Nesbit's books, and in the adventures of the Swallows and Amazons. No writer past Kipling writes forthrightly of the need to actively educate youth to lead the empire, but perhaps no writer has to: their child characters have incorporated imperial values quite thoroughly into their play and into their imaginations.

Only in writers writing beyond World War I are there any suggestions that children may not grow up to be participants in the world the adults around them knew as both children and adults. Milne's Christopher Robin must leave the Hundred Acre Wood, must leave childhood, presented by Milne as a sad but inevitable loss. Christopher Robin is growing up into a world where he is expected to make sense of what, to him, appear to be disconnected bits of knowledge of exports and equations and that education should weave together for him. But Milne, unlike Kipling, Burnett, or Nesbit, gives no sense of the kind of adult Christopher Robin might grow into, in a world that after World War I seemed as fragmented as the list of topics Christopher studies in school. Kipling often fast-forwards his characters into adulthood so that the reader can see the benefits of imperial education; Burnett's little girls grow up to rule household empires supported by imperial enterprise; the Bastables and Walkers and Blacketts will, their stories suggest, grow into proper middle-class gentlemen and ladies who have bourgeois, if not conservative, values. Christopher Robin's future seems less sure, and Milne provides fewer clues than earlier writers would have. The best prediction we can make is that he will grow up into some of the same attitudes of leadership and patronage that he shows to his stuffed animals. When Christopher Robin goes off to school, he vanishes into unknown territory, just as the England Milne returned to after the war was unknown territory. Milne had difficulty navigating post-war Britain, and the insularity of his fantasy world is suggestive of this unease. His contemporary, Hugh Lofting, seems even more unsure than Milne of the world children are now facing, to the point of very nearly excluding children from his stories altogether. Tommy Stubbins as narrator does not appear until the second volume, and he is not present as narrator in all of the succeeding Doctor Dolittle books. When we meet him in *The Voyages of Doctor Dolittle* we meet him as an adult looking back on childhood, not as a child character. As a child, Tommy had much in common with adventuring children of empire, wanting to "seek [his] fortune in foreign lands—Africa, India, China, and Peru!" Yet it is not fortune he finds with Doctor Dolittle, but rather the problematics of imperial intervention in Africa and elsewhere.

In other words, none of these authors can imagine an adult life for the children in their books that is not substantially similar to the lives of the adult authors: there is a failure to imagine any sort of changing world, despite the evidence of World War I that the world had, indeed, already changed irrevocably. None of the children is in any kind of substantial disagreement with the adults in their lives, nor do they rebel against reasonable adult authority. The adults who imagined them imagined, if you will, good colonial subjects who might cause mischief and trouble, but who were educable and—since they are British children and not native colonial subjects—will grow into suitable adult imperial leaders, of their own (future) children as well as of Britain. Nostalgia for an ideal childhood is bound up with nostalgia for empire in these novels.

Children's books—children themselves—are often discounted as not being serious, as undeserving of close critical attention. Children's literature is often marginalized in academe, and older children's literature suffers from this more than contemporary children's literature does. Most students who study children's texts today are future teachers—future conveyors of adult ideology to their students. University courses in children's literature tend to emphasize contemporary books for children, books children today actually read. If the cultural import of children's books is discussed at all, it is usually done in the spirit of multiculturalism or feminism or censorship: does this book accurately and respectfully convey a different culture? is this book free of sex-role stereotyping? is *Heather and Her Two Mommies* or *Weetzie Bat* too controversial to be in a school library? Must we ban *Harry Potter* because it seems to endorse pagan magic? The deeper ideologies of children's books are rarely tackled. And classic children's books, when taught at all, tend to be taught in an historical context, as examples of what genres looked like then and how they grew into the now of contemporary children's books.

But children's texts provide a cultural mirror for adult fears and desires. They are important cultural artifacts and can have a lasting effect upon the beliefs of children who read them. This is especially true of the classic British children's texts I have examined here, which not only influenced child readers in the past, but continue to influence contemporary children, through both their continued availability in print and, even more importantly, in their strong influence upon writers of more contemporary texts that children today are more likely to read.

Children today may be more interested in the way the empire strikes back in *Star Wars* than they are in how the British Empire reigned in the past. But issues of empire are still with us, both in science fiction fantasies and in our real lives. That issues and questions of empire linger on one hundred years beyond the height of the British Empire speaks eloquently to the importance of and desire for empire in Britain's past—and in her present.

## NOTES

[1]Fred Inglis, *The Pursuit of Happiness: Value and Meaning in Children's Fiction* (Cambridge: Cambridge University Press, 1981), 158.

[2]J. R. R. Tolkien, "Foreword," *The Fellowship of the Rings* (New York: Ballantine, 1969), xi.

[3]Rosemary Sutcliff, *Dawn Wind* (New York: Henry Z. Walck, 1962).

[4]Phillipa Pearce, *Tom's Midnight Garden* (London: Oxford, 1958), 1.

[5]Lucy Boston, *The Children of Green Knowe* (New York: Harcourt, 1954), 39.

[6]Michael D.C. Drout, "Reading the Signs of Light: Anglo-Saxonism, Education, and Obedience in Susan Cooper's *The Dark is Rising*," *Lion and Unicorn* 21:2 (1997): 230–50.

[7]Lynn Reid Banks, *The Mystery of the Cupboard* (New York: Avon, 1993), 11. For a more complete discussion of this series and its links with other contemporary British fantasies, see my "Thatchers and Thatcherites: Lost and Found Empires in Three British Fantasies," *Lion and Unicorn* 22:2 (1998): 196-210.

[8]Lynn Reid Banks, *The Return of the Indian* (New York: Avon, 1986), 9.

[9]Michael Nevin, *The Age of Illusions: The Political Economy of Britain 1968–82* (New York: St. Martin's, 1983), 48.

# Bibliography

**PRIMARY SOURCES**

Ballantyne, R. M. *The Coral Island*. Oxford: Oxford University Press, 1991.
Banks, Lynn Reid. *The Return of the Indian*. New York: Avon, 1986.
———. *The Mystery of the Cupboard*. New York: Avon, 1993.
Boston, Lucy M. *The Children of Green Knowe*. New York: Harcourt Brace, 1955.
Buchan, John. *Prester John*. 1910. Oxford: Oxford University Press, 1994.
Burnett, Frances Hodgson. *A Little Princess*. 1905. London: Puffin, 1994.
———. *The Secret Garden*. 1911. New York: HarperCollins, 1990.
Conrad, Joseph. "Heart of Darkness," In *Youth and Two Other Stories,* New York: Doubleday 1908.
Cooper, Susan. *The Dark Is Rising*. New York: Macmillan, 1973.
Kipling, Rudyard. *Something of Myself*. Garden City, NY: Doubleday, 1937.
———. *The Complete Stalky & Co.* 1899. London: Oxford, 1987.
———. *The Jungle Books*. 1894,1895. London: Penguin, 1987.
———. *Puck of Pook's Hill*. 1906. London: Penguin, 1990.
———. *Kim*. 1901. London: Penguin, 1989.
Lofting, Hugh. *The Story of Doctor Dolittle*. Philadelphia: Lippincott, 1920.
———. *The Voyages of Doctor Dolittle,* rev. ed. New York: Dell, 1988.
———. *Doctor Dolittle's Post Office*. Philadelphia: Lippincott, 1926.
———. *Doctor Dolittle and the Secret Lake*. Philadelphia: Lippincott, 1948.
———. *The Story of Doctor Dolittle,* rev. ed. New York: Dell, 1988.
———. *The Voyages of Doctor Dolittle*. Philadelphia: Lippincott, 1922.
Milne, A. A. *Autobiography*. New York: E.P. Dutton, 1939.
———. *Winnie-the-Pooh*. 1926. New York: Puffin, 1992.
———. *The House at Pooh Corner*. 1928. New York: Puffin, 1992.
Nansen, Fridtjof. *Farthest North*. New York: Harper, 1898.
Nesbit, E. *The Story of the Treasure Seekers*. London: Puffin, 1994.
———. *The Wouldbegoods*. 1901. London: Puffin, 1987.
———. *New Treasure Seekers*. 1899. London: Puffin, 1996.
Pearce, Philippa. *Tom's Midnight Garden*. 1958. HarperCollins, 1992.

Ransome, Arthur. *Missee Lee*. 1941. London: Puffin, 1983.
————. *Swallows and Amazons*. 1930. Boston: Godine, 1985,
————. *Swallowdale*. 1931. Boston: Godine, 1985.
————. *Winter Holiday*. 1933. London: Puffin, 1983.
Sutcliff, Rosemary. *Dawn Wind*. New York: Henry Z. Walck, 1961.
Tolkien, J.R.R. *The Fellowship of the Ring*. New York: Ballantine, 1972.

## SECONDARY SOURCES

Adams, Gillian. "Secrets and Healing Magic in *The Secret Garden.*" In *Triumphs of the Spirit in Children's Literature,* edited by Francelia Butler. Hamden, CT: Library Professional Publications, 1986.

Anderson, Celia Catlett. "Kipling's Mowgli and Just So Stories: The Vine of Fact and Fantasy." In *Touchstones: Reflections on the Best in Children's Literature,* edited by Perry Nodelman, 113–23. West Lafayette, IN: Children's Literature Association, 1985.

Armstrong, Judith M. "The Semiotics of *Fin de siècle: Stalky and Co.* and *Cyrano de Bergerac.*" *Essays in Poetics* 17, no. 2 (1992): 47–60.

Avery, Gillian and Julia Briggs, eds. *Children and Their Books: A Celebration of the Work of Iona and Peter Opie*. Oxford: Clarendon, 1989.

Bangie, Chris. *Exotic Memories: Literature, Colonialism, and the Fin de Siècle*. Stanford: Stanford University Press, 1991.

Bivona, Daniel. *Desire and Contradiction: Imperial Visions and Domestic Debate in Victorian Literature*. Manchester: Manchester University Press, 1990.

Bixler, Phyllis. "Gardens, Houses, and Nurturant Power in *The Secret Garden.*" In *Romanticism and Children's Literature in Nineteenth–Century England,* edited by James Holt McGavran, Jr. Athens, GA: University of Georgia Press, 1991.

Brantlinger, Patrick. *Rule of Darkness: British Literature and Imperialism, 1830–1914*. Ithaca: Cornell University Press, 1988.

Briggs, Julia. "Women Writers and Writing for Children: From Sarah Fielding to E. Nesbit." In *Children and Their Books: A Celebration of the Work of Iona and Peter Opie,* edited by Julia Briggs, Gillian Avery, 221–50. Oxford: Clarendon, 1989.

Bush, Julia. "Edwardian Ladies and the 'Race' Dimensions of British Imperialism." *Women's Studies International Forum* 21, no. 3 (1998): 277–89.

Bush, Julia. *Edwardian Ladies and Imperial Power*. London: Leicester University Press, 1999.

Cadden, Mike. "Home is a Matter of Blood, Time, and Genre: Essentialism in Burnett and McKinley." *Ariel* 28, no. 1 (1997): 53–67.

Carpenter, Humphrey. *Secret Gardens: The Golden Age of Children's Literature*. Boston: Houghton Mifflin, 1985.

Connell, Eileen. "Playing House: Frances Hodgson Burnett's Fairy Tale." In *Keeping the Victorian House: A Collection of Essays,* edited by Vanessa D. Dickerson. New York: Garland, 1995.

Crews, Frederick C. *The Pooh Perplex: A Freshman Casebook*. New York: E. P. Dutton, 1963.

Crouch, Marcus. *Treasure Seekers and Borrowers: Children's Books in Britain 1900–1960.* London: Library Association, 1962.

Crouch, Marcus. *The Nesbit Tradition: The Children's Novel in England, 1945–1970.* Totowa, NY: Rowman and Littlefield, 1972.

Darcy, Jane. "The Representation of Nature in *The Wind in the Willows* and *The Secret Garden.*" *Lion and Unicorn* 19 (1995): 211–222.

Darton, F.J. Harvey. *Children's Books in England: Five Centures of Social Life.* Cambridge: Cambridge University Press, 1932.

David, Deidre. "Children of Empire: Victorian Imperialism and Sexual Politics in Dickens and Kipling." In *Gender and Discourse in Victorian Literature and Art,* edited by Beverly Taylor and Antony H. Harrison. DeKalb, IL: Northern Illinois University Press, 1992.

David, Deirdre. *Rule Britannia: Women, Empire, and Victorian Writing.* Ithaca: Cornell University Press, 1995.

Dingley, R.J. "Beetle's Responsibility: The Ending of *Stalky & Co.*" *The Kipling Journal* 58, no. 230 (1984): 9–17.

Dowling, William C. *Jameson, Althusser, Marx: An Introduction to the Political Unconscious.* Ithaca: Cornell University Press, 1984.

Drout, Michael D.C. "Reading the Signs of Light: Anglo–Saxonism, Education, and Obedience in Susan Cooper's *The Dark Is Rising.*" *Lion and Unicorn* 21.2 (1997): 230–50.

Egoff, Sheila, ed. *Only Connect: Readings on Children's Literature.* 2nd. ed. Toronto: Oxford University Press, 1980.

Eldridge, C.C. *The Imperial Experience: From Carlyle to Forster.* New York: St. Martin's, 1996.

Evans, Gwyneth. "The Girl in the Garden: Variations on a Feminine Pastoral." *Children's Literature Association Quarterly,* no. 11, Spring (1994): 20–24.

Field, Elinor Whitney, ed. *Horn Book Reflections: On Children's Books and Reading.* Boston: Horn Book, 1969.

Flynn, Richard. "Kipling and Scouting: Or, 'Akela, We'll Do Our Best.'" *Children's Literature Association Quarterly* 16, no. 2 (1991): 55–58.

Foster, Shirley; Simons, Judy. *What Katy Read: Feminist Re–Readings of "Classic" Stories for Girls.* Iowa City: University of Iowa, 1995.

Fromm, Gloria G. "E. Nesbit and the Happy Moralist." *Journal of Modern Literature* 11, no. 1 (1984): 45–65.

Giddings, Robert, ed. *Literature and Imperialism.* New York: St. Martin's, 1987.

Gilbert, Elliott. *Kipling and the Critics.* New York: New York University Press, 1965.

Girouard, Marc. *The Return to Camelot.* New Haven: Yale University Press, 1981.

Green, Roger Lancelyn. *Kipling and the Children.* London: Elek, 1965.

Green, Martin. *Dreams of Adventure, Deeds of Empire.* New York: Basic Books, 1979.

Green, Roger Lancelyn. "Mowgli's Jungle." *The Kipling Journal* 57, no. 227 (1983): 29–35.

Gunther, A. "*The Secret Garden* Revisited." *Children's Literature in Education* 25, no. 3 (1994): 159–168.

Hai, Ambreen. "On Truth and Lie in a Colonial Sense: Kipling's Tales of Tale-Telling." *ELH* 64, no. 2 (1997): 599–625.

Hammond, Dorothy and Alta Jablow. *The Myth of Africa.* New York: Library of Social Science, 1977.

Hardyment, Christina. *Arthur Ransome and Captain Flint's Trunk.* London: Jonathan Cape, 1984.

Harrison, James. "Kipling's Jungle Eden." In *Critical Essays on Rudyard Kipling,* edited by Harold Orel, 151–64. Boston: G. K. Hall, 1985.

Hatch, John. *The History of Britain in Africa: From the Fifteenth Century to the Present.* New York: Praeger, 1969.

Hinchcliffe, Peter. "Coming to Terms With Kipling: *Puck of Pook's Hill, Rewards and Fairies,* and the Shape of Kipling's Imagination." *University of Toronto Quarterly* 45 (1975): 75–90.

Horwitz, Richard P. "Just So Stories of Ethnographic Authority." In *When They Read What We Write: The Politics of Ethnography,* edited by Caroline B. Brettell, 131–143. Westport, CT: Bergin & Garvey, 1993.

Hunt, Peter, ed. *Children's Literature: An Illustrated History.* Oxford: Oxford University Press, 1995.

Inglis, Fred. *The Promise of Happiness: Value and Meaning in Children's Fiction.* Cambridge: Cambridge University Press, 1981.

Jameson, Frederic. *The Political Unconscious: Narrative as a Socially Symbolic Act.* Ithaca: Cornell University Press, 1981.

Kemp, Sandra. *Kipling's Hidden Narratives.* Oxford: Basil Blackwell, 1988.

Keyser, Elizabeth. "'Quite Contrary': Frances Hodgson Burnett's *The Secret Garden." Children's Literature* 11 (1983): 1–13.

Keyser, Elizabeth Lennox. "'The Whole of the Story' Frances Hodgson Burnett's *A Little Princess."* In *Triumphs of the Spirit in Children's Literature,* edited by Francelia Butler and Richard Roberts. NY: Library Professional Publications, 1986.

Kiernan, V. G. *The Lords of Human Kind: Black Men, Yellow Men, and White Men in an Age of Empire.* Boston: Little, Brown, 1969.

Knoepflmacher, U. C. "The Balancing of Child and Adult: An Approach to Victorian Fantasies for Children." *Nineteenth-Century Literature* 37, no. 4 (1983): 497–530.

————. "Of Babylands and Babylons: E. Nesbit and the Reclamation of the Fairy Tale." *Tulsa Studies in Women's Literature* 6, no. 2 (1987): 299–325.

Knox, Robert. *The Races of Men: A Fragment.* Philadelphia: Lea and Blanchard, 1850.

Kohl, Herbert. *Should We Burn Babar?* New York: The New Press, 1995.

Kutzer, M. Daphne. "'Thatchers and Thatcherites': Lost and Found Empires in Three British Fantasies." *Lion and Unicorn* 22, no. 2 (1998): 196–210.

LaCapra, Dominick, ed. *The Bounds of Race: Perspectives on Hegemony and Resistance.* Ithaca: Cornell University Press, 1991.

McBratney, John. "Imperial Subjects, Imperial Space in Kipling's *Jungle Book. Victorian Studies* 35, no. 3 (1992): 277–93.

McCutchan, Corinne. "Puck & Co.: Reading *Puck of Pook's Hill* and *Rewards and Fairies* as a Romance." *Children's Literature* 20 (1992): 69–89.

McGavran, James Holt, Jr., ed. *Romanticism and Children's Literature in Nineteenth-Century England.* Athens: University of Georgia, 1991.

McGillis, Roderick. " 'Secrets' and 'Sequence' in Children's Stories." *Studies in the Literary Imagination* 17 (1985): 35–46.

McGillis, Roderick. *A Little Princess: Gender and Empire.* Edited by Robert Lecker. Vol. 159, Twayne's Masterwork Studies. NY: Twayne, 1996.

McGillis, Roderick. *The Nimble Reader: Literary Theory and Children's Literature.* New York: Twayne, 1996.

Mackenzie, John M., ed. *Imperialism and Popular Culture.* Manchester: University of Manchester, 1986.

McMaster, Juliet. "The Trinity Archetype in *The Jungle Books* and *The Wizard of Oz.*" *Children's Literature* 20 (1992): 90–110.

Magnan, J. A. *The Games Ethic and Imperialism.* New York: Viking, 1986.

Maher, Susan Naramore. "Recasting Crusoe: Frederick Marryat, R.M. Ballantyne and the Nineteenth-Century Robinsonade." *Children's Literature Association Quarterly* 13, no. 4 (1988): 169–75.

Mallett, Phillip. *Kipling Considered.* New York: St. Martin's, 1989.

Manlove, Colin N. "Fantasy as Witty Conceit: E. Nesbit." *Mosaic* 10, no. 2 (1977): 109–30.

Meyer, Susan. *Imperialism at Home: Race and Victorian Women's Fiction.* Ithaca: Cornell University Press, 1996.

Moore, Doris. *E. Nesbit: A Biography.* Philadelpha: Chilton, 1966.

Morris, Jan. *Coronation Everest.* London: Faber and Faber, 1958.

Moss, Robert F. *Rudyard Kipling and the Fiction of Adolescence.* New York: St. Martin's, 1982.

Moss, Anita. "*The Story of the Treasure Seekers:* The Idiom of Childhood." In *Touchstones: Reflections of the Best in Children's Literature,* edited by Perry Nodelman, 188–97. W. Lafayette, IN: Children's Literature Association, 1985.

Moss, Anita. "E. Nesbit's Romantic Child in Modern Dress." In *Romanticism and Children's Literature in Nineteenth-Century England,* edited by James Holt McGavran, Jr. Athens, GA: University of Georgia Press, 1991.

Murray, John. "The Law of The Jungle Books." *Children's Literature* (1992): 1–14.

Nelson, Claudia. *Boys Will Be Girls: The Feminine Ethic and British Children's Fiction, 1857–1917.* New Brunswick, NJ: Rutgers University Press, 1991.

Nevin, Michael. *The Age of Illusions: The Political Economy of Britain, 1968–1982.* New York: St. Martin's, 1983.

Nières, Isabelle. "Writers Writing a Short History of Children's Literature within Their Texts." In *Aspects and Issues in the History of Children's Literature,* edited by Maria Nikolajeva. Westport, CT: Greenwood, 1995.

Nikolajeva, Maria. "Children's Literature as a Cultural Code: A Semiotic Approach to History." In *Aspects and Issues in the History of Children's Literature,* edited by Maria Nikolajeva. Westport, CT: Greenwood, 1995.

Nodelman, Perry, ed. *Touchstones: Reflections on the Best in Children's Literature.* Vol. 1. W. Lafayette, IN: Children's Literature Association, 1985.

Nodelman, Perry. "The Other: Orientalism, Colonialism, and Children's Literature." *Children's Literature Association Quarterly* 17, no. 1 (1992): 27–32.

Orel, Howard, ed. *Critical Essays on Rudyard Kipling.* Boston: G.K. Hall, 1989.

Pakenham, Thomas. *The Scramble for Africa: White Man's Conquest of the Dark Continent from 1876–1912.* New York: Avon, 1991.

Pafford, Mark. *Kipling's Indian Fiction*. New York: St. Martin's, 1989.

Petzold, Dieter. "Fantasy Out of Myth and Fable: Animal Stories in Rudyard Kipling and Richard Adams." *Children's Literature Association Quarterly* 12, no. 1 (1987): 15–19.

Phillips, Jerry. "The Mem Sahib, the Worthy, the Rajah, and His Minions: Some Reflections on the Class Politics of *The Secret Garden.*" *Lion and Unicorn* 17 (1993): 168–194.

Plotz, Judith A. "The Empire of Youth: Crossing and Double-Crossing Cultural Barriers in Kipling's *Kim.*" *Children's Literature* 20 (1992): 111–131.

Plotz, Judith A. "Latin for Empire: Kipling's 'Regulus' as a Classics Class for the Ruling Classes." *Lion and Unicorn* 17, no. 2 (1993): 152–67.

Rahn, Suzanne. "News from E. Nesbit: *The Story of the Amulet* and the Socialist Utopia." *English Literature in Transition* 28, no. 2 (1985): 124–44.

Randall, Don. "Post-Mutiny Allegories of Empire in Kipling's *Jungle Books.*" *Texas Studies in Literature and Language* 40, no. 1 (1998): 97–120.

Rawlins, Dennis. *Peary at the North Pole: Fact or Fiction?* Washington & New York: Robert Luce, 1973.

Robson, W.W. "E. Nesbit and *The Book of Dragons.*" In *Children and Their Books: A Celebration of the Work of Iona and Peter Opie,* edited by Gillian Avery, 251–269. Oxford: Clarendon, 1989.

Rose, Jacqueline. *The Case of Peter Pan: The Impossibility of Children's Fiction.* London: Macmillan, 1984.

Rosenthal, Lynne M. "Boy-Society in Rudyard Kipling's *Stalky & Co.*" *Lion and Unicorn* 2, no. 2 (1978): 16–26.

Rutherford, Jonathan. *Forever England: Reflections on Race, Masculinity, and Empire*. London: Lawrence & Wishart, 1997.

Said, Edward. *Orientalism.* New York: Vintage, 1979.

Said, Edward. *Culture and Imperialism.* NY: Vintage, 1993.

Sale, Roger. *Fairy Tales and After: From Snow White to E. B. White.* Cambridge MA: Harvard University Press, 1979.

Schmidt, Gary D. "The Craft of the Cobbler's Son: Tommy Stubbins and the Narrative Form of the Doctor Dolittle Series." *Children's Literature Association Quarterly* 12, no. 1 (1987): 19–23.

Scott, Patrick. "The Schooling of John Bull: Form and Moral in Talbot Baines Reed's Boys' Stories and in Kipling's *Stalky & Co.*" *Victorian Newsletter* 60 (1981): 3–8.

Scott, Carole. "Limits of Otherworlds: Rules of the Game in *Alice's Adventures* and the *Jungle Books.*" In *Work and Play in Children's Literature: Selected Papers from the 1990 Children's Literature Association Conference,* edited by Susan R. Gannon, Ruth Anne Thompson, 1990.

Sharpe, Jenny. *Allegories of Empire: The Figure of Woman in the Colonial Text.* Minneapolis: University of Minnesota Press, 1993.

Singh, Minnie. "The Government of Boys: Golding's *Lord of the Flies* and Ballantyne's *Coral Island.*" *Children's Literature* 25 (1997): 205–213.

Stewart, D.H. "Stalky and the Language of Education." *Children's Literature* 20 (1992): 36–51.

Sullivan, Zorah T. *Narratives of Empire: The Fictions of Rudyard Kipling.* Cambridge: Cambridge University Press, 1993.

Swann, Thomas Burnett. *A.A. Milne.* Edited by Sylvia E. Bowman. Vol. 113, Twayne's English Authors Series. New York: Twayne, 1971.

Swarley, Ariel. "Television Focuses on Africa's Human History." *New York Times,* 24 October 1999, 2:1, p 46.

Taylor, Anthony H. Harrison and Beverly, ed. *Gender and Discourse in Victorian Literature and Art.* DeKalb, IL: Northern Illinois University Press, 1992.

Thwaite, Anne. *Waiting for the Party: The Life of Frances Hodgson Burnett, 1849–1924.* NY: Scribner, 1974.

Tiffin, Chris and Alan Lawson, ed. *De-Scribing Empire: Post-colonialism and Textuality.* London: Routledge, 1994.

Tinkler, Penny. "Introduction to Special Issue: Women, Imperialism and Identity." *Women's Studies International Forum* 23, no. 3 (1998): 217– 222.

Tuson, Penelope. "Mutiny Narratives and the Imperial Feminine: European Women's Accounts of the Rebellion in India in 1857." *Women's Studies International Forum* 21, no. 3 (1998): 291–303.

Twells, Alison. " 'Happy English Children': Class, Ethnicity, and the Making of Missionary Women in the Early Nineteenth Century." *Women's Studies International Forum* 21, no. 3 (1998): 235–245.

Unsworth, Walt. *Everest: A Mountaineering History.* Boston: Houghton Mifflin, 1981.

Wilson, Anita. "Milne's Pooh Books: The Benevolent Forest." In *Touchstones: Reflections on the Best in Children's Literature,* edited by Perry Nodelman, 163–172. W. Lafayette, IN: Children's Literature Association, 1985.

# Index